MORE FAMILY FAVORITES

By Mary Beth Roe

Published by FLP Publications
Post Office Box 208
Long Prairie, Minnesota 56347

Item No. F-14927

Cover: Hair and Make-up by David Stephens; Food Stylist, Aliza Green

ACKNOWLEDGEMENTS

First of all, I want to express my gratitude and sincere appreciation to the more than 275,000 people who purchased my first cookbook! I am overwhelmed and humbled by the response to my first cookbook, and I am grateful for the many letters I have received telling me how much everyone is enjoying using it! I hope that this cookbook will be enjoyed as much!

I bring this second volume to you because of the many requests for another one. It has taken two years to put this one together, because all of these recipes are different from the ones in volume one. It includes many more low fat recipes and some interesting informational tidbits I thought you would enjoy. Of course, these are still down-to-earth, everyday recipes that I'm known for - - - the perfect cookbook for the busy woman, wife, mother, grandmother, and men who like to cook, too! Also, due to requests, it includes more recent family photos and information about the people who mean the most to me in my life.

I want to say thank you to several people who helped with this book: my friends, Sherrie, Lynne, Sally, Linda, Paula, Marlene, my sisters and sisters-in-law who added a few recipes, my mom, Lois, my dad, Irving, and my mother-in-law, Orva, all of whom are great cooks and have taught me a lot about cooking and about life! I could not have put this book together without the dedication of my two sisters and best friends, Faith and Diane! We are like the three musketeers: All for one and one for all!

Most importantly, I want to thank my husband, Mark, and my three boys, Eric, Cory and Ryan for eating whatever I put on the table with minimal complaints! Mark did a lot of taste-testing, and he was a good sport about it!

When I do a project like this, I do it for two reasons: to give you something to enjoy and to give to others who need financial help. My portion of the proceeds will be going to various charities, primarily those which help children! I thank my Lord Jesus Christ for the opportunity to give back some of which He has blessed me with! I leave you with my "life" verse: Proverbs 3: 5-6 *"Trust in the Lord with all your heart, and lean not on your own understanding. In all your ways acknowledge Him, and He will direct your paths."*

Mary Beth Roe

TABLE OF CONTENTS

Appetizers & Beverages

Appetizers

Beverages

Dips

Pesto Dip

2 cups lightly packed fresh basil leaves
1/4 cup grated parmesan cheese
1 clove garlic, minced
3/4 cup nonfat sour cream

1/2 tsp. salt
1/2 tsp. pepper
1 cup plain nonfat yogurt

In food processor, combine basil, cheese, garlic, salt and pepper; process until minced, scraping down sides of bowl once or twice. Add yogurt and sour cream and pulse until just evenly combined. Cover and chill at least one hour or up to 1 day for flavors to mellow.

New Wave Onion Dip

3 small red onions, finely chopped
1 can beef broth
1 1/2 Tbsp. minced ginger
1 tsp. balsamic vinegar
1 cup nonfat sour cream

3 cloves garlic, minced
1/2 tsp. dried thyme
1/8 tsp. salt
1/8 tsp. pepper

Boil onions, broth, ginger, garlic, thyme, salt and pepper. Cook 15 minutes, stirring, until almost dry (watch toward end of cooking time to avoid scorching). Transfer to bowl and stir in vinegar. Let cool. When cool, stir in sour cream.

Hamburger Cheese Dip

2 lbs. hamburger
2 - 15 oz. cans tomato sauce

1 or 2 cans chopped green chiles
2 lbs. Velveeta cheese

Brown hamburger. Add tomato sauce and green chiles. Heat to hot and bubbly. Add cheese and stir until melted. Serve with Tostito chips.

Corn Dip

1 - 12 oz. can shoe peg corn
    (tiny white kernel)
3/4 lb. grated sharp cheese

3 - 4 jalepeno peppers chopped
1/2 white onion chopped
1 cup mayonnaise

Mix all ingredients together and serve with Tostito chips.

Crab Dip

4 oz. cream cheese
2 oz. crab meat, shredded
4 tsp. lemon juice

2 Tbsp. chopped green onion tops
1 Tbsp. milk

Combine all ingredients together. Serve with crackers.

Yogurt Vegetable Dip

1 cup plain yogurt
3 green onions, chopped
1/2 tsp. curry powder

1/2 tsp. garlic powder
1/2 tsp. pepper

Combine all ingredients in a medium bowl. Mix well. Refrigerate several hours before serving. Serve with vegetables. Makes 1 cup.

Mexican Mild Salsa

6 oz. can tomato paste
1 3/4 cups water
2 large tomatoes or 3 medium, chopped
1/4 medium onion, chopped
1 medium green pepper, chopped
18 green olives, chopped, (optional)

2 Tbsp. chili powder
1 tsp. salt
1 tsp. lemon juice
2 tsp. basil
1 tsp. chopped chives
1 tsp. garlic powder

Combine all ingredients. Makes 5 - 6 cups. Store in refrigerator.

Salsa Reuben Dip

8 oz. cream cheese, softened
1 cup sour cream
1 cup thick 'n chunky salsa
4 oz. chopped cooked corned beef

3 oz. shredded swiss cheese
1/2 cup sauerkraut, rinsed, drained, chopped
1 - 2 garlic cloves, minced
salt and pepper

Combine cream cheese, sour cream and salsa; beat on low speed until well blended. Add all remaining ingredients. Beat on low speed until well blended. Spoon mixture into ungreased pie pan. Bake at 350 degrees for 20 - 30 minutes or until thoroughly heated. Serve warm with cocktail rye bread, tortilla chips or cut-up fresh vegetables for dipping. Store in refrigerator.

Hot Crab Dip

6 oz. crabmeat
1/2 cup sour cream
3 oz. cream cheese
1 Tbsp. lemon juice

1 tsp. prepared horseradish
2 Tbsp. minced green pepper
1 Tbsp. minced pimento
dash worcestershire sauce

Drain crabmeat, set aside. In a medium saucepan, combine sour cream, cream cheese, lemon juice and horseradish, stirring to blend. Add green pepper, pimento, worcestershire sauce and crabmeat. Stir over low heat until bubbly. Serve with French bread or crackers. Yields 2 cups.

Fresh Mushroom Dip

12 oz. pkg. bacon
1 lb. fresh mushrooms, sliced
1 large red onion, chopped
2 cloves garlic, pressed
2 Tbsp. flour
8 oz. cream cheese

2 tsp. worcestershire sauce
2 tsp. soy sauce
1/2 to 2/3 cup sour cream
salt and white pepper to taste
bread sticks or crackers

Cook bacon until crisp, remove and drain on paper towel. Discard all but 1 Tbsp. bacon grease. Add onions and saute for several minutes over medium heat. Add garlic and mushrooms, continue cooking until mushrooms begin to turn dark. Sprinkle flour over mushroom mixture and stir for one minute. Reduce heat to low and add cream cheese, worcestershire sauce, soy sauce, salt and white pepper to taste. Stir until cream cheese is melted. Remove from heat and add sour cream. Stir in bacon. Serve warm with breadsticks or crackers. May be made ahead and refrigerated. Serves 25.

Zesty Seafood Spread

16 oz. cream cheese
3/4 cup seafood (cocktail) sauce

4 1/2 oz. can shrimp

Beat softened cream cheese until fluffy. On serving plate, spread cheese into 8 inch circle. Chill at least 1 hour. Just before serving, top with chilled cocktail sauce, then shrimp which have been drained and rinsed. Garnish as desired. Serve with assorted crackers. Refrigerate leftovers.

Nacho Belle Grande

16 oz. salsa
16 oz. cream cheese
shredded lettuce
green onions, diced

tomatoes, diced
shredded cheddar cheese
sliced black olives
tortilla chips

Combine salsa and cream cheese, mixing with electric mixer until fairly smooth. Spread on platter. Layer remaining ingredients in order. Serve with tortilla chips

Olive Cheese Nuggets

1 pkg. sharp cracker barrel cheese
1/2 cup butter
1 1/2 cups flour

1 tsp. paprika
50 to 60 stuffed olives

Let cheese and butter get soft, then mix together with flour and paprika, and knead like dough. Flatten small portion in palm of hand, put olive in center, and make a ball, covering olive. Bake in preheated 400 degree oven for 15 - 20 minutes until browned. Excellent!

Cheese Krispies

1 lb. sharp grated cheese (2 cups)
2 sticks butter
2 cups plain flour

1/2 tsp. cayenne pepper
2 cups Rice Krispies

Grate cheese and let cheese and butter come to room temperature. Using dough hooks on mixer, combine cheese and butter and add flour, 1/2 cup at a time. Add cayenne pepper. Blend in rice krispies with dough hooks. Form into small balls on a cookie sheet and flatten with fork tines. Bake at 325 degrees for 10 minutes. Only let them begin to brown on the bottom. Let cool on wax paper and store in tight tin box. These freeze well.

Cheese Snack Rounds

5 oz. jar sharp cheese spread
1/2 cup Bisquick

2 Tbsp. sesame or poppy seeds

Mix cheese spread and bisquick. Shape in 1 inch diameter roll. Roll in sesame/poppy seeds. Chill for at least 2 hours. Cut into 1/4" thick pieces. Place on lightly greased cookie sheet. Bake at 375 degrees for 8 - 10 minutes.

Mini Bagel Italian Pesto Cheese Puffs

1 pkg. frozen mini bagels, thawed, split
1 1/2 cups shredded cheddar cheese
3 Tbsp. prepared pesto

1 egg white
1/2 cup diced ham
3 Tbsp. pine nuts or chopped walnuts

Arrange bagels, cut side up, on foil-lined baking sheet. Combine 1 cup cheese, pesto and egg white in food processor. Pulse 3 times to combine. Add ham; pulse 6 times or until ham is finely chopped. Spread mixture evenly over cut sides of bagels. Top with remaining 1/2 cup cheese, and sprinkle with nuts. Puffs may be covered and refrigerated up to 2 hours before baking. Bake at 450 degrees 8 - 10 minutes or until puffed and golden brown. Serve warm or at room temperature. Makes 20 appetizers.

French Onion Cheese Toasts

1 Tbsp. olive oil
1 large onion, thinly sliced (2 cups)
1 tsp. dried rosemary, crushed
1/4 tsp. salt

1/4 tsp. black pepper
12 slices French bread
1 1/2 Tbsp. Dijon mustard
1 1/2 cups shredded swiss cheese

In large skillet, heat oil over medium-high heat; add onions and cook 5 minutes, stirring occasionally. Reduce heat to medium-low and continue cooking onions 15 minutes or until browned and very soft, stirring frequently. Stir in rosemary, salt and pepper. Spread bread slices evenly with mustard. Top with cheese. Divide onion mixture evenly over cheese. Place on foil-lined baking sheet; bake at 425 degrees 10 minutes or until cheese is melted.

Curried Chicken Wings

1 cup honey
2/3 cup Dijon-style mustard
2 Tbsp. butter

3 to 5 tsp. curry powder
2 1/2 lbs. chicken wings

In small saucepan, combine honey, butter, mustard and curry. Cook and stir over medium heat until blended. Arrange chicken in a 9 x 13 pan. Drizzle with honey mixture. Cover with foil and bake at 350 degrees for 30 minutes. Remove foil and bake 30 minutes longer. Turn after 15 minutes.

Stuffed Mushrooms

1 lb. mushrooms, small to medium size
1 onion, chopped
1/4 cup green pepper
1/2 of the mushroom stems, chopped fine
8 slices of bacon, cooked & drained

4 oz. cream cheese
1/2 cup grated cheddar cheese
seasonings to taste: celery salt, garlic salt
  curry, white pepper

Remove stems from mushrooms and chop half of them. Rinse and dry mushrooms. Add butter to skillet and saute chopped onions, green pepper and stems until onions are transparent. Let cool slightly. In bowl mix onions, green pepper, stems and cream cheese. When well mixed add crumbled bacon and cheddar cheese. Season to taste. Stuff each mushroom with mixture. Place mushrooms in a buttered baking dish and bake at 350 degrees for 15 minutes or until mixture is melted. Watch closely so not to over cook. Serve hot. You may stuff mushrooms early in day. Cover and refrigerate until ready to cook. Serves 20 to 25.

Cream Cheese and Olive Appetizer Tree

Cream Cheese Mixture:
2 (8 oz.) pkg. cream cheese
1/2 cup chopped green onion
1/2 cup chopped green olives,
    (with pimentos)
1/4 tsp. garlic powder

Garnish:
2 Tbsp. sliced pimento
1 Tbsp. chopped fresh parsley
1 Tbsp. chopped green onions
1 star shape cut from red bell pepper

In medium bowl, combine all cream cheese mixture ingredients; mix well. On serving platter, shape mixture into pine tree shape, about 1/2 inch thick. Decorate tree with pimentos, parsley and onions. Place star shape on top of tree. Refrigerate 30 minutes or until firm. Serve with crackers.

Honey Garlic Spareribs

3 lbs. pork spareribs
garlic salt to taste
1/2 cup honey
1/4 cup soy sauce

3 Tbsp. cider vinegar
3 to 5 cloves garlic, minced
1/4 tsp. pepper

Season spareribs with garlic salt. Arrange in 9 x 13 pan. Cover with foil and bake at 325 degrees for 1 hour until tender. Drain all liquid. Combine remaining ingredients in saucepan and simmer 5 minutes. Drizzle honey mixture over spareribs and bake uncovered at 350 degrees for 30 minutes. Baste every 10 minutes.

Cheesy Sun Crisps

2 cups shredded cheddar cheese
1/2 cup grated parmesan cheese
1/2 cup butter
3 Tbsp. water

1 cup flour
1/4 tsp. salt
1 cup quick-cooking oats
2/3 cup roasted salted sunflower nuts

Beat cheddar cheese, parmesan cheese, butter and water with electric mixer until well blended. Add flour and salt; mix well. Stir in oats and sunflower nuts, and mix until well combined. Shape dough into 12 inch long roll; wrap securely in plastic wrap. Refrigerate at least 4 hours, or may be refrigerated up to one week. Cut roll in 1/4-inch slices and bake 8 to 10 minutes at 400 degrees until edges are light golden brown. Cool.

Water Chestnut Wrap-ups

2 - 6 1/2 oz. cans water chestnuts, drained
1 lb. bacon
12 oz. ketchup
1/2 cup sugar

1/2 cup brown sugar, packed
juice of one lemon
2 Tbsp. worcestershire sauce
2 Tbsp. dark molasses

Cut bacon strips in half and wrap around whole chestnuts, secure with toothpicks. Place chestnuts on a roasting rack and cook bacon until crisp. (Broil for 5 minutes, turn over, broil another 5 minutes.) Mix remaining ingredients and place in a shallow glass serving dish. Place chestnuts in the sauce and cook until sauce is thoroughly heated (about 20 minutes at 350 degrees).

Special Scallops

1 lb. bacon, cut in half, crosswise
2 lb. small sea scallops
1/2 cup olive oil
1 tsp. garlic powder

1 tsp. pepper
1/2 tsp. onion powder
dash oregano
fresh parsley, chopped

Wrap 1 bacon piece around each scallop, securing with wooden toothpick if necessary. Combine olive oil, garlic powder, pepper, onion powder, oregano and parsley, and pour over wrapped scallops. Marinate, covered, in refrigerator at least 4 hours. Remove scallops from marinade and place on broiler pan. Broil 4 inches from heat for 7 to 10 minutes until bacon is brown. Turn over, brown other side five minutes or until scallops are opaque. Remove toothpicks and arrange on platter.

Spinach Balls

3 1/2 lbs. frozen chopped spinach,
   thawed and well drained
2 cups seasoned bread crumbs
10 oz. freshly grated parmesan cheese
1 cup butter, melted

10 green onions, chopped
5 - 6 eggs, lightly beaten
2 Tbsp. Dijon mustard
1/4 tsp. nutmeg
1/2 tsp. white pepper

Combine all ingredients in large bowl. Form into small l-inch balls and place on an ungreased cookie sheet. Bake in a 350 degree oven for 15 to 20 minutes or until lightly browned. Serve with Dijon mustard. Spinach balls may be frozen and heated before serving. Serves 25.

Party-Time Popcorn

2 Tbsp. vegetable oil
1 cup popcorn kernels
3 cups shoestring potatoes
1 cup salted mixed nuts or peanuts
1/4 cup butter, melted

1 tsp. dill weed
1 tsp. worcestershire sauce
1/2 tsp. lemon-pepper seasoning
1/4 tsp. garlic powder
1/4 tsp. onion salt

Heat oil and pop popcorn, without adding butter or salt. Combine popcorn, shoestring potatoes and nuts in large roasting pan. Set aside. Combine butter, dill, worcestershire sauce, lemon-pepper seasoning, garlic powder and onion salt in small bowl. Pour evenly over popcorn mixture, stirring until evenly coated. Bake 8 to 10 minutes at 325 degrees, stirring once. Let stand at room temperature until cool. Store in airtight containers.

Tropical Smoothie

8 oz. vanilla yogurt
1 cup orange juice
1 medium banana, sliced
1 cup sliced strawberries

Optional - substitute 1/2 cup of pineapple
pieces for 1/2 cup of strawberries

Place all ingredients in blender and blend until smooth. Serve with a strawberry or
pineapple garnish on the glass. Serve cold.

Watermelon Cooler

3 cups watermelon, chunked and seeded
1/2 pint lemon sorbet

1/2 tray ice cubes
2 Tbsp. grape juice

Place all ingredients in a blender. Pulse blender until ice is chopped, then process at high
speed until smooth.

Special Summer Lemonade

1 cup lemon juice
1 cup orange juice
3/4 cup light corn syrup
2 cups sparkling water, chilled

2 cups ginger ale, chilled
16 oz. frozen whole strawberries or
    1 pt. fresh strawberries

Combine lemon juice, orange juice and corn syrup. Add chilled sparkling water and ginger
ale. Serve over ice with strawberries.

Banana Strawberry Yogurt Shake

1 cup frozen whole strawberries
8 oz. plain yogurt
1 ripe banana

2 Tbsp. honey
1/4 cup milk
1/2 tsp. vanilla

Place all ingredients in blender and blend until smooth and frothy.

Punch and Judy

2 Tbsp. malted milk powder
1 tsp. cocoa

1 tsp. sugar
3/4 cup milk

Mix malted milk powder and dry cocoa and sugar. Add milk and mix thoroughly in the blender.

Festive Punch

3 cups cranberry juice
1 cup orange juice
1 cup pineapple juice

1/2 cup grapefruit juice
2 large bottles ginger ale

Combine all fruit juices and mix well. Pour over ice in punch bowl. Fill bowl with ice cold ginger ale. Garnish with orange slices. Makes about 30 punch cup servings.

Patio Punch

1 pkg. cherry Kool-Aid
1 pkg. strawberry Kool-Aid
2 cups sugar
2 quarts cold water

1 6 oz. can frozen orange juice concentrate
1 6 oz. can frozen lemonade concentrate
1 pint (12 oz.) ginger ale

Combine Kool-Aid and sugar. Add water and stir. Add frozen concentrate. Chill. Add ginger ale. Pour over ice cubes. Makes 4 quarts.

Punch Favorite

2 pkgs. lemon Kool-Aid
1 pkg. orange or raspberry Kool-Aid
1 qt. sherbet (flavor to match Kool-Aid)

1 pt. vanilla ice cream
1 qt. ginger ale
ice ring made of Kool-Aid

Mash 1 pt. of sherbet in bottom of punch bowl and add Kool-Aid made according to directions on package. Make small balls of remaining sherbet and ice cream with a melon scoop and float on punch. Put in ice ring. Pour in ginger ale carefully to preserve fizz just before serving.

Frozen Fruit Punch

4 cups sugar
6 cups water
1 (46 oz.) can pineapple juice
24 oz. frozen orange juice, undiluted

12 oz. frozen lemonade, undiluted
5 bananas mashed
6 qt. ginger ale

Measure sugar and water into saucepan. Heat, stirring until sugar dissolves. Bring to boiling and boil 1 minute. Refrigerate until cold. Mix chilled mixture with pineapple juice, orange juice, lemonade and bananas. Pour into containers, cover and freeze. At serving time, partially thaw mixture and add ginger ale.

Punch

1 pkg. cherry Kool Aid
1 pkg. strawberry Kool Aid
2 cups sugar
3 qts. water

6 oz. can frozen orange juice
6 oz. frozen lemon juice
1 or 2 qts. ginger ale

Dissolve Kool Aid in sugar and water. Add frozen juices. Stir in ginger ale just before serving. Makes 1 1/2 gallons.

Almost Pink Champagne

1 bottle white grape juice, chilled
1 bottle pink grape juice, chilled

1 bottle club soda, chilled
1 Tbsp. lemon juice

Combine all ingredients in punch bowl. Stir to blend and serve immediately.

Chocolate Eggnog

7 cups milk
3/4 cup chocolate syrup
4 egg yolks
1/2 cup creamy peanut butter (opt)

2 tsp. vanilla
4 egg whites
1 cup whipping cream, whipped
cinnamon

Process 3 1/2 cups of milk, chocolate syrup, egg yolks, peanut butter and vanilla in a blender until foamy; pour into punch bowl. Stir in remaining milk. Beat egg whites until stiff peaks form and fold into milk mixture. Fold in whipped cream. Sprinkle lightly with cinnamon. Serve in punch cups.

Coffee Nog

2 tsp. instant coffee
1 Tbsp. hot water
1 qt. eggnog
1/4 cup powdered sugar

1/4 tsp. allspice
1/2 cup whipping cream, whipped
1/8 tsp. allspice

In large pitcher, dissolve coffee in hot water. Add eggnog, powdered sugar and 1/4 tsp. allspice. Blend well. Refrigerate until serving time. To serve, top each serving with whipped cream and sprinkle with allspice.

Lemon Ice Cubes

lemon juice

water

Fill ice tray with water. Then put 5 to 8 drops of lemon juice in each square. Put tray in freezer for 2 to 3 hours or until frozen. Serve with water, tea or just eat them plain.

Soup & Sandwiches

Sandwiches

Soups

Vegetable Cheese Soup

2 cups diced potatoes
1 1/2 cups onion, chopped
1 cup sliced carrots
1 cup chopped celery
2 1/4 cups water
1/4 cup butter

6 cubes chicken bouillon
2 cups milk
1/2 cup flour
3 cups shredded cheddar cheese
1 tsp. dry mustard
1/8 tsp. pepper

Combine potatoes, onion, carrots, celery, water, butter, and bouillon, bring to boil, reduce heat and simmer for 30 minutes. Combine milk and flour, beat until smooth and blend into veggie mixture. Add cheese, mustard and pepper and stir to melt. Do not boil.

Norwegian Spinach Soup

2 pkg. frozen spinach
8 cups chicken stock
3 Tbsp. butter
2 Tbsp. flour

1 tsp. lemon juice
1/4 tsp. pepper
1/8 tsp. nutmeg
thin slices of lemon

Cook spinach (defrosted and drained) in chicken stock for 10 minutes. Melt butter, and stir in flour with wire whisk. Add paste to soup and bring to a boil. Season with lemon, pepper and nutmeg. Garnish with lemon slices.

Harvest Bisque

1 - 2 lb. butternut squash, peeled and cubed
4 cups chicken stock
2 McIntosh apples, peeled and quartered

2 Tbsp. lemon juice
salt and pepper to taste
1 cup milk or cream

Cook the squash in chicken stock until tender (about 10 minutes). Add the apples, cook until soft. Puree squash and apples in processor. Reheat in stock, adding the lemon juice and seasonings to taste. Stir in milk or cream. Heat thoroughly, but do not boil. Serves 6.

Pumpkin Bisque

1 Tbsp. butter
2 Tbsp. finely minced shallots
    or white part of scallions
2 cans condensed chicken broth, undiluted
    or 2 1/2 cups homemade chicken
    broth

1 can (1 lb.) pumpkin puree
1/4 tsp. dried thyme leaves
1/8 tsp. pepper
dash ground allspice
dash nutmeg
1 cup heavy cream

In 3 qt. saucepan, over medium-low heat, melt butter. Add shallots; saute until tender, about 5 minutes. Stir in broth, pumpkin, thyme, pepper, nutmeg and allspice. Simmer, uncovered, stirring occasionally, 5 minutes. Add cream, and cook until soup is hot but not boiling. Serves 6.

Oyster Stew

2 cans oysters
1/2 cup butter
1 Tbsp. worcestershire sauce

1 qt. milk
salt and pepper to taste

In saucepan, combine oysters (including juice), butter and worcestershire sauce and boil for 2 minutes. Add milk, salt and pepper, and simmer for 1/2 hour or more.

Beef Barley Soup

1 Tbsp. vegetable oil
1 lb. beef stew meat, cut into 1/2" cubes
8 cups water
2 beef flavored bouillon cubes
1/2 cup hot water
14 oz. can stewed tomatoes
1 cup sliced carrots

1 cup sliced celery
1/4 cup parsley
1 cup chopped onion
1/2 cup barley
1/2 tsp. salt
1 1/2 tsp. pepper

In large sauce pot, heat oil over medium heat. Add beef, cook, stirring often until browned. Add 8 cups water. Bring to boil. Reduce heat, cover and simmer 1 hour. With slotted spoon, remove meat. In cup, dissolve bouillon in the hot water. Add to sauce pot with remaining ingredients. Stir in meat. Cover and simmer 2 hours or until vegetables are tender.

Hamburger Soup

1 lb. hamburger, browned
1 big can V-8 veg. juice
1 pkg. mixed frozen vegetables

1 pkg. frozen hash browns
1 pkg. onion soup mix
1 can tomatoes

Place all ingredients in crockpot and fill with water to make 2 1/2 quarts. Cook on slow all day.

Lasagna Soup

1 lb. ground beef
1 large onion, chopped
1/2 green pepper, chopped
2 celery ribs, chopped
1 cup sliced fresh mushrooms
2 garlic cloves, minced

2 tsp. Italian seasoning
salt and pepper to taste
1 can (28 oz.) crushed tomatoes
1 can (15 oz.) tomato sauce
1 lb. lasagna noodles

Brown beef, onion, green pepper, celery and mushrooms until the beef is no longer pink. Add garlic, Italian seasoning, salt, pepper, tomatoes and tomato sauce (mixture should be thick). Simmer. Meanwhile, break each noodle into bite-sized pieces, and cook according to package directions. When noodles are tender, drain off about half the water. Stir in meat sauce and heat through.

Venus DeMilo Soup

1 lb. hamburger, browned and drained
1 pkg. frozen mixed vegetables
1 can crushed tomatoes

5 cups water
1 pkg. dry onion soup mix
1 cup pasta - shells, rings or elbows

Combine all ingredients except pasta in large pot and bring to a boil. Add pasta and simmer until pasta is cooked.

Vegetable-Burger Soup

1 lb. ground beef
1 16 oz. can sliced stewed tomatoes
1 8 oz. can tomato sauce
2 cups water

1 16 oz. can mixed vegetables
1 envelope dry onion soup mix
1 tsp. sugar

Brown ground beef and drain. Add the other ingredients. Simmer and serve.

Quick and Easy Chili

1 lb. ground beef
2/3 cup chopped onions
1/2 cup chopped green pepper
1/2 cup water
1 can condensed beef broth

1 - 8 oz. can tomato sauce
1 - 6 oz. can tomato paste
2 cans kidney beans, drained, rinsed
3 tsp. chili powder

Brown ground beef with onions and green pepper. Drain. Stir in remaining ingredients. Bring to a boil. Reduce heat, simmer 15 minutes, stirring occasionally. Cover and refrigerate; use within 3 days. Individual servings can be heated in microwave.

Hearty Chicken-Broccoli Soup

2 pkg. (10 oz. each) frozen cut broccoli
with cheese flavored sauce in a pouch
1/2 cup chopped onion
1/2 cup chopped celery
1/4 cup margarine
3 Tbsp. flour
1 Tbsp. dry mustard

1/4 tsp. salt
1/4 tsp. pepper (white pepper is preferred)
3 cups milk
2 tsp. lemon juice
1 1/2 cups diced cooked chicken

Place unopened broccoli pouches in warm water to partially thaw or cut slit in center of pouch and thaw in microwave on DEFROST for 7 minutes.

In large sauce pan, saute onion and celery in margarine until crisp-tender. Mix flour, mustard, salt and pepper together and stir into the onions and celery. Cook until bubbly and smooth. Gradually add milk. Cook until mixture boils and thickens, stirring constantly. Slowly stir in lemon juice. Add chicken and broccoli. Simmer until thoroughly heated, stirring occasionally. Makes 6 cups.

Chicken Chili Soup

2 Tbsp. olive oil
1 cup chopped onion
4 oz. chopped green chilis
15 oz. can crushed tomatoes
4 cups chicken broth
1 tsp. lemon pepper
2 tsp. worchestershire sauce
1 tsp. chili powder

1 tsp. cumin
1/2 tsp. hot sauce, optional
4 Tbsp. flour
1/2 cup water
1 lb. chicken, cooked and diced
tortillas
sour cream to garnish

Saute the onions in the oil. Add the green chilis, tomatoes, chicken broth, pepper, worchestershire sauce, chili powder, cumin and hot sauce, depending on how spicy you like it. In a separate bowl, mix the flour and water, then whisk the mixture into the soup and bring it to a boil. Keep stirring. After it thickens a bit, then add the chicken pieces. Simmer for 20 minutes and serve. Garnish soup with a dab of low fat sour cream on top of the bowl of soup. Cut tortillas into strips, and put strips in oven for 8 - 10 minutes at 350 degrees to make them crispy. Put in bowls and serve with soup. Very low fat and low calories.

Corn, Sausage and Bell Pepper Chowder

2 Tbsp. butter
1 1/2 cups chopped onion
1 red bell pepper, chopped
1/2 green bell pepper, chopped
1 1/2 tsp. chopped garlic
2 cans chicken broth
1 lb. red-skinned potatoes, diced

1/4 tsp. pepper
1/4 tsp. ground cumin
3 cups frozen corn, thawed
4 oz. fully cooked kielbasa sausage, sliced
    and halved
1 cup milk
1/2 pint whipping cream

Melt butter in large dutch oven over medium heat. Add onion, both bell peppers, and garlic, and saute until tender, about 15 minutes. Add broth, potatoes, pepper and cumin. Bring to a boil. Reduce heat and simmer about 30 minutes, until potatoes are tender. Add corn, sausage, milk and cream, and simmer another 20 minutes. Add salt and pepper as desired.

Tortellini Chowder

3 cans chicken broth
1 1/2 cups thick 'n chunky salsa
1/2 tsp. grated orange peel
18 oz. refrigerated tortellini
dash salt

1 lb. pkg. frozen vegetables
   (corn, broccoli & red peppers)
1 can evaporated milk
parsley or cilantro to garnish

Combine broth, salsa and orange peel. Bring to a boil, then reduce heat and simmer 3 minutes. Stir in tortellini and vegetables. Cook over medium heat 6 - 8 minutes or until tortellini and vegetables are tender. Stir in milk and salt. Cook 1 - 2 minutes or just until thoroughly heated, stirring occasionally. Do not boil. Serve; garnish each serving with parsley or cilantro.

Zesty Clam Chowder

6 slices bacon, chopped
1 large onion, chopped
2 large potatoes, peeled and diced
1 red bell pepper, chopped
3 - 10 oz. cans baby clams, drained, liquid
reserved

2 cups milk
1/2 cup bottled clam juice
2 - 15 oz. cans cream style corn
1 Tbsp. thyme
salt and pepper

Cook chopped bacon in large saucepan until brown. Add onions and saute about 10 minutes. Add potatoes and red pepper and saute one minute. Add reserved liquid from clams, milk and bottled clam juice. Simmer chowder about 15 minutes. Add corn and clams and simmer another 5 minutes. Add in thyme, salt and pepper to desired taste. Let simmer another 20 minutes.

Creamy Crab Soup

1 pkg. crabmeat, thawed
2 Tbsp. butter
1/2 cup chopped onion
1/2 cup chopped celery
2 Tbsp. flour
dash cayenne

1/2 tsp. salt
2 cups milk
1 cup whipping cream
1 Tbsp. pale dry sherry, optional
1 tsp. lemon juice
chopped parsley

Drain crab and remove any bits of shell or cartilage. Cut the crabmeat in pieces. Saute onion and celery in butter about 10 minutes. Blend in flour and seasonings. Add milk, stir and cook until smooth and thick. Add crab and cream. Stir and heat. Mix in sherry and lemon juice, sprinkle with parsley and serve.

Shrimp Soup

2 Tbsp. butter
1/3 cup chopped green onions
3 Tbsp. flour
1/2 tsp. salt
1/2 tsp. thyme
1/4 tsp. ground red pepper
2 cans chicken broth

1 lb. pkg. frozen vegetables with pasta
1/2 lb. fresh or frozen cooked small shrimp,
thawed, shelled and deveined
1 cup whipping cream
1/4 cup grated parmesan cheese
2 Tbsp. chopped green onions

Cook onions in butter until tender. Stir in flour, salt, thyme, red pepper and 1/4 cup chicken broth. Stir until smooth and stir in remaining chicken broth. Bring to a boil. Stir in vegetables with pasta and return to a boil. Reduce heat and simmer 3 - 5 minutes or until vegetables are crisp-tender. Stir in shrimp and cream. Cook 2 - 3 minutes until thoroughly heated, stirring occasionally. Do not boil. Top each serving of soup with parmesan cheese and green onions.

Hearty Italian Bean Soup

1 Tbsp. vegetable oil
1/4 lb. cooked ham
2 celery stalks
2 medium carrots
1 medium onion
1 medium zucchini
2 cups water

2 - 15 oz. can white kidney beans
1/2 tsp. dried basil leaves
1/4 tsp. pepper
14 oz. can stewed tomatoes
13 1/2 oz. can chicken broth
1 cup chopped fresh spinach
grated parmesan cheese

In Dutch oven heat vegetable oil. Cut up and add cooked ham, celery, carrots, onion and zucchini. Open cans of white kidney beans. Rinse and drain. Remove 1 1/2 cups of beans and mash. Cook ham, vegetables, basil leaves and pepper about 15 minutes until tender. Stir in stewed tomatoes, chicken broth, chopped spinach, mashed white beans and water. Heat to boiling. Reduce heat to low. Cover and simmer 15 minutes. Stir in remaining beans. Spoon into bowls. Sprinkle each serving with grated parmesan cheese.

Cabbage Soup with Cheese

1/2 lb. bacon, chopped
1 onion, chopped
1 bunch green onions, chopped
1/2 head cabbage, chopped
2 potatoes, peeled & diced
5 cups chicken broth
1 tsp. marjoram
1 tsp. savory
1 tsp. thyme

1 tsp. sweet basil
pinch of crushed sage
salt & pepper to taste
4 oz. swiss cheese, shredded
2 oz. sharp cheddar cheese, shredded
1/2 tsp. dried dill
3/4 cup heavy cream
1/8 tsp. cayenne pepper

Saute bacon in Dutch oven over medium heat until partially crisp. Pour off all but 3 or 4 Tbsp. fat. Add onions and cabbage to pan. Saute for 5 minutes or until onions are soft. Stir in potatoes, then broth, herbs, salt and pepper. Bring to boil. Immediately reduce heat and simmer, uncovered, 30 minutes or until potatoes are quite tender. Just before serving, slowly add cheese, stirring until melted, but do not boil. Add remaining ingredients and adjust seasoning.

Cream of Spinach Soup with Cheese

3 Tbsp. butter
3 Tbsp. oil
1 small onion, minced
20 oz. frozen chopped spinach, thawed
    and drained
2 cups strong chicken broth

2 cups cream
1/2 tsp. white pepper
1/4 tsp. nutmeg
1/2 lb. cooked bacon, crumbled
1 cup grated cheddar cheese

Melt butter and oil in large saucepan over medium heat. Add onion and cook for 5 minutes. Add spinach to onions and cook for 3 minutes, stirring frequently. Blend in broth and simmer for 10 minutes. Stir in cream, pepper and nutmeg. Continue to simmer for 5 minutes. Add bacon and cheese. Serve at once.

Easy Vegetable Chowder

1 Tbsp. butter
1/2 cup chopped onion
1 can cream of potato soup

2 cups milk
1/4 tsp. dried thyme leaves
1 lb. frozen vegetables

Melt butter and add onion; cook and stir 2 to 3 minutes until tender. Stir in soup, milk and thyme. Cook until very hot, but do not boil. Add vegetables and cook 12 to 14 minutes or until vegetables are tender, stirring occasionally. Salt and pepper to taste.

Julius' Wild Rice Soup

1 cup wild rice, cooked
1/2 lb. bacon, cut up and fried
1/2 onion, diced
1 lb. Velveeta cheese, diced

1 qt. half & half
3 cans cream of potato soup
fresh mushrooms

Combine all ingredients in a crockpot. Serve with breadsticks.

Chilled Blueberry Soup

3 cups water
1 qt. blueberries
3/4 cup sugar
2 Tbsp. cornstarch

1 1/2 - 2 Tbsp. water
cinnamon
sour cream or yogurt

Add blueberries, sugar and cinnamon to 3 cups boiling water. Cook for several minutes to dissolve sugar. Set aside. Mix 1 1/2 to 2 Tbsp. water to cornstarch. Add to warm mixture and bring to boil again. Cool, cover and refrigerate. Serve well chilled with Tbsp. of yogurt or sour cream and sprinkle of cinnamon on top.

Summertime Pea Soup

10 oz. pkg. frozen tiny green peas
1 1/2 cups chicken broth
1 cup sour cream + for garnish

1 tsp. salt
1/2 tsp. pepper

Thaw peas in colander under running water. Reserve 2 Tbsp. peas for garnish. In blender, puree peas, broth and 1 cup of the sour cream. Strain soup through coarse sieve into bowl, and season with salt and pepper. Refrigerate. To serve, ladle soup into 4 bowls. Garnish with sour cream and reserved peas.

Ham Filled Sandwiches

1/2 lb. cooked ham
1 large dill pickle
4 hard cooked eggs

salt and pepper
1 tsp. mustard
1 or 2 Tbsp. mayonnaise

Grind together the ham, pickle and eggs. Season with pepper and mustard. Moisten with mayonnaise to spreadable consistency.

Fajitas

1 lb. round steak	1 cup diced tomatoes
1/3 cup lime juice	1/2 cup sliced green onions
1 1/2 tsp. garlic powder	1/2 cup shredded cheddar cheese
1/2 tsp. pepper	flour tortillas
1 cup shredded lettuce	sour cream or yogurt

Trim excess fat from round steak. Pound steak to 1/4 inch thickness. Put in covered bowl. Sprinkle both sides with lime juice, garlic powder and pepper. Marinate in refrigerator for 6 to 8 hours. Drain marinade and discard. Broil steak over med-hot coals 2 to 3 minutes each side or pan broil over medium heat 5 to 7 minutes, turning occasionally. Carve across the grain into thin slices. To serve, warm flour tortillas and pile on lettuce, tomatoes, onion, cheese, meat strips and sour cream or yogurt.

Sloppy Joes

1 lb. ground beef	1 1/2 tsp. worcestershire sauce
1/2 cup chopped onion	1 Tbsp. vinegar
1/2 cup chopped celery	1 8 oz. can tomato sauce
1 Tbsp. sugar	1/2 cup ketchup

Fry together beef, onion, celery and sugar. Add remaining ingredients and simmer on stove until done.

Open Faced Grilled Cheese

bread, lightly toasted	mustard
sliced American cheese	stuffed olives for garnish
bacon strips	parsley for garnish

Place a slice of cheese on each slice of toasted bread, which has been spread with mustard. Cross two strips of bacon on cheese and grill under low flame until bacon is crisp and cheese melted. Garnish with stuffed olives and parsley.

Easy Pizza Burgers

1/2 lb. extra-lean ground beef
1/4 cup finely chopped onion
1 - 6 oz. can tomato paste
3/4 tsp. dried Italian seasoning

1 - 4 oz. can mushrooms, drained
4 English muffins, halved
1 cup shredded mozzarella cheese

Brown ground beef and onion; drain. Stir in tomato paste, Italian seasoning and mushrooms. Mix well. Cover and refrigerate; use within 3 days. Spread about 1/4 cup beef mixture on muffin half. Sprinkle 2 Tbsp. cheese over top. Place on paper towel and microwave on HIGH for 1 to 2 minutes or until beef mixture is hot and cheese is melted. To prepare in oven, place sandwiches on baking sheet and bake at 400 degrees for 10 to 15 minutes or until beef mixture is hot and cheese is melted.

Chicken Rolls

6 chicken breasts, cooked, diced
2 pkg. crescent rolls
8 oz. cream cheese

3/4 stick butter
1 tsp. pepper
3 slices bread, made into crumbs

Mix chicken pieces with cream cheese, butter and pepper. Flatten out crescent rolls. Put 1 heaping Tbsp. in center and seal it in the roll. Dip in melted butter and then bread crumbs. Bake at 350 degrees for 20 - 30 minutes or until golden brown. Top with chicken gravy or onion-mushroom sauce.

Hot Tuna Buns

8 hamburger buns
1 can tuna
1 small onion, chopped
salad dressing

3 hardboiled eggs, chopped
1/4 lb. Velveeta cheese, diced
salt and pepper to taste

Mix all ingredients, using enough salad dressing to moisten. Fill hamburger buns and wrap each sandwich in foil. Bake at 350 degrees for 15 to 20 minutes.

Hawaiian Pita Sandwiches

8 - 10 oz. ham, diced
8 oz. can pineapple tidbits
1/2 cup chopped carrots
1/4 cup salad dressing

1 Tbsp. honey mustard
3 pocket (pita) breads, halved
6 lettuce leaves

Combine all ingredients except pocket breads and lettuce. Mix well. Line each pocket bread half with lettuce leaf. Fill with ham salad.

Fresh Veggie Pitas

1/4 cup shredded carrots
3/4 cup shredded cucumber
3/4 cup sliced mushrooms
1 1/4 cups diced tomatoes

1/4 tsp. thyme
2 Tbsp. finely chopped onion
2 Tbsp. grated parmesan cheese
4 pocket (pita) breads

Cook carrot, cucumber and mushrooms in microwave until tender (2 - 4 minutes). Add remaining ingredients, except pocket breads. Divide warm filling among the 4 pitas and stuff filling in pockets.

Salads

Fruit Salads

Meat Salads

Vegetable Salads

Salad Dressings

Snicker Salad

3 apples, diced
4 bananas, sliced
lemon juice

4 large Snickers candy bars, diced
16 oz. Cool Whip

Mix apples, bananas, candy bars and Cool Whip together. Serve immediately. To mix up ahead of time, rinse the diced apples and sliced bananas in lemon juice, and then they can be held in the refrigerator for several hours until time to serve. Mix the ingredients together just before serving.

Creamy Cookie Salad

2 cups buttermilk
2 - 3 oz. pkg. vanilla instant pudding
16 oz. Cool Whip

15 oz. can mandarin oranges, drained
11 oz. pkg. Keebler Fudge Striped Cookies

Beat together buttermilk and pudding. Stir in cool whip and oranges. Break cookies into bite size pieces and add to mixture. Chill for one hour and serve.

Frosted 7-Up Salad

2 pkg. lemon jello
2 cups boiling water
2 cups 7-Up
20 oz. can crushed pineapple, drained
1 cup small marshmallows
1 can mandarin oranges
1 cup pineapple juice

1/2 cup sugar
1 egg, beaten
2 Tbsp. flour
2 Tbsp. butter
1 cup whipped cream
grated cheese

Dissolve jello in boiling water. Add 7-up and let partly set. Add crushed pineapple, marshmallows and oranges. Chill until set. Mix together pineapple juice, sugar, egg and flour. Cook until thick. Cool slightly and add butter. When chilled, fold in whipped cream and spread over jello that is set. Sprinkle with grated cheese and serve on a lettuce leaf.

Orange Ice Cream Salad

1 pkg. (3 oz.) orange jello
6 oz. frozen orange juice
1 can mandarin oranges, drained

1 cup hot water
1 cup vanilla ice cream

Dissolve jello in hot water. Add the frozen orange juice. Let cool. When mixture starts to gel, beat until creamy and add ice cream, which has softened enough to mix. Add the orange sections. Pour into mold and refrigerate overnight or at least 6 hours. Serves 6 - 8.

Frozen Salad

2 large cans crushed pineapple
3 oz. pkg. lime jello
10 oz. pkg. mini marshmallows

1 pint cream, whipped
small pkg. of crushed pillow mints
1 can fruit cocktail, drained.

Mix the pineapple, jello and marshmallows and let stand overnight in the refrigerator. Then add the whipped cream, pillow mints and fruit cocktail. Put in a 9 x13 pan and freeze. Serve frozen on lettuce leaves.

Fruit Divine

4 large bananas
1 1/2 cups fresh blueberries
1/2 cup butter, melted

3/4 cup brown sugar
1 cup sour cream

Heat oven to 375 degrees. Slice banana into 1/2" thick slices and put into the bottom of a glass or ceramic pie plate. Pour washed blueberries over the bananas. Sprinkle brown sugar over the fruit, and then pour the melted butter over that. Bake for 20 to 30 minutes, and you will want to gently stir after 15 minutes. Spread sour cream over the top after removing from the oven. Serve warm.

Bing Cherry Salad

1 pkg. cherry gelatin
1 cup boiling water or juice
1 cup pineapple juice
3 oz. pkg. cream cheese

1 cup chopped pecans
1 cup drained, crushed pineapple
1 cup canned bing cherries, pitted

Dissolve gelatin in hot liquid, add cream cheese softened with a little gelatin mixture and pineapple juice. Stir until smooth, chill until syrupy, beat until fluffy. Fold in nuts, cherries, and pineapple. Pour in mold and refrigerate.

Cherry Whipped Salad

1 pkg. cherry jello
1 cup boiling water
1 can pitted bing cherry sauce

1 cup miniature marshmallows
1/2 cup whipping cream, whipped
3/4 cup walnuts

Dissolve jello in boiling water. Add juice from cherry sauce and marshmallows. Let set. When partially set, beat. Add whipped cream, cherries, nuts and place in mold. Chill.

Cranberry Salad

3 oz. pkg. red jello
2 Tbsp. lemon juice
boiling water
1 can jellied cranberry

1 cup cream, whipped
1/4 cup mayonnaise
1/4 cup powdered sugar

Combine lemon juice with boiling water to make one cup. Dissolve jello in juice and water. While hot, add cranberries. Beat with egg beater until well blended. Pour into 8x8 pan. Chill. Combine whipped cream, mayonnaise, and powdered sugar. Spread over set jello, and sprinkle with finely chopped nuts.

Cranberry Salad

1 cup cranberries, cut up
2 cups sugar
1 small orange, ground up, rind & sections
3 oz. pkg. lemon jello

2 cups hot water
1 cup mini marshmallows
1 cup chopped celery
1 cup chopped apple

Add sugar to cranberries and orange and let stand overnight. Dissolve jello in hot water, let partially set, add cranberries and rest of ingredients and chill.

Marshmallow Cranberry Salad

3 cups whole frozen raw cranberries,
    ground coarse
3/4 cup sugar
2 1/3 cups miniature marshmallows

8 1/2 oz. can crushed pineapple, drained
1/2 cup chopped nuts
1 cup whipping cream, whipped

Add sugar to cranberries and chill 2 hours. Then add marshmallows, pineapple and nuts and lastly fold in whipped cream. Freeze or set overnight in refrigerator. Makes a 10x8 pan or ring mold.

Pineapple Strawberry Bavarian

3 oz. pkg. strawberry jello
1 cup boiling water
1/2 cup pineapple tidbits, drained

1/2 cup pineapple syrup
1 cup heavy cream, whipped
1/2 cup sliced strawberries, fresh or frozen, drained

Dissolve jello in boiling water. Drain pineapple tidbits, reserving syrup. Add syrup to the jello mixture. Chill until slightly thickened. Set bowl firmly in bowl of ice. Whip jello until light and fluffy. Fold in whipped cream, pineapple tidbits and strawberries. Chill until firm.

Pink Champagne Salad

16 oz. cream cheese
1 1/2 cups sugar
20 oz. frozen strawberries with juice

2 cans crushed pineaapple, drained
16 oz. Cool Whip
4 bananas

Beat cream cheese and sugar together. Add in strawberries and pineapple, and mix well. Fold in Cool Whip, and add bananas last.

Patriotic Gelatin Salad

2 3 oz. pkg. berry blue flavored gelatin
2 3 oz. pkg. strawberry gelatin
4 cups boiling water, divided
2 1/2 cups cold water, divided
2 env. unflavored gelatin

2 cups milk
1 cup sugar
2 cups sour cream
2 tsp. vanilla extract

In four separate bowls, dissolve each package of gelatin in 1 cup boiling water. Add 1/2 cup cold water to each and stir. Pour one bowl of blue gelatin in an oiled 10 in. fluted tube pan. Chill until almost set, about 30 minutes. Set other three bowls of gelatin aside at room temperature. Soften unflavored gelatin in remaining cold water; let stand 5 minutes. Heat milk in a saucepan over medium heat just below boiling. Stir in softened gelatin and sugar until sugar is dissolved. Remove from heat; stir in sour cream and vanilla until smooth. When blue gelatin in pan is almost set, carefully spoon 1 1/2 cups sour cream mixture over it. Chill until almost set, about 30 minutes. Carefully spoon one bowl of strawberry gelatin over cream layer. Chill until almost set. Carefully spoon 1 1/2 cups cream mixture over strawberry layer. Chill until almost set. Repeat, adding layers of blue gelatin, cream mixture and strawberry gelatin, chilling in between each. Chill several hours or overnight. This salad takes time to prepare since each layer must be almost set before the next layer is added, but it looks wonderful and is very special when completed.

Ribbon Salad

3 oz. pkg. lime jello
3 oz. pkg. lemon jello
15 large marshmallows, cut up
1 cup whipping cream, whipped

1 cup crushed pineapple, drained
1/2 cup sugar
3 oz. pkg. cream cheese
3 oz. pkg. cherry jello

Make lime jello according to package directions and set until firm. (Put in 9 x 13 pan.) Make lemon jello according to package directions, adding marshmallows with the hot water and stirring until marshmallows are dissolved before adding cold water. Set aside until syrupy. Beat together cream cheese and sugar, add pineapple and whipped cream. Add mixture to syrupy lemon jello. Pour on top of lime jello and chill until firm. Make cherry jello according to package directions and set aside until cool and syrupy. Pour on top of lemon jello mixture. Chill.

Perfection Salad

1 1/2 cups lemon gelatin
5 cups hot water
5 cups cold water
5 cups finely shredded cabbage
5 cups finely diced celery

5 jars chopped pimentos
6 chopped sweet pickles
5 tsp. salt
10 Tbsp. lemon juice

Dissolve gelatin in hot water, then add cold water. Let jello start to thicken and then add remaining ingredients. Serves 40.

Sunshine Salad

3 oz. pkg. orange jello
3 oz. pkg. lemon jello
1 cup pineapple juice
8 oz. cream cheese

2/3 cup whipping cream, whipped
1 large can crushed pineapple, drained
grated cheddar cheese

Dissolve orange jello in 2 cups boiling water. Chill until firm. Dissolve lemon jello in 1 cup boiling pineapple juice mixed with 1 cup water. Let cool. Fold in softened cream cheese, the whipped cream, and pineapple. Pour this over the set orange jello. Sprinkle with grated cheese. Chill.

Peach Salad

1 1/2 cups orange jello
2 cups hot water
2 cups cold water
3/4 cup sugar

3 cups drained & diced peaches
1/2 tsp. almond flavoring
2 cups whipping cream, whipped

Dissolve jello in hot water. Add sugar, flavoring, cold water, peaches and whipped cream at one time. Put in 9 x 13 pan. Cool.

Strawberry Pineapple Jello Salad

6 oz. pkg. strawberry jello
1 cup hot water
1 lb. box sweetened sliced strawberries

8 oz. can crushed pineapple with juice
8 oz. sour cream
chopped pecans

Dissolve jello in hot water. Add strawberries and crushed pineapple. Pour half of jello mixture into 8-inch square dish. Chill. (Leave other half of jello mixture at room temperature.) Cover the chilled jello with sour cream. Add the remaining jello mixture and chill. Sprinkle chopped pecans over the top.

Cranberry Cream Jello Salad

3 oz. box cherry jello
1 cup hot water
16 oz. can whole cranberry sauce

1/2 cup diced celery
1/4 cup chopped walnuts
1 cup sour cream

Dissolve jello in water. Cool, then add remaining ingredients. Pour into quart mold and chill.

Jello Salad

2 - 3 oz. pkg. lemon jello
3 1/2 cups boiling water
2 or 3 bananas
1 can mandarin oranges, drained
48 small colored marshmallows
1 large can crushed pineapple, drained
    (reserve juice)

1 cup pineapple juice and water
1/2 cup sugar
1 egg, beaten
2 Tbsp. flour
2 Tbsp. butter
1 cup cream, whipped

Combine jello and boiling water and set slightly. Add bananas, oranges, marshmallows and pineapple to jello mixture and chill until firm. Combine pineapple juice and water, sugar, egg, flour and butter. Cook until it coats spoon. Cool and add whipped cream. Unmold salad and spread custard on top.

Speedy 24-Hour Salad

3 oz. pkg. instant vanilla pudding
2 cups milk
1 cup cream, whipped
14 oz. can fruit cocktail

11 oz. can mandarin oraanges
4 oz. jar maraschino cherries
6 oz. pkg. miniature marshmallows
2 medium bananas, sliced

Prepare pudding mix with milk, according to package directions. Fold in whipped cream. Drain liquid from fruit and fold fruit into pudding mixture along with marshmallows and bananas. Chill thoroughly.

Pineapple Float

2 cans crushed pineapple
1 1/2 bags (15 oz.) mini marshmallows

4 pints whipping cream

Combine pineapple and marshmallows in large bowl overnight in refrigerator. The next day, whip the whipping cream and fold into the mixture.

Sudden Fruit Salad

1 can lemon pie filling
1 can fruit cocktail, drained

1 cup whipping cream
1 cup mini marshmallows

Whip cream stiff, add marshmallows. Fold in lemon filling and fruit cocktail. Chopped nuts are optional. Can make a day ahead.

Cottage Cheese Salad

1/2 lb. cottage cheese
1/2 cup sour cream
1/2 bunch radishes

2 tsp. salt
1/2 medium cucumber
1/2 green pepper

Slice radishes, dice cucumber and chop pepper fine. Mix vegetables, add salt and sour cream to cheese and combine vegetables and cheese.

Quick Salad

12 oz. cottage cheese, small curd
4 1/2 oz. Cool Whip

1 large can crushed pineapple, drained
3 oz. pkg. orange jello, or any flavor

Mix all ingredients together in bowl. (Do not add any water to jello). This may be frozen if desired.

Sin Salad

1 8 oz. carton Cool Whip
1 can sweetened condensed milk
1 can cherry pie filling

2 cups marshmallows
1 med. can crushed pineapple
Small amount of nuts and coconut

Mix first 2 ingredients in a large bowl. Add pie filling and crushed pineapple. Do not drain. Add rest of ingredients. Chill.

Pretzel Salad

1 cup crushed pretzels
1/2 cup butter, melted
1/3 cup sugar
8 oz. cream cheese

1/2 cup sugar
20 oz. can crushed pineapple, drained
8 oz. Cool Whip

Mix pretzels, butter, and 1/3 cup sugar together and spread on a cookie sheet. Roast at 400 degrees for 5 minutes. Mix together the cream cheese and 1/2 cup sugar, then add the pineapple and Cool Whip. Just before serving, mix in the pretzels.

Glorified Rice

1 cup rice
1 large can crushed pineapple, drained
1 cup heavy cream, whipped

1 lb. marshmallows, quartered
   or mini marshmallows

Boil rice in salted water just until tender. Add pineapple and marshmallows and let stand several hours. Before serving, add whipped cream.

Curried Rice Salad

1 cup cooked long-grain rice
1/2 cup chopped celery
1/4 cup finely chopped green onions
1/4 cup chopped sweet red pepper

2 Tbsp. slivered almonds, toasted
1/4 cup fat-free Italian dressing
2 tsp. vinegar
1 tsp. curry powder

Combine first 5 ingredients in a medium bowl. Combine Italian dressing, vinegar and curry powder and add to rice mixture and toss well. Cover and chill.

Rotini Pasta Salad

1 box Rotini
1/2 cup oil
1/2 cup soy sauce
2 Tbsp. honey, melted
2 Tbsp. lemon juice
pepper to taste
2 cups Miracle Whip
1 cup sugar

4 Tbsp. vinegar
broccoli, cut up
carrots, cut up
celery, diced
onions, chopped
black olives, chopped
radishes, sliced

Cook box of Rotini in water, 1/4 cup oil and 1/4 cup soy sauce. Drain. While warm, add to Rotoni 1/4 cup oil, 1/4 cup soy sauce, honey, lemon juice and pepper. This may be stored in refrigerator for quite a while, if desired. Then add Miracle Whip, sugar and vinegar, and vegetables in desired amounts. This serves many!

Broccoli Pasta Salad

Dressing:
1/3 cup extra-virgin olive oil
1/4 cup red wine vinegar
1 clove garlic, crushed
1/2 tsp. salt
1/2 tsp. oregano
1/2 tsp. pepper

15 oz. can white kidney beans, rinsed,
   drained
2 tomatoes, chopped
1/2 lb. (2 1/2 cups) pasta twists
1 bunch broccoli, trimmed, thinly sliced,
   and tops in florets

Whisk together all dressing ingredients. Stir in beans and parsley. Let stand. Cook pasta in plenty of boiling salted water about 8 minutes or until almost cooked. Stir in all the broccoli. Cook 4 minutes or until pasta and broccoli are done and firm to the bite. Drain pasta. Add to dressing along with tomatoes. Gently toss. Let cool to room temperature, stirring occasionally. Serve at room temperature.

Macaroni Pasta Salad

2 boxes macaroni shells
1 cup grated cheddar cheese
1 cup chopped sweet pickles
2/3 cup diced onion
2 cups Miracle Whip

10 oz. frozen peas
1 1/2 tsp. salt
1/2 tsp. pepper
3/4 tsp. minced garlic

Cook macaroni shells, rinse in cold water. Add remaining ingredients. Refrigerate several hours or overnight, and serve.

Bowtie Tomato Pasta Salad

4 cups uncooked bowtie pasta
1/2 cup shredded parmesan cheese
6 plum tomatoes, diced
1 cup frozen peas, thawed

2 tsp. dried basil leaves
1 Tbsp. olive oil
1 tsp. minced garlic

Cook pasta to desired doneness as directed on package. Drain, and keep warm. Combine 1/4 cup of cheese and remaining ingredients. Mix well. Add cooked pasta to tomato mixture and toss gently. Sprinkle with remaining cheese.

Frog Eye Salad

16 oz. Acini de Pepe pasta
1 cup sugar
2 Tbsp. flour
2 1/2 tsp. salt
1 3/4 cups pineapple juice
2 eggs, beaten
1 Tbsp. lemon juice

1 Tbsp. oil
3 cans mandarin oranges
2 cans pineapple chunks
1 can crushed pineapple
16 oz. cool whip
1 cup miniature marshmallows

Combine sugar, flour and 1/2 tsp. salt. Gradually add pineapple juice and beaten egg. Cook mixture over medium heat until thickened. Add lemon juice. Cool mixture. Boil 3 qts. of water and remaining 2 tsp. salt and oil. Add pasta. Cook until done. Drain pasta. Rinse with water. Drain again. Cool to room temperature. Combine egg mixture with pasta. Mix lightly but thoroughly. Refrigerate overnight in tight container. Drain oranges, pineapple chunks and crushed pineapple. Add oranges, pineapple, cool whip and miniature marshmallows to egg and pasta mixture. Mix lightly and thoroughly. Refrigerate until chilled in air tight container. Makes 25 servings.

Spaghetti Salad

1/2 lb. spaghetti (angel hair), cooked and
drained
1 large bottle zesty Italian dressing
Salad Supreme seasoning to taste
1 onion, chopped

2 tomatoes, chopped
1 cucumber, chopped (optional)
1 green pepper, chopped

Mix all together. This should be made a day ahead of time, and it can be kept in the refrigerator for up to two weeks.

Apricot Turkey Salad

4 cups cooked pasta - shells, rings or
    elbows
1 cup diced turkey or chicken
1 cup diced apricots
1 cup sliced almonds

diced scallions to taste
1 cup yogurt
1/4 cup apricot jam
1 Tbsp. mustard

Mix together pasta, turkey, apricots, almonds and scallions. Mix separately the yogurt, apricot jam, and mustard. Then combine both mixtures together and chill several hours before serving.

Chicken Wild Rice Salad

1 cup wild rice, washed & drained
3 cups chicken broth
1 cup chopped celery
1/4 cup chopped green pepper
1 bunch green onions & tops
2 Tbsp. diced pimento

1/4 cup sweet pickle relish
1/2 cup slivered almonds or cashews
8 oz. frozen peas, thawed
2 cups cooked chicken, cubed
Miracle Whip salad dressing

Place rice and broth in a 3 quart covered casserole dish. Bake at 350 degrees for 1 1/2 hours. Chill rice. Add the remaining ingredients. Mix all together and chill overnight. May need to add more salad dressing before serving. Very good served with grapes and melon.

Strawberry Spinach Chicken Salad

4 cups torn prewashed fresh spinach or
    mixed greens
2 cups cooked chicken, cut into strips
2 cups fresh strawberries, halved
1 1/2 cups seedless green grapes

1/4 cup Italian salad dressing
1/4 cup orange juice
1 tsp. Dijon mustard
1 tsp. finely grated orange peel, optional
2 Tbsp. sliced almonds, toasted

Arrange spinach on 4 chilled plates. Place chicken strips in the center of the plates, arranging the strawberries and grapes around the chicken. Combine the salad dressing, orange juice, mustard and orange peel and mix well. Drizzle over salads. Sprinkle with almonds.

Baked Seafood Salad

7 1/2 oz. crabmeat (1 can), drained
4 1/2 oz. shrimp (1 can), or fresh, cooked
1 1/2 cup chopped celery
1/4 cup chopped green pepper
1/4 cup chopped onion
1/4 cup chopped pimento

1/2 cup mayonnaise
juice of 1/2 lemon
1/2 tsp. worcestershire sauce
1/2 tsp. salt
dash of red pepper (liquid)

Topping:
1 1/4 cup crushed Ritz crackers
    or bread crumbs
1 Tbsp. grated onion

1/2 tsp. worcestershire sauce
2 cloves garlic, crushed

Combine all ingredients in casserole. Mix ingredients for topping and cover mixture in casserole. Bake at 350 degrees for 25 minutes. Good with rice and crusty sourdough bread.

Shrimp Salad

1 cup shrimp
1 cup chopped celery
2 cups chopped hard boiled eggs
1 Tbsp. chopped onion
chopped nuts, optional

1 cup chopped stuffed olives
1 Tbsp. chopped green pepper
4 Tbsp. mayonnaise
1 cup whipping cream, whipped

Mix and serve on lettuce. Sprinkle with chopped nuts.

Pasta Shrimp Salad

Dressing:
1/3 cup mayonnaise
1/3 cup plain low-fat yogurt
1 tsp. dried basil
1/4 cup chopped onion
1 clove garlic, chopped
1 1/2 tsp. red wine vinegar

1/2 lb. (3 cups) pasta shells
1 cup frozen green peas, thawed
3/4 lb. cooked, cleaned medium shrimp
1 cup ripe avocado, diced
1/2 cup sliced scallions
*   (white & green parts)*

In blender, puree all dressing ingredients until smooth. Cook pasta according to package directions. Stir in peas and cook 30 seconds. Drain, and add to dressing. Cool to room temperature, stirring. Stir in shrimp, avocado and sliced scallions. Serve at room temperature.

HELPFUL HINT - How to peel and dice an avocado: Using a paring knife, slice avocado in half lengthwise, cutting around the pit. Separate halves by twisting in opposite directions. Carefully peel off the skin with your fingers (or a sharp paring knife). Using the edge of a spoon, gently lift out the pit. Cut each half lengthwise into thin slices. Next, cut crosswise at 1/2 inch intervals. To prevent discoloration, toss with lemon juice.

Layered Shrimp Salad

14 oz. frozen cooked shrimp, peeled,
deveined
2 cups shredded lettuce
1/4 cup finely chopped green onion
1 cup thinly sliced celery
1 cup coarsely grated carrots
1 cup frozen peas
1/2 cup grated cheddar cheese

2/3 cup natural yogurt
2 Tbsp. mayonnaise
1 Tbsp. lemon juice
2 tsp. honey
1 Tbsp. finely chopped chives
1/4 tsp. dill weed

Thaw shrimp and drain well. In a large glass bowl, layer lettuce, onion, celery, carrots, peas, shrimp and cheese. Refrigerate for several hours. Combine remaining ingredients and serve with the salad.

Marinated Shrimp and Vegetables

1 lb. raw medium shrimp
1 cup fresh cauliflowerets
4 oz. small fresh mushrooms
1 cup sliced zucchini
1 large green pepper
1 large red pepper
3/4 cup lemon juice

1 Tbsp. green onion
2 tsp. sugar
1 tsp. salt
1/2 tsp. dried dill weed
5 drops hot pepper sauce
3/4 cup vegetable oil

Cook, peel and devein shrimp. Slice zucchini. Cut peppers into squares. Place shrimp, cauliflower, mushrooms, zucchini and peppers in large shallow dish. In small bowl combine all remaining ingredients except oil; mix well. Add oil; shake well. Pour over shrimp mixture. Cover; chill 6 hours or overnight, stirring occasionally. Garnish as desired. Refrigerate leftovers.

Sesame Beef and Veggie Salad

3 Tbsp. soy sauce
2 Tbsp. sesame oil
1 Tbsp. vinegar
1 tsp. grated ginger root
1 garlic clove, minced
1/8 tsp. crushed red pepper flakes
1 lb. boneless top sirloin beef steak

1 tsp. garlic salt
1 lb. pkg. frozen vegetables
     (broccoli, carrots & water chestnuts)
4 cups shredded napa cabbage or lettuce
2 Tbsp. sesame seed, toasted
1/4 cup thinly sliced green onions

Combine soy sauce, sesame oil, vinegar, ginger root, garlic, and red pepper to make dressing. Blend well. Sprinkle steak with garlic salt and broil to desired doneness. Meanwhile prepare frozen vegetables according to package directions; drain. Line large serving platter with cabbage. Cut steak diagonally into small slices. Combine steak and vegetables. Pour dressing over and toss to combine. Spoon mixture over cabbage. Sprinkle with toasted sesame seed and onions. (Toast sesame seeds by stirring in skillet over medium heat about 5 minutes.)

Asian Chicken Salad

2 cups deli cream-style coleslaw
2 - 5 oz. cans chunk white chicken,
    drained, flaked
8 oz. can pineapple tidbits, drained

1/4 tsp. ginger
8 leaf lettuce leaves
1 cup chow mein noodles

Combine coleslaw, chicken, pineapple and ginger; mix well. Arrange lettuce leaves on 4 individual serving plates. Spoon coleslaw mixture over lettuce. Sprinkle each with 1/4 cup chow mein noodles. Serve immediately.

Light Fiesta Potato Salad Ole'

2 lbs. red potatoes, cooked, peeled, cubed
2 cups shredded cheddar cheese
2/3 cup diced red bell pepper
2/3 cup canned black beans, rinsed,
drained
1/2 cup thinly sliced celery

1/3 cup thinly sliced green onions
2 Tbsp. chopped fresh cilantro
1/2 tsp. salt
3/4 cup fat free ranch dressing
1/2 cup prepared chunky salsa
fresh cilantro sprigs, optional

Combine potatoes, 1 1/2 cups cheese, pepper, beans, celery, green onions, cilantro and salt. Combine dressing and salsa. Pour over potato mixture. Toss gently to coat. Chill at least 1 hour before serving. Serve salad topped with remaining 1/2 cup cheese, and garnish with cilantro sprigs, if desired.

Parmesan Tossed Salad

1 - 2 heads lettuce, torn
1 head cauliflower, cut up
chopped onion
1 lb. bacon, cooked and crumbled

Dressing:
1 cup mayonnaise
1/2 cup parmesan cheese
1/4 tsp. garlic powder
1 Tbsp. white vinegar
1/4 cup sugar

Mix salad ingredients together. Toss with dressing just before serving.

Tropical Garden Salad

1 head lettuce, torn
2 cans tropical fruit salad, drained

1 1/2 tsp. poppy seed
1/3 cup purchased Honey Dijon dressing

Break up lettuce to bite size pieces. Add fruit salad and poppy seed. Just before serving, toss with dressing. Serve immediately. So easy and quick, but a delicious change of pace from regular tossed salad.

Finnish Fresh Mushroom Salad

1/2 lb. thin-sliced fresh mushrooms
1 cup water
1 Tbsp. lemon juice
1/4 cup sour cream

2 Tbsp. grated onion
1/2 tsp. salt
dash black pepper
Romaine lettuce

Boil water and lemon juice. Add mushrooms, cover. Simmer 2 - 3 minutes. Remove and drain. Combine sour cream, onion, salt and pepper. Toss mushrooms carefully in sauce. Serve on crisped romaine leaves.

Spinach Salad

1 pkg. fresh spinach, washed and drained
3 hard boiled eggs, sliced
1/2 to 3/4 lb. bacon, cooked and crumbled
1 can bean sprouts, drained
1 can water chestnuts, drained and sliced

Dressing:
1 cup oil
3/4 cup sugar
1/3 cup ketchup
1/4 cup vinegar
2 Tbsp. worcestershire sauce
1 small onion, chopped

Mix ingredients for dressing in blender. Dressing can be made a day or two ahead for flavors to blend. Mix salad ingredients and toss with dressing when ready to serve.

Mandarin Orange Garden Salad

1 head of lettuce	Dressing:
leaf lettuce	1/4 cup oil
romaine lettuce	2 Tbsp. sugar
spinach greens	2 Tbsp. vinegar
any other greens desired	1 Tbsp. snipped parsley
2 large cans mandarin oranges	1/2 tsp. salt
	dash pepper
	dash tabasco

Mix greens and desired amount of mandarin oranges together. Mix all ingredients for dressing and shake well. Just before serving, drizzle dressing over the greens and toss.

Pea Salad

1/2 cup Miracle Whip	1 cup peanuts
1/4 cup Kraft Italian dressing	6 slices bacon (browned & crumbled)
10 oz. frozen peas	1/4 cup red onion, chopped
1 cup celery, diced	pimento if desired

Mix all ingredients and serve when peas have thawed.

Broccoli Salad

1 large head broccoli, chopped	1 cup mayonnaise
4 - 5 green onions, sliced	1/4 cup white sugar
1/2 cup golden raisins	2 Tbsp. vinegar
10 strips bacon, cooked crisp and crumbled	

Mix all ingredients. Refrigerate at least 4 hours before serving.

Broccoli and Grape Salad

3 bunches broccoli, cut up
3 - 4 cups red grapes, cut in half
4 green onions, chopped

1 cup mayonnaise
1 Tbsp. vinegar
2 Tbsp. sugar

Mix together onions, mayonnaise, vinegar and sugar, and pour over grapes and broccoli. Let stand several hours.

Oriental Salad

1 head cabbage, shredded
4 green onions, chopped
3/4 cup sunflower seeds
1 cup sliced almonds
3/4 cup oil
2 Tbsp. sugar

2 pkg. chicken flavored Ramen noodles
flavoring packets from noodles
1 box frozen pea pods
1/2 tsp. pepper

Mix cabbage and onions. Cover and refrigerate. Toast seeds and nuts on baking sheet at 350 degrees for 7 minutes. Crumble Ramen noodles. Mix dressing: oil, sugar, pepper and chicken flavoring packets. Just before serving, toss together the cabbage, nuts and seeds, ramen noodles, thawed pea pods, and dressing.

State Fair Cole Slaw

1 head cabbage
1 green pepper
1 red pepper
parsley
1 small onion

Sauce:
2 cups vinegar
2 Tbsp. butter
1 cup water
1 cup brown sugar
1 cup white sugar
2 Tbsp. pickling spice

Cut cabbage, green and red peppers, parsley and onion fine. Mix all this together. Cook all sauce ingredients together. Put spice in a bag or else strain it out. This sauce will keep a long time in refrigerator. Put enough sauce on cabbage mixture just to moisten.

Best Ever Coleslaw

1 head shredded cabbage
1/2 chopped green pepper
2 cups water
4 tsp. salt
1 cup sugar

1/2 cup water
1 tsp. mustard seed
1/2 cup vinegar
1 small can pimento
3 ribs of celery, chopped

Soak cabbage and pepper in brine made of 2 cups of water and 4 tsp. salt for 1/2 hour. Drain. Cook together sugar, water, mustard seed and vinegar. Cool. Add to cabbage along with can of pimento and chopped celery. Store in refrigerator. Drain and serve. This keeps for days.

Coleslaw

4 cups chopped cabbage
1 Tbsp. chopped onion
1/2 cup grated carrots
1 Tbsp. chopped green pepper
1 tsp. salt

1/4 tsp. pepper
1/4 tsp. celery seed
1/4 tsp. white mustard seed
2 Tbsp. sugar
3/4 cup mayonnaise.

Mix together and let stand for 12 hours before serving.

Ham Apple Coleslaw

3 cups shredded cabbage
1 1/2 cups cooked slivered ham
2 medium apples, cored and diced

1/3 cup mayonnaise
2/3 Tbsp. vinegar

Chill ham and cabbage. Just before serving, add the apples and stir in mayonnaise and vinegar. Makes 6 servings.

Hubbel House Salad Dressing

1 can tomato soup
2/3 cup salad oil
2/3 cup brown sugar
1/2 cup ketchup
1/4 cup vinegar
1 tsp. salt

1 tsp. paprika
1 tsp. mustard
2 Tbsp. mayonnaise
1 small onion, cut fine
1 Tbsp. green pepper, cut fine

Put all ingredients in a bowl and beat well. Do not cook. Keep in a covered jar in refrigerator.

Marge's French Dressing

1/2 cup powdered sugar
1/2 cup catsup
1/4 cup vinegar
1/2 cup to 1 cup salad oil

1 tsp. salt
1/2 tsp. paprika
1 small onion, diced

Beat well until thoroughly blended.

Thousand Island Dressing

1 cup mayonnaise
1/2 cup chili sauce
2 hard boiled eggs, chopped
2 Tbsp. green pepper, chopped
2 Tbsp. celery, chopped

1 1/2 Tbsp. finely chopped onion
1 tsp. paprika
1/2 tsp. salt
1/4 cup chopped green olives

Combine all ingredients. Mix well. Makes 1 1/2 cups.

Cucumber Dressing

1/2 cup mayonnaise
1/2 cup sour cream
1 tsp. chopped chives
1/4 tsp. salt

dash pepper
1/2 tsp. dill seed
3/4 cup sliced cucumbers

Mix all ingredients and chill well.

Honey Dressing for Fruit

2/3 cup sugar
1 tsp. dry mustard
1 tsp. paprika
1 tsp. celery seed
1/4 tsp. salt

1/3 cup honey
5 Tbsp. vinegar
1 Tbsp. lemon juice
1 tsp. grated onion
1 cup salad oil

Mix dry ingredients, add honey, vinegar, lemon juice, and onion. Pour oil into mixture, very slowly, beating constantly with electric mixer. Store in refrigerator. Very good on mixed fruit. Serve in pitcher.

Oil Dressing for Cabbage & Lettuce Salad

1 pt. cooking oil
1 pt. vinegar
2 cups sugar

2 tsp. salt
2 tsp. celery seed
2 Tbsp. grated onion

Mix all together. Refrigerate.

Vegetables

Vegetables

Vegetable Casserole

1 1/2 lbs. fresh asparagus
1 1/2 lbs. fresh broccoli
3/4 lb. fresh mushrooms
1/4 cup butter, melted
1/4 tsp. nutmeg

salt and white pepper to taste
3/4 cup gruyere cheese, grated
1 cup thin sliced ham, cut up
5 eggs, beaten
1/3 to 1/2 cup grated parmesan cheese

Trim and cook asparagus and broccoli and cut into l-inch pieces. Slice and saute mushrooms. Place asparagus, broccoli, and mushrooms in a large buttered baking dish. Pour melted butter over vegetables. Season with nutmeg, salt, and pepper. Sprinkle with Gruyere cheese and ham. Cover with beaten eggs. Top with parmesan cheese and bake at 350 degrees for 30 minutes or until eggs are set and top is golden brown.

Curly Vegetables

3 cups water
2 - 3 oz. pkg. ramen noodles, chicken
       flavored
1 lb. pkg. frozen vegetables
4 green onions, diced

1 red or yellow bell pepper, sliced
1 Tbsp. cornstarch
1 tsp. sugar
1/2 tsp. ginger
2 Tbsp. dry sherry, optional

Bring water to a boil, and add ramen noodles, reserving seasoning packets. Boil for 3 minutes or until noodles are tender, stirring frequently. Drain noodles, saving water. Add frozen vegetables to same boiling water and return to a boil. Reduce heat and simmer 4 minutes, then add onions and bell peppers. Combine cornstarch, noodle soup seasoning packets, sugar, ginger and sherry, mixing until smooth. Add to the vegetable mixture and coor 1 to 2 minutes or until thickened and bubbly, stirring constantly. Serve over noodles on serving platter or toss with noodles in serving bowl.

Asparagus au Gratin

1 can (15 oz.) green asparagus
milk
Schillings white sauce mix
4 hard boiled eggs, sliced

2 - 3 cups croutons
1 cup shredded cheese
paprika

Drain asparagus and reserve juice, adding milk to make 1 cup. Make white sauce according to package directions. Layer ingredients in baking dish, starting with asparagus, then eggs, then croutons, and then cheese. Pour white sauce over and sprinkle with paprika. Bake at 350 degrees for about 15 minutes, or until cheese melts.

Creamy Asparagus Pasta

1 lb. fresh asparagus, cut diagonally into
    2 inch pieces
1 lb. linguinie or fettucine
1 pint light cream
2 Tbsp. butter

1 tsp. salt
1 tsp. pepper
1 lemon
1 clove minced garlic

Put asparagus into 4 quarts boiling water for 3 - 4 minutes. In separate frypan, saute butter, garlic and then add drained asparagus. Add cream and let simmer for 10 minutes. Take the water that asparagus boiled in and cook your pasta according to box directions. Cut the lemon in half, remove the seeds, and squeeze the juice from both halves into simmering asparagus. After pasta is cooked, drain and put into big pasta bowl. On top of the pasta, pour the asparagus and cream over it, then sprinkle 1 tsp. of grated rind from the lemon over the pasta and asparagus. Serves 4 - 6 people.

Cheesy Zucchini Casserole

2 tomatoes, peeled, cut into wedges
2 small zucchini, sliced
2 small yellow squash, sliced
1/8 tsp. thyme
1/2 tsp. basil

dash garlic powder
1/2 cup shredded cheddar cheese
1/2 cup grated parmesan cheese
1/3 cup bread crumbs
1 cup shredded mozzarella cheese

Combine tomatoes, zucchini, squash, seasonings, and cheddar cheese. Place in 1 1/2 quart casserole. Top with parmesan cheese and bread crumbs. Bake at 350 degrees about 45 minutes until vegetables are tender. Sprinkle with mozzarella cheese. Let stand 5 minutes before serving. Serves 6 - 8.

Zucchini Bake

1 lb. grated zucchini (raw)
1 Tbsp. grated onion
1/2 cup cracker crumbs
2 beaten eggs

1/2 tsp. salt & pepper (each)
1/4 cup melted butter
1/2 cup cheddar cheese

Combine all ingredients and place in buttered dish. Bake for 35 minutes covered and 10 minutes uncovered at 350 degrees. Serves 4 - 6.

Scalloped Zucchini

6 cups thinly sliced zucchini
1 cup boiling water
2 eggs, beaten
1 tsp. salt
1/2 tsp. worcestershire sauce
1 tsp. finely chopped onion
1/4 cup finely ground dry bread crumbs
1 Tbsp. butter or margarine, melted

White Sauce:
1 or 2 Tbsp. butter
2 Tbsp. flour
1/4 tsp. salt
1 cup milk

To make white sauce, melt butter in a saucepan. Blend in flour until mixture is smooth. Add salt. Add milk slowly while stirring rapidly to prevent lumping. Bring mixture to a boil, stirring constantly. Reduce heat and cook one minute, stirring constantly. Remove from heat.

Cook zucchini in boiling water or steam it until tender; drain well. Stir a small amount of white sauce into eggs, then gradually stir eggs into remaining sauce. Stir in salt, worcestershire sauce, onion and cooked squash. Place mixture in a greased 1-quart casserole. Mix bread crumbs with butter and sprinkle over squash mixture. Bake at 325 degrees for about 35 minutes.

Zucchini Bars

1 cup pepperoni, sliced thin and cut in quarters
3 cups grated zucchini
1 cup Biscuit mix
1/2 cup grated parmesan cheese
1/2 cup chopped onion
1/2 tsp. salt
1/2 tsp. oregano

1 chopped garlic clove
2 tsp. parsley
1/2 green pepper, diced
1/2 cup skim milk
6 eggs, beaten
2 Tbsp. oil
1/2 cup grated mozzarella cheese

Mix all ingredients except mozzarella cheese. Bake in 9 x 13 pan at 350 degrees for 30 - 35 minutes. Halfway through baking, sprinkle mozzarella cheese on top. Let stand 5 minutes before cutting into bars. Serves six.

Spinach Casserole

2 - 10 oz. pkgs. frozen, chopped spinach,
   thawed and drained
2 cups creamed style cottage cheese
1/4 cup butter, cut into pieces

1 1/2 cups American cheese, cubed
3 eggs, beaten
1/4 cup flour
1 tsp. salt

Thoroughly combine all ingredients in mixing bowl. Pour into greased crock pot. Cover and cook on high 1 hour, then low for 4 or 5 hours. In the oven, bake 1 hour at 350 degrees to brown top and heat through and then low heat until served.

Baked Corn

1 can whole corn, drained
1 can creamed corn
1 box Jiffy corn muffin mix

1/2 cup butter or margarine, melted
1 egg
8 oz. sour cream

Mix all ingredients together, and put in 2 qt. baking dish. Bake at 350 degrees for one hour or more.

Swedish Red Cabbage

1/4 cup unsalted butter
4 tart green apples (Granny Smith)
   peeled, cored, coarsely chopped
1 large onion, thinly sliced
2 lbs. red cabbage, shredded
1/4 cup packed brown sugar

2 Tbsp. cider vinegar
1 tsp. salt
1/4 tsp. ground cloves
1/4 tsp. ground allspice
1/3 cup dry red wine
2 Tbsp. red or black currant jelly

Melt butter in heavy large Dutch oven over medium-high heat. Add chopped apples and onion and saute until tender, about 10 minutes. Stir in cabbage and cook until slightly wilted, stirring frequently, about 8 minutes. Stir in sugar, cider vinegar, salt, cloves and allspice. Cover and cook until cabbage is crisp-tender, stirring occasionally, about 10 minutes. Uncover, add dry red wine and jelly and cook 5 minutes longer. Season to taste with salt and pepper. Serve warm, room temperature or chilled. (This can be prepared 1 day ahead. Cover and refrigerate. Reheat over low heat if serving warm.)

Squash Casserole

6 cups diced yellow squash
1 small onion, diced
2 cans cream of chicken or mushroom
    soup, undiluted

1 cup (8 oz.) sour cream
1/2 cup butter or margarine, melted
1 bag (12 ounces) stuffing mix

In a skillet, saute the squash and onion; drain. Place half in a greased 3-qt. baking dish.
Combine soup, sour cream and butter; pour half over squash and onion. Sprinkle with half
of the stuffing mix. Repeat layers. Bake, uncovered, at 350 degrees for 40 minutes.

Broccoli Casserole

1 onion, diced
1/2 stick margarine
1 pkg. (9 oz.) chopped broccoli
1 can cream of chicken soup

1/4 cup water
3/4 cup Minute Rice
1/2 cup Cheese Whiz (or cheese chunks)

Saute onion and butter. Add the broccoli, soup, water and rice. Then stir in the cheese.
Mix all together and pour in casserole dish and bake, covered, at 350 degrees for 30 - 40
minutes.

Snow Peas Oriental

1 tsp. light sesame oil
1/2 lb. fresh snow pea pods, trimmed
1/2 cup sliced carrots
1/4 cup sliced water chestnuts

1/2 cup chicken broth, undiluted, no-salt
1 tsp. low-sodium soy sauce
1 tsp. cornstarch

Coat a nonstick skillet with cooking spray. Add oil, and place over medium-high heat until
hot. Add snow peas and carrots. Saute 2 minutes. Add water chestnuts and broth.
Bring to a boil. Cover, reduce heat, and simmer 5 minutes or until vegetables are
crisp-tender. Combine soy sauce and cornstarch, stirring until cornstarch dissolves. Add
to vegetable mixture. Cook over medium heat, stirring constantly, until sauce thickens.
Serve immediately.

Peas and Mushrooms

2 Tbsp. butter
1/4 cup chopped celery
2 Tbsp. finely chopped onion

4 oz. can sliced mushrooms
1 pkg. frozen peas
1 small jar diced pimento

Melt butter, and add celery and onion, and cook until tender. Add remaining ingredients and cook until thoroughly heated. This recipe can be easily done in the microwave also.

Carrot Coins

2 lbs. carrots
1 medium onion, chopped
1 green pepper, chopped
1 can tomato soup
1/2 cup salad oil
1 cup sugar

3/4 cup cider vinegar
1 tsp. dry mustard
1 tsp. salt
1 tsp. worcestershire sauce
1 tsp. pepper

Peel carrots and slice into 1/4 inch coins. Cook carrots about 20 - 25 minutes until tender, then drain. Combine carrots with all ingredients while warm. Marinate at least 12 hours in refrigerator. Serve cold.

Scalloped Carrots

4 cups sliced carrots
1 medium onion, chopped
3 Tbsp. butter
1 can cream of celery soup
1/2 tsp. salt

1/8 tsp. pepper
1/2 cup grated cheddar cheese
1/3 cup herb bread crumbs
1/3 cup butter

Cook carrots, drain. Cook onion in butter until soft. Stir in soup, salt, pepper, cheese and carrots. Place in greased 2 quart casserole. Toss bread crumbs with 1/3 cup of butter. Spoon over carrots. Bake at 350 degrees until thoroughly heated, about 20 minutes.

Sour Cream Cucumbers

2 medium cucumbers, sliced
1 small onion, sliced
1/2 cup sour cream

1 Tbsp. vinegar
1 tsp. sugar
1/2 tsp. salt

Combine cucumbers and onions. Stir together sour cream, vinegar, sugar and salt. Toss with vegetables. Cover and chill, stirring occasionally. Makes 3 to 4 cups.

Sweet Potato Souffle

3 cups sweet potatoes, baked & mashed
1 cup sugar
2 or 3 eggs
1 cup evaporated milk
1 stick margarine
1 tsp. vanilla

1 cup chopped pecans
1/2 cup flour
1 cup brown sugar
1 stick margarine, melted

Mix sweet potatoes, sugar, eggs, evaporated milk, 1 stick margarine and vanilla, and pour into buttered casserole. Mix pecans, flour, brown sugar, and melted margarine and put on top of casserole mixture. Bake at 350 degrees for 30 - 35 minutes.

Orange-Glazed Sweet Potatoes

6 cooked sweet potatoes
1 1/4 cups brown sugar
1/2 cup orange juice

2 Tbsp. orange rind
4 Tbsp. melted butter

Peel the cooked potatoes. Slice in half lengthwise and place in a shallow baking pan. Sprinkle the sugar over them and add the other ingredients. Bake at 400 degrees 45 minutes to 1 hour. If basted during baking, they are more attractive.

Baked Stuffed Sweet Potatoes

6 sweet potatoes
butter or margarine
1/2 tsp. salt

1/4 cup orange juice
1/2 cup butter or margarine
1 Tbsp. grated orange rind

Scrub potatoes; dry; rub lightly with margarine; prick well with fork. Bake at 350 degrees for one hour or until tender. Remove from oven; cut in half and scoop out potatoes leaving shells intact. Mash potatoes; add salt, 1/2 cup butter or margarine, orange rind and juice. Fill shells with mixture. Return potatoes to oven for 15 minutes and heat through. Potatoes may be garnished with sliced oranges, if desired. Serves 6.

Twice Baked Potatoes

12 potatoes, baked
3/4 cup milk
3/4 cup butter
8 oz. cream cheese

4 tsp. chives
1/4 tsp. garlic powder
1 tsp. thyme
1 tsp. salt

While baked potatoes are still hot, cut in half, scoop out potato, and leave half shells intact to fill later. Melt butter and milk together. Beat potatoes with electric mixer, adding melted butter/milk mixture and remaining ingredients. Beat well. Fill potato shells with potato mixture. Sprinkle with paprika and chives. Reheat in oven at 325 degrees to serve hot. These can be done a day ahead, refrigerated and warmed up to serve. If cold, it takes about 30 - 45 minutes to heat. Do not overheat, or potato mixture will "boil" out of the shells. Shredded cheese can be sprinkled on top to melt while reheating if desired.

Potato Spinach Casserole

6 - 8 lg. potatoes, peeled, cooked &
    mashed
1 cup sour cream
2 tsp. salt
1/4 tsp. pepper

2 Tbsp. chopped chives or green onion tops
1/4 cup butter
1 pkg. frozen chopped spinach
    (thaw & drain)
1 cup (4 oz.) shredded cheddar cheese

Combine all ingredients except cheese. Spoon into greased 2 qt. casserole. Bake uncovered at 400 degrees for 15 minutes. Top with cheese and bake 5 minutes longer. Makes 6 - 8 servings.

New Potatoes and Peas

10 - 12 small new potatoes
1 lb. pkg. frozen peas
1 Tbsp. butter
1 Tbsp. flour

1/2 tsp. salt
1/8 tsp. pepper
1 cup milk

In medium saucepan, bring water to boil, enough to cover potatoes. Add potatoes and cook 12 - 15 minutes until tender, adding peas for the last 5 minutes. Drain and cover to keep warm. Melt butter, then blend in flour, salt and pepper, mixing until smooth. Gradually add milk, and cook and stir 6 to 8 minutes or until mixture boils and thickens, stirring constantly. Add cooked potatoes and peas, and heat through. Delicious with a new harvest of potatoes and fresh from the garden peas!!

Cheesy Potatoes

1/2 pkg. frozen hash browns,
    O'Brien style
3/4 cup frozen peas

4 oz. Cheese Whiz, Mexican flavor
1/4 cup chopped salami

Mix all ingredients in pan and cook about 10 minutes or until potatoes are done. This can be baked in the oven for 30 minutes at 350 degrees instead of on the stove. Use regular Cheese Whiz for a milder flavor.

Confetti Scalloped Potatoes

1/2 cup butter or margarine
1/2 cup chopped onion
1 pkg. (16 oz.) frozen hash brown
    potatoes
1 can cream of mushroom soup, undiluted
1 soup can milk

1 cup (4 oz.) shredded cheddar cheese
1 small green pepper, cut into strips
2 Tbsp. chopped pimento
dash of pepper
1 cup cheese cracker crumbs, divided

In a skillet, melt butter over medium heat. Saute onion until tender. Stir in potatoes, soup and milk. Add cheese, green pepper, pimento, pepper and 1/2 cup of the crumbs. Pour into shallow casserole; top with remaining crumbs. Bake at 375 degrees for 35-40 minutes.

Scalloped Potatoes

8 medium sized potatoes, thinly sliced
1/4 cup chopped green pepper
1/4 cup minced onion
1 tsp. salt

1/8 tsp. pepper
1 can cream of mushroom soup
1 cup milk

Alternate layers of potatoes, green pepper and onion in greased baking dish, season each layer with salt and pepper. Mix mushroom soup and milk; pour over potatoes. Cover and bake at 350 degrees for 1 1/2 hours.

Buffet Potatoes

1/4 lb. butter
1 cup onion, chopped
1 cup green pepper, chopped
1/3 cup flour
1 tsp. salt
1/2 tsp. white pepper
3 cups milk or half & half

1 1/2 lb. Gruyere cheese, grated
12 cups cubed cooked potatoes
8 oz. pimentos, chopped
3 Tbsp. fresh parsley, chopped
4 cups bread crumbs
2/3 cup butter, melted
bacon, cooked, crumbled

Preheat oven to 375 degrees. In large pot, melt 1/4 lb. butter. Add onion and green pepper. Cook over medium heat until tender, stirring occasionally. Blend in flour, salt and pepper (use additional seasonings if desired). Add milk, stir constantly over medium-high heat until mixture thickens. Stir in cheese and remove from heat. Place potatoes in large baking dishes. Sprinkle pimentos over potatoes and mix lightly. Divide thickened sauce among baking dishes, pouring over each dish. In a medium bowl mix bread crumbs, parsley and 2/3 cup melted butter. Sprinkle crumb mixture over potatoes. Bake 30 to 40 minutes until heated through. Serve hot. Serves 25.

Latkes

6 medium potatoes
1 small onion
2 eggs, beaten
2 Tbsp. all-purpose flour
1/3 tsp. baking powder

1 tsp. salt
vegetable oil
applesauce, optional
parsley sprigs, optional

Peel and shred potatoes. Place shredded potatoes in a colander; rinse with cold water. Squeeze potatoes between paper towels to remove excess moisture. Combine potatoes, eggs, onion, flour, baking powder and salt. Pour oil to depth of 1/4 inch into a large heavy skillet. Drop 1/4 cup potato mixture at a time into hot oil; press into 3-inch rounds with the back of a fork. Fry over high heat until golden brown, turning once. Drain on paper towels. Serve with applesauce, and garnish with parsley sprigs, if desired. Yield: 10 latkes.

Old Fashioned Baked Beans

1 1/2 cup dried beans
1/4 cup onion, chopped
1/4 lb. salt pork
1 tsp. ginger

1 tsp. dry mustard
1 tsp. salt
1 scant cup sugar

Soak beans overnight and drain. Cover with water and ginger and bring to boil, then simmer slowly until done. Drain. Mix onion, salt pork, mustard, salt, and sugar and mix with beans. Put in baking dish, cover, and bake 6 - 8 hours at 200 degrees. Uncover beans the last hour.

Baked Beans

28 oz. can Bush's Baked Beans
1/2 lb. bacon
1 1/2 tsp. mustard
1/4 cup ketchup

1/4 cup chopped onion
1/4 cup brown sugar
1 Tbsp. vinegar

Combine all ingredients and put in electric roaster. Bake for 2 hours at 350 degrees.

Portabella Crimini Stir Fry

1 1/2 lbs. portabella mushrooms	1/4 - 1/2 tsp. garlic powder
2 medium onions	2 oz. vegetable oil
2 stalks celery	1/2 cup chicken stock
2 green peppers	2 Tbsp. soy sauce
8 oz. crimini mushrooms sliced	2 tsp. cornstarch mixed with 2 tsp. water
1 tsp. ginger	

Roast portabella mushrooms for 15 minutes at 375 degrees; let cool. Slice mushrooms into 1/4" strips. Slice onions from stem to bottom into strips. Cut celery on 45 degree angle, cut peppers top to bottom into strips. Slice crimini mushrooms. Saute onions, green peppers, celery, ginger and garlic in oil until tender. Add chicken stock and soy sauce, simmer one minute. Thicken with cornstarch mixture. Simmer 2 - 5 minutes. Add both kinds of mushrooms. Simmer 5 minutes and serve over rice or linguini.

Gourmet Mushroom Fettuccini

1 pkg. fettuccini florentine	3 cloves garlic, minced
3 Tbsp. extra virgin olive oil	1/2 cup pine nuts
1 pkg. Phillips Gourmet Mushroom Blend	3 oz. sun dried tomatoes, soft and minced

Cook fettuccini according to package directions. Heat oil and saute remaining ingredients 2 - 3 minutes. Remove from heat; toss with hot cooked fettuccini.

Breads

Breads

Coffeecake, Rolls

Waffles, Pancakes

Light & Fluffy Waffles

1 3/4 cups flour
1/2 tsp. salt
1/2 tsp. soda
2 tsp. baking powder

2 cups buttermilk
2 egg yolks - reserve whites
1/2 cup oil

Sift dry ingredients together. Add buttermilk, egg yolks and oil. Whip egg whites and fold into batter.

Waffles Supreme

4 eggs, separated
2 cups milk
3 cups sifted flour
5 tsp. baking powder

1 tsp. salt
1 Tbsp. sugar
2/3 cup butter, melted

Beat egg yolks one minute. Add milk gradually with sifted dry ingredients. Add shortening. Fold in stiffly beaten egg whites last. Makes 8 waffles.

Norwegian Pancakes

1 cup sugar
4 eggs
1/2 tsp. salt

2 cups milk
2 cups flour
Pam cooking spray

Mix batter in large bowl. Heat a medium frying pan and apply a thin coat of Pam spray. Pour a thin layer of batter into frying pan. Flip pancake after it bubbles and browns lightly. Remove from frying pan. Add butter, sugar, jelly or jam or anything else you might like. Roll into a tube, then enjoy it.

Banana Pancakes

2 tsp. baking soda
2 cups buttermilk
2 cups flour
2 eggs

3 Tbsp. melted butter
2 tsp. salt
2 cups sliced bananas (4 to 5 med. bananas)
Maple syrup

In large bowl dissolve baking soda in buttermilk. Add flour, eggs, butter and salt; stir lightly. Batter should be streaky and lumpy. Gently fold in bananas. Drop by spoonful onto hot, lightly oiled griddle or skillet. Turn when bubbles begin to break. Cook until golden brown. Serve with maple syrup.

Strawberry-Filled French Toast

8 oz. cream cheese, softened
12 slices bread
1/2 cup strawberry jam
3 eggs
1/2 cup milk

1/2 tsp. vanilla
1/4 tsp. nutmeg
1/4 cup butter
maple syrup
fresh fruit

Spread cream cheese on 6 bread slices. Spread jam over cream cheese. Top with remaining bread slices. Cut diagonally. Beat together eggs, milk, vanilla and nutmeg. Set aside. Place butter in 15 x 10 pan. Place under broiler until melted. Dip each triangle in egg mixture and place in baking pan. Broil 5 - 6 inches from heat for 2 - 3 minutes per side. Serve with maple syrup and fresh fruit. Serves six.

Baked Orange French Toast

1 1/2 cup orange juice
8 eggs
2 loaves French bread

1 cup butter
1 1/2 cup sugar
1 1/4 tsp. cinnamon

Mix butter, sugar and cinnamon, and spread on greased cookie pans. Beat together eggs and orange juice. Slice French bread, dip in egg mixture, and lay in mixture on cookie sheet. Bake at 325 degrees for 25 minutes. Flip bread over about 10 minutes before finished. After baking, let set for one minute. Serve with honey or syrup.   Serves about 10 people.

Banana French Toast

1 egg, slightly beaten
2 egg whites
1 Tbsp. honey
1/4 tsp. cinnamon

1/4 cup skim milk
1 ripe banana, mashed
non-stick vegetable spray
10 slices whole wheat bread

Heat griddle or skillet to medium heat (350 degrees). In a shallow bowl or pie pan, combine egg, egg whites, honey, cinnamon, milk, and banana; mix well. Spray non-stick vegetable spray onto the griddle. Dip bread in the egg mixture, turning to coat both sides. Cook on griddle, about four minutes on each side, or until golden brown. Serve. If desired, serve with reduced-calorie syrup; 3/4 cup has about 120 calories. 5 servings of 2 slices each. Nutrient Analysis per serving: 189 calories, 55 mg cholesterol, 4 gm fat, 359 mg sodium.

Banana Chocolate Brunch Cake

Cake:
1 pkg. Banana Quick Bread Mix
3/4 cup water
3 Tbsp. oil
3 eggs
3/4 cup chopped banana
1/2 cup chocolate chips

Topping:
1/3 cup reserved quick bread mix
1/3 cup chopped pecans
3 Tbsp. sugar
2 Tbsp. butter
Glaze:
3 Tbsp. chocolate chips
1 tsp. oil

Spray springform pan with nonstick cooking spray. Reserve 1/3 cup quick bread mix for topping. Combine remaining quick bread mix, water, oil and eggs. Stir with spoon until mix is moistened. Pour half of batter into pan. Sprinkle with banana and chocolate chips. Spoon remaining batter over chips and carefully spread to cover. Combine reserved quick bread mix, pecans and sugar. Add butter and mix until crumbly. Sprinkle over batter. Bake at 375 degrees for 30 - 40 minutes or until golden brown and edges start to pull away from sides of pan. Cool 10 minutes. Remove sides of pan. Melt glaze ingredients over low heat, stirring constantly until smooth. Drizzle over cake. Cool 20 minutes. Serve warm or cool.

Frosted Orange Rolls

dough for rolls (breadmaker or frozen)　　　*4 Tbsp. orange juice*
6 Tbsp. soft butter　　　*3 cups powdered sugar*
2 Tbsp. grated orange rind

Combine all ingredients (except dough) to make orange frosting. Roll out dough just like for cinnamon rolls, except spread dough with creamy orange frosting. Use 1/2 of frosting on dough and make rolls. Bake for 25 - 30 minutes at 375 degrees. Spread rest of frosting on rolls after they are baked. Enough frosting for six dozen rolls.

Bear Claws

1 egg　　　*1/2 tsp. almond extract*
3/4 cup ground almonds　　　*1 pkg. refrigerated crescent rolls*
2 Tbsp. flour　　　*2 Tbsp. sliced almonds*
1 Tbsp. powdered sugar　　　*1 - 2 Tbsp. sugar*
1 Tbsp. butter

Beat egg, and reserve 1 Tbsp. separately. Set aside. Stir in ground almonds, flour, powdered sugar, butter and almond extract. Refrigerate the mixture 15 minutes for easier handling. Unroll dough into 2 long rectangles, and firmly press perforations together to seal. Roll half of almond filling into long rope, and place lengthwise down center of dough rectangle. Repeat with remaining filling and dough. Fold dough over almond filling lengthwise, pressing unfolded edges to seal. Cut each strip crosswise into 4 pieces. Cut 4 slashes in each piece from unfolded edge to center. Curve each piece slightly to fan out and form claw shape. Brush tops with reserved beaten egg, and sprinkle with sliced almonds and sugar. Bake at 375 degrees for 13 - 15 minutes. Serve warm.

Quick Coffee Rolls

2 pkg. refrigerator biscuits　　　*1/2 cup orange marmalade*

Spread marmalade in bottom of a layer 9" pan which has been well greased. Take packages of refrigerator biscuits, separate them and roll in melted butter. Put the biscuits in pan and bake at 400 degrees for 20 minutes. Remove from oven and let stand 3 minutes before turning over on a serving plate.

Darlene's Cherry Cheese Danish

2 cans crescent rolls
8 oz. cream cheese
1/3 cup powdered sugar

1 egg, separated
1/2 tsp. vanilla
1 can cherry pie filling

Beat cream cheese, powdered sugar, egg yolk, and vanilla until smooth.   Lay crescent roll rectangles out flat on a cookie sheet in two long rows, with the edges hanging off the edge of the cookie sheet. Spread cream cheese mixture on the "bottom" half of the crescent rolls. Put pie filling on top of the cream cheese mixture. Fold the crescent rolls in half, bringing the edges hanging off the pan over towards the center. Seal edge. Brush dough with beaten egg white. Bake for 30 minutes at 350 degrees. Drizzle with powdered sugar glaze.

Cinnamon Swirl Coffee Cake

1 stick butter
1 cup sugar
2 eggs
2 cups flour
1 tsp. baking powder
1 tsp. baking soda

1/4 tsp. salt
2 cups sour cream
1 tsp. almond extract
1/4 cup sugar
1 tsp. cinnamon
1/2 cup chopped walnuts

Cream together butter and 1 cup sugar. Add eggs, flour, baking powder, baking soda and salt. Then add sour cream and almond extract. Mix topping together of 1/4 cup sugar, cinnamon and walnuts. Pour half of batter into greased and floured tube pan. Sprinkle half of topping over it. Add rest of batter, and sprinkle remaining topping over it. Swirl batter with knife. Bake at 350 degrees for 45 minutes to one hour.

Double Toffee Coffee Cake

2 cups flour
2 tsp. baking powder
1 cup sugar
1 tsp. salt
3 oz. pkg. instant vanilla pudding
3 oz. pkg. instant butterscotch pudding
1 cup water

3/4 cup oil
1 tsp. vanilla
4 eggs
Topping:
1 1/2 cups brown sugar
1 Tbsp. cinnamon
1 cup chopped nuts

Beat all ingredients together for 2 minutes. Pour 1/3 batter in 9 x 13 greased and floured pan. Sprinkle 2/3 part of topping on batter. Add rest of batter and top with remaining topping. Bake at 350 degrees for 40 - 45 minutes.

Night-Before Coffee Cake

2/3 cup soft butter
1 cup sugar
1/2 cup brown sugar
2 eggs
2 cups flour
1 tsp. baking powder

1 tsp. soda
1 tsp. cinnamon
1/2 tsp. salt
1 cup buttermilk
1/2 cup chopped dates

Topping:
1/2 cup brown sugar
1/2 tsp. cinnamon
1/4 tsp. nutmeg
1/2 cup chopped nuts

Cream butter and sugars until light. Add eggs and beat well. Add dry ingredients alternately with buttermilk. Beat until smooth. Stir in dates, and pour in 9 x 13 pan. Sprinkle topping over top of mixture. Cover with foil, and refrigerate overnight, or may be baked immediately after preparing. Bake for 35 - 40 minutes at 350 degrees.

Favorite Coffee Cake

3 cups flour
1 1/2 cups sugar
5 tsp. baking powder
1 1/2 tsp. salt
1/2 cup shortening
1 1/2 cups milk
2 eggs
1/2 tsp. vanilla
1/2 tsp. almond extract

Topping:
2/3 cup packed brown sugar
1/2 cup flour
1 tsp. cinnamon
6 Tbsp. firm butter
Frosting:
1 cup powdered sugar
3 Tbsp. melted butter
1 tsp. almond extract

Heat oven to 375 degrees. Grease a 9 x 13 pan. Blend all ingredients for coffee cake and mix for 1/2 minute vigorously. Pour into pan. Make topping and put on top of coffee cake. Bake for 25 -30 minutes. Make frosting. Add a few teaspoons of milk to make correct consistency. Pour on coffee cake after it is out of oven.

Cranberry Coffee Cake

1/2 cup butter, softened
1 1/2 cups sugar
2 eggs
1 tsp. vanilla extract
1 1/2 tsp. almond extract
1 cup sour cream

2 cups flour
1 tsp. baking soda
1 tsp. baking powder
1 tsp. salt
1 cup whole berry cranberry sauce

Preheat oven to 350 degrees. Cream butter and sugar in large bowl. Beat in eggs and extracts until well blended. In another bowl mix flour, baking powder, baking soda and salt. Add flour mixture to creamed mixture, alternating with sour cream. Pour half of batter into greased tube or Bundt pan. Spoon cranberry sauce over batter. Top with remaining batter. Bake 55 to 60 minutes or until toothpick inserted in center comes out clean. Cool in pan 10 minutes. If desired, glaze with l cup confectioners sugar mixed with 3 Tbsp. milk and 1/2 tsp. almond extract. Serves 14 to 16.

Blueberry Buckle

3/4 cup sugar
1/4 cup soft butter
1 egg
1/2 cup milk
2 cups flour
2 tsp. baking powder
1/2 tsp. salt
2 cups blueberries

Crumb Mixture:
1/2 cup sugar
1/3 cup sifted flour
1/2 tsp. cinnamon
1/4 cup soft butter

Mix sugar, butter and egg. Stir in milk. Sift together dry ingredients and stir into mixture. Gently stir in berries. Top with crumb mixture. Bake 45 minutes in greased and floured 9 x 13 pan at 350 degrees.

Working Girl Rolls

1 pkg. dry yeast
2 cups warm water
1/4 cup sugar

1 egg
1/4 cup oil
4 cups self-rising flour

Dissolve yeast in warm water and set aside. Mix sugar, egg and oil. Add flour alternately with yeast mixture. Drop by spoonful into greased muffin tins. Bake at 425 degrees until golden brown.

Oven Doughnuts

5 Tbsp. butter	1/4 tsp. nutmeg
1/2 cup sugar	1/2 cup milk
1 beaten egg	Topping:
1 1/2 cups flour	6 Tbsp. butter
2 1/2 tsp. baking powder	1/2 cup sugar
1/4 tsp. salt	1 tsp. cinnamon

Cream together 5 Tbsp. butter, 1/2 cup sugar and egg. Set aside. Mix together flour, baking powder, salt and nutmeg. Add dry ingredients alternately with milk to first mixture. Place in greased muffin tins. Fill 1/2 full. Bake at 350 degrees for 20 to 25 minutes. Melt 6 tbsp. butter. Dip tops in butter and roll in mixture of 1/2 cup sugar and 1 tsp. cinnamon. Makes 1 dozen.

Doughnuts

1 1/2 cups sugar	1 3/4 cups buttermilk
3 Tbsp. oil	1 tsp. vanilla
3 eggs	1 tsp. salt
1/2 tsp. nutmeg	1 1/2 tsp. baking soda
2 tsp. baking powder	4 cups flour

Use a doughnut maker. Makes 4 dozen.

Butter Scones

2 cups self-rising flour	1 small onion, chopped fine
1/2 tsp. salt	1/4 tsp. garlic powder
2 Tbsp. butter	1/2 cup sourdough starter
1/2 cup cheddar cheese, grated	1/4 cup milk (approximately)
1 jar pimento	1/3 cup butter, melted

Combine flour and salt. Cut in butter. Add cheese, pimento, onion, garlic powder and sourdough starter. Mix with enough milk to make a soft but not sticky dough. Line bottom of 8-inch baking dish with waxed paper. Pat out mixture in dish. Bake at 450 degrees for 10 minutes or until done. Remove mixture from oven and pour melted butter over it. Let set 5 minutes. Cut it into 1-1/2 x 3 inch fingers. Serve them warm.

Lizanne's Grandmother's Scones

4 cups flour
4 tsp. baking powder
3 Tbsp. sugar
1/2 tsp. salt

1/4 lb. softened butter
2 cups raisins
1 3/4 cups milk
1 egg

Sift dry ingredients. Knead softened butter into mixture. Add raisins. Beat egg in milk and add to mixture. Coat top of cake with milk before baking. Bake at 350 degrees for 1 hour in a greased and floured round cake pan.

Scottish Scones

1 1/4 cups flour
1/2 tsp. baking soda
1 tsp. cream of tartar
1 tsp. sugar
1/8 tsp. salt

1 slightly beaten egg
1/2 cup milk
1/2 tsp. dried yeast
1/4 cup hot water
1 tsp. sugar

Combine flour, baking soda, cream of tartar, 1 tsp. sugar and salt. Make a hole in the center and add egg, milk, and the yeast dissolved in the hot water with 1 tsp. sugar. Mix together. Pat out on a lightly floured cloth into a circle 1/2 inch thick. Cut into wedges. Bake on a lightly oiled grill until brown on both sides, turning once. (Or these may be dropped by the large serving spoon on to the griddle.) Split and serve with butter and jam. Makes 6.

Baking Powder Biscuits

1 3/4 cups flour
1/2 tsp. salt
3 Tbsp. baking powder

4 - 6 tsp. butter or margarine
3/4 cup milk

Sift together flour, salt and baking powder. Cut butter into dry ingredients. Make a well in the center of the mixture and add the milk. Stir until the dough is fairly free from the sides of the bowl. Turn the dough onto a lightly floured board. Knead gently. Roll with floured rolling pin until the dough has the desired thickness. Cut with biscuit cutter dipped in a very little flour. Brush with milk or melted butter. Place on an ungreased cookie sheet. Bake for 12 - 15 minutes at 450 degrees. Yields 24 1-1/2 inch biscuits.

Apple Ricotta Brunch Biscuits

1/2 cup sugar
1 cup ricotta cheese
1 egg
1/2 tsp. cinnamon

1/4 cup sliced almonds
1 can refrigerator biscuits
1 small apple, peeled, cut into 8 wedges

Spray 8 muffin cups with nonstick cooking spray. Combine sugar, cheese and egg, beating at high speed for 1 minute. In small bowl, combine cinnamon and almonds. Separate dough into 8 biscuits. Press each biscuit evenly in bottom and up sides of muffin cups. Place 1 wedge of apple in each cup. Spoon 2 Tbsp. cheese mixture over each apple wedge and sprinkle with cinnamon mixture. Bake at 375 degrees for 20 - 25 minutes or until biscuits are deep golden brown and apples are crisp-tender. Remove biscuits and cool 15 minutes. Serve warm.

Peanut Butter Crescents

Rolls:
1/4 cup packed dark brown sugar
1/4 cup creamy peanut butter
2 Tbsp. butter
2 cans crescent rolls

Glaze:
1 cup powdered sugar
1 Tbsp. creamy peanut butter
1/8 tsp. vanilla
1 - 2 Tbsp. milk

Combine brown sugar, peanut butter and butter. Blend well. Unroll dough into rectangles and spread peanut butter mixture evenly over dough. Separate into triangles. Roll up and place point side down on greased cookie sheet; curve into crescent shape. Bake at 375 degrees for 10 - 14 minutes or until golden brown. Cool 10 minutes. Meanwhile, combine all glaze ingredients, adding enough milk for glaze consistency. Blend until smooth. Drizzle over warm rolls.

Walnut Date Coconut Crescents

1/2 cup walnuts	1 can crescent rolls
1/4 cup chopped dates	1 egg white, slightly beaten
2 Tbsp. brown sugar	3/4 cup coconut
1/2 tsp. cinnamon	powdered sugar
1 Tbsp. butter	

Combine walnuts and dates, both finely chopped. Add brown sugar, cinnamon and butter, and blend well. Separate dough into triangles. Spread 1 Tbsp. walnut mixture evenly over each triangle. Loosely roll up, then dip top and sides of each roll in egg white. Coat with coconut. Place on sprayed cookie sheet and curve into crescent shape. Bake at 350 degrees for 15 - 20 minutes or until golden brown. Remove from cookie sheet. Cool 5 minutes. Lightly sprinkle with powdered sugar.

Pumpkin Roll

3 eggs	2 tsp. cinnamon
1/3 cup honey	1 tsp. ginger
1 cup pumpkin	Filling:
1 tsp. lemon juice	1/4 cup honey
1/2 cup whole-wheat flour	8 oz. cream cheese
1/2 cup white flour	4 Tbsp. butter
1 tsp. baking powder	3/4 tsp. vanilla

Beat eggs on high speed for 5 minutes. Gradually beat in honey. Stir in pumpkin and lemon juice. Stir together flours, baking powder, cinnamon and ginger. Fold into pumpkin mixture. Spread on well greased and floured 15 x 10 x 1- inch pan. Bake 15 minutes in 375 degree oven. Turn out on towel. Starting at narrow edge, roll towel and cake together. Let cool, unroll and spread with filling, roll again and chill. Slice thinly. To make filling, combine honey, cream cheese, butter and vanilla. Beat until smooth.

Cranberry Jewel Muffins

3/4 cup cranberries cut in fourths	1 cup milk
1/2 cup confectioner's sugar	2 Tbsp. sugar
2 cups Bisquick	1 egg

Cover cranberries with confectioner's sugar and let stand overnight. Mix all ingredients and put in muffin cups. Bake at 350 degrees until done.

Cranberry Muffins

1 1/2 cup flour
3 tsp. baking powder
1/4 tsp. salt
1/4 cup sugar
1/4 cup vegetable oil

1 egg, slightly beaten
1 cup orange juice
1 Tbsp. grated orange peel
1 1/2 cup chopped fresh cranberries

Sift flour, salt and baking powder. Beat oil and sugar together until light. Add beaten egg and beat until smooth. Add orange juice and orange peel, then add cranberries. Add flour and stir, just until mixed. Fill greased muffin pans 2/3 full. Bake at 400 degrees for 20 - 25 minutes. Makes 10 - 12 muffins.

Pumpkin Muffins

1 1/2 cups flour
1/2 cup sugar
2 tsp. baking powder
1/2 tsp. salt
1/2 tsp. cinnamon
1/2 tsp. nutmeg

1/2 cup raisins
1 egg
1/2 cup milk
1/2 cup pumpkin puree
1/4 cup melted butter
2 Tbsp. molasses

Combine dry ingredients, then add raisins, egg, milk, pumpkin, butter, and molasses. Put in muffin cups. Bake at 400 degrees for 18 - 20 minutes. While hot, sprinkle or roll tops in sugar. Makes 1 dozen.

Orange Blueberry Muffins

1 cup uncooked oatmeal
1 cup orange juice
3 cups flour
4 tsp. baking powder
1 tsp. salt
1/2 tsp. baking soda
1 cup sugar
1 cup vegetable oil

3 eggs, beaten
1 1/2 cups blueberries
1 Tbsp. grated orange peel

Topping:
1/2 cup finely chopped walnuts
1/3 cup sugar
1 tsp. cinnamon

Combine oatmeal and orange juice. Set aside. In large bowl, combine flour, baking powder, salt, soda and sugar. Make a well in the center and add oatmeal mixture, oil and eggs. Stir until moistened. Carefully fold in blueberries and orange peel. Spoon batter into greased muffin tins. Combine topping ingredients and sprinkle over muffins. Bake at 400 degrees for 15 minutes. Makes 24 muffins.

Blueberry Orange Muffins

1 1/2 cups flour
3/4 cup sugar
2 tsp. baking powder
1/2 tsp. salt
1/2 cup milk

1 stick butter or margarine
1 large egg
1 cup fresh blueberries or frozen unsweet
2 tsp. grated orange peel

Grease muffin tin or line with twelve paper liners. Combine flour, 1/2 cup sugar, baking powder and salt in large bowl. Whisk milk, 1/2 stick of butter (melted), and egg in medium bowl. Add to dry ingredients and stir. Stir in blueberries and orange peel. Spoon batter into muffin cups and bake until golden, about twenty minutes, at 400 degrees. Brush tops with remaining 1/2 stick butter, melted. Place remaining 1/4 cup sugar in small bowl. Dip muffin tops in sugar and serve.

Chocolate Banana Muffins

2 oz. unsweetened chocolate
1 cup buttermilk
1/3 cup oil
1 pkg. Banana Quick Bread Mix

1/4 cup cocoa
6 oz. chocolate chips
2 eggs, slightly beaten

Grease muffin cups or line with baking cups. Over low heat, melt unsweetened chocolate, stirring constantly. Stir in 3 Tbsp. of buttermilk and 1 Tbsp. of the oil. Blend well. Combine quick bread mix and cocoa. Add remaining buttermilk, remaining oil, chocolate mixture, chocolate chips and eggs. Stir just until dry ingredients are moistened. Spoon batter into muffin cups. Bake at 400 degrees for 18 - 22 minutes or until tops spring back when lightly touched. Immediately remove from pan. Serve warm or cool.

Applesauce Muffins

1 1/2 cups sugar
1/2 cup butter or margarine, softened
2 eggs
2 cups flour
1 tsp. baking powder

1 tsp. ground cinnamon
1/2 tsp. baking soda
1/2 tsp. ground cloves
1/4 tsp. salt
1 cup applesauce

Cream sugar and butter together. Add eggs, one at a time, beating well. Add flour, baking powder, cinnamon, baking soda, cloves, salt and applesauce. Mix just until combined. Fill muffin cups 2/3 full. Bake at 350 degrees 20-25 minutes. Cool on a wire rack.

Orange Nut Bread

3 cups flour
1 1/3 Tbsp. baking powder
1/4 tsp. salt
1 cup sugar
1/2 cup chopped pecans

1 egg slightly beaten
1/2 cup orange rind grated
1 cup orange juice
1/3 cup melted shortening or salad oil

Mix dry ingredients and pecans together. Beat together the egg, rind, juice and shortening. Add to the dry ingredients and mix to moisten. Put in greased loaf pan. Bake at 350 degrees for about 1 hour. Remove from pan and cool. Delicious served with cream cheese. Slices better on the second day.

Butterscotch Nut Bread

2 eggs, beaten
2 cups brown sugar
2 cups sour milk
1 1/4 tsp. baking soda

1 tsp. baking powder
1/2 tsp. salt
1 cup chopped walnuts
4 cups flour

Mix all ingredients, and put in 2 loaf pans. Bake at 350 degrees for 50 - 60 minutes.

Date Nut Bread

2 cups boiling water
2 cups chopped dates
1 tsp. baking soda
2 cups brown sugar
2 eggs
1 tsp. butter

1 tsp. vanilla
3 1/2 cups flour
1 tsp. baking powder
pinch of salt
1 cup nuts, chopped

Mix together the boiling water, dates and soda, and let them cool. Mix together the sugar, eggs, butter and vanilla, and then the dry ingredients, date mixture, and the nuts. Bake for 1 hour at 350 degrees.

Lemon Bread

1 cup sugar
1/4 cup butter
2 eggs
1/2 cup milk
1 1/2 cups flour
pinch of salt

1 tsp. baking powder
grated rind of 1 lemon
1/2 cup chopped nuts
Glaze:
juice of 1 lemon
2/3 cup sugar

Cream butter and sugar. Add eggs and beat. Add milk, beat, and add the rest of the ingredients. Bake in a greased loaf pan for 50 minutes at 350 degrees. Cool 5 minutes. Glaze with the juice of one lemon mixed with 2/3 cup sugar.

Rhubarb Bread

1 1/2 cups rhubarb
1 1/2 cups brown sugar (packed)
1/2 cup nuts
2/3 cup oil
1 egg

1 cup sour milk
1 tsp. baking soda
Pinch of salt
1 tsp. vanilla
2 1/2 cups flour

Mix in order given and pour into two well greased and floured tins. Sprinkle on top of raw dough the following topping : 1/2 cup sugar and 1 Tbsp. butter, mixed together. Bake at 350 degrees for 55 or 60 minutes.

Cherry Nut Bread

2 eggs
1 cup sugar
1 1/2 cups flour
1 1/2 tsp. baking powder

1/2 tsp. salt
4 oz. bottle cherries (cut up) and juice
1/2 cup chopped nuts

Mix ingredients in order, and bake in greased loaf pan 1 hour at 325 degrees.

Cranberry Bread

1/4 cup butter
1 cup sugar
1/2 tsp. salt
1 egg
3/4 cup fresh orange juice
1 3/4 cups flour

1/2 tsp. baking soda
1 1/2 tsp. baking powder
grated rind of 1/2 orange
1/2 cup chopped nuts
1 cup cranberries, cut in half

Blend butter, sugar, and salt. Add egg and beat with mixer. Add dry ingredients alternately with juice. Add rind, nuts and berries last. Grease sides and line bottom of loaf pan. Bake at 350 degrees for 35-40 minutes. Makes 2 small or 1 regular loaf.

Banana Sour Cream Walnut Loaf

2/3 cup butter or margarine
1 1/2 cups sugar
2 eggs
1 1/2 cups mashed bananas (about 3)
2 3/4 cups flour

1 tsp. baking powder
1 tsp. baking soda
1/2 tsp. salt
1/2 cup dairy sour cream
1 cup chopped walnuts

Cream butter and sugar until light and fluffy. Add eggs and bananas and beat until well blended. Sift together flour, baking powder, soda and salt. Add alternately with sour cream to banana mixture, stirring just to blend. Stir in walnuts. Spoon batter into greased and floured loaf pan. Bake at 350 degrees for 90 minutes or until cake tester comes out clean. Let stand in pan on rack for 20 minutes. Remove from pan and cool thoroughly.

Cardamon Bread

2 cups flour
3/4 cup oatmeal
3/4 tsp. salt
3 Tbsp. powdered milk
1/4 cup sugar

1 tsp. ground cardamon
1 egg & enough water to make 1 cup
2 Tbsp. butter
1 tsp. yeast

Mix in order in bread baking machine.

Basic Pizza Crust

1 pkg. yeast
1/2 cup warm water
4 cups plus 4 Tbsp. flour
1 1/3 cups hot water

4 Tbsp. oil
4 Tbsp. sugar
2 tsp. salt

Dissolve yeast in warm water. Set aside. Mix remaining ingredients together with fork. Add to yeast mixture. Let rise about 20 to 30 minutes. Grease fingers and work dough into pan, shaping up over pan sides. Prebake crust 10 to 12 minutes at 375 degrees before filling. Makes enough for two crusts.

Basic Bread Recipe

1 tsp. honey
1 cup lukewarm water
2 Tbsp. yeast
2 cups very hot water

1/4 cup sunflower oil
1/4 cup honey
1 Tbsp. salt
8 - 9 cups flour

Dissolve honey in warm water. Stir in yeast. Let rise about 10 minutes while you are mixing the rest of the ingredients. Mix the remaining ingredients in the order given. Begin mixing the flour in with an electric mixer. When the dough gets heavy add in the yeast mixture. Continue beating until mixture gets too stiff, then knead in the remainder of the flour by hand. Knead until all air bubbles are gone. Cover the bowl with greased waxed paper. Set in your sink which has been partially filled with hot water. Allow to rise until double its bulk. Punch down, knead and form into loaf shapes. Put into greased loaf pans and put in a warm place to rise. (Your oven which has been turned on for about one minute and then off again provides a good warm place for the rising. Leave the light on, and that will furnish enough heat to keep the oven warm.) When loaves are about double their bulk, turn the oven on to 350 degrees and bake the bread until nicely browned on top. Turn out of pans to partially cool. Wrap in plastic bags to finish cooling. Store in the refrigerator or freeze.

Basic Bread: Pan Buns

one recipe basic bread dough

Form dough into round shapes and place in a greased pan. About 9 buns to an 8" square pan. Allow to rise. Bake at 350 degrees for 20 minutes.

Basic Bread: Bowknots

one recipe basic bread dough

Cut off pieces of dough and roll under your hand to form a cylinder 1/2" thick and 6" long. Tie in a knot without stretching the dough. Place on a greased baking sheet. Allow to rise and bake at 350 degrees for 20 minutes or so.

Basic Bread: Twirls

one recipe basic bread dough   *melted butter*

With greased rolling pin, roll dough out to rectangle 12" x 6" x 1/4" thick. (It will be easier to roll this shape if dough is first squeezed into a long roll with hands.) Cut into 1/2" strips, 6" long. Twist. Hold one end of the twisted strip down on the baking sheet with finger. Wind strip around and tuck the end underneath. Rise, and bake at 350 degrees for 20 minutes or so. Brush with melted butter or oil when done.

Basic Bread: Crescents

one recipe basic bread dough   *melted butter*

Roll ball of dough into circular shape 1/4" thick. Cut into 12 pie shaped pieces. Brush with melted butter or oil and roll up, beginning with the wide end. Seal point to bun with fingers. Place on baking sheet with sealed point underneath. Curve into crescents. Rise, bake at 350 degrees for 20 minutes or so and brush with butter.

Basic Bread: Cloverleaf Rolls

one recipe basic bread dough   *oil*

Grease muffin tins. Snip off small pieces of dough with greased scissors. Shape into 3 little balls for each muffin cup. Dip into oil before placing in pans. Rise and bake at 350 degrees for 20 minutes or so.

Basic Bread: Chelsea Buns

one recipe of basic bread dough
1/4 cup butter, melted
1 tsp. cinnamon

1 cup brown sugar
1/2 cup raisins

Roll out 1/4 of the dough into 9x12 rectangle. Brush with melted butter. Mix cinnamon and brown sugar, and sprinkle evenly over the dough. Sprinkle raisins over the sugar. Roll up the dough like a jelly roll. Seal the edge of the roll with fingers. Slice with a sharp knife into 9 pieces (each about 2"). Arrange slices of the dough cut side down in a greased 8" square pan. While rising, cover pan with greased wax paper. Temperature should be 75 - 85 degrees for rising. Bake at 350 degrees for 20 minutes or so.

Basic Bread: Hot Cross Buns

one recipe basic bread dough
1/4 - 1/2 cup extra honey or sugar
2 tsp. cinnamon
1/2 tsp. allspice
1/2 tsp. cloves
1 cup raisins or currants
1 cup candied mixed fruit or chopped peel

Glaze:
2 Tbsp. sugar
2 Tbsp. water
Icing:
1 egg white
1 1/3 cups icing sugar
1/4 tsp. vanilla

Mix in honey and spices with the flour when making up the bread recipe. Stir in fruits at the end. After first rising, shape pieces of dough into balls about 1 1/2" in diameter. Rise, bake at 350 degrees for 20 minutes or so, then brush with glaze. Make a cross on top of each with white icing, made by whipping the three icing ingredients together.

Basic Bread: Butterscotch Pecan Rolls

one recipe basic bread dough
butter
1 tsp. cinnamon
1 cup brown sugar

brown sugar
chopped nuts

Roll out 1/4 of the dough into 9x12 rectangle. Brush with melted butter. Mix cinnamon and 1 cup brown sugar. Sprinkle evenly over the dough. Roll up the dough like a jelly roll. Seal the edge of the roll with fingers. Cut dough into slices about 1" thick and place into muffin tins which have been prepared as follows: grease each muffin tin, and cover bottom of each muffin tin with 1/2 tsp. melted butter, 1 tsp. brown sugar and a few chopped nuts. Place the cut portion of the dough on top of the nut mixture. Raise, bake at 350 degrees for 20 minutes or so, and turn pan upside down on rack and leave for a minute until butterscotch mixture runs down over each roll.

Basic Bread: French Peasant Ring

one recipe basic bread dough
1/4 cup butter, melted

date filling

Roll out 1/4 of the dough into 9x12 rectangle. Brush with melted butter and spread date filling on dough. Roll up the dough like a jelly roll. Seal the edge of the roll with fingers. Form into a ring on a greased baking sheet. Keep sealed edge to bottom. Cut with scissors through ring almost to center in slices 1" wide, making an even number of slices. Lift every other slice to the center of the ring. Raise and bake at 350 degrees for 20 minutes or so.

Butter Batter Bread

3 cups whole wheat flour
2 pkg. yeast
2 1/2 cups buttermilk
1/4 cup molasses
1/4 cup honey
1 tsp. salt

1/3 cup butter
1 1/2 cups oats
2 eggs
2 1/2 - 3 cups flour
2 Tbsp. melted butter

Combine wheat flour and yeast. Heat the buttermilk, molasses, honey, salt and butter until warm. Add oats, then the wheat flour and yeast mixture and the eggs. Blend until moist. Stir in the other flour. Top with melted butter. Let rise for one hour or until double in size. Punch down and put in two loaf pans. Let rise for 45 minutes, then bake for 25 - 35 minutes at 375 degrees.

Rye Bread

1 cake compressed yeast	8 cups white flour
2 cups lukewarm milk	1 Tbsp. salt
2 cups lukewarm water	1/2 cup sugar
4 cups rye flour	1/2 cup molasses

Dissolve yeast in 1/2 cup of the lukewarm water. Let stand 5 minutes. Mix with the rest of the water and milk. Add sugar, salt and 4 cups of the flour. Stir the molasses into mixture. Add the rest of the flour and knead. Place in a greased, covered bowl to rise, overnight, (or use 2 cakes of yeast for 4 hour rising). Room temperature is all right. Knead again in the morning and let rise until light. Then shape into 3 loaves. Let rise until double in bulk. Bake in a moderate for 45 minutes. Brush with melted shortening.

Challoh

2 cups white bread flour	1 egg yolk, beaten
1 Tbsp. sugar	1/2 tsp. poppy seeds
1 tsp. salt	1/2 cup water
2 1/2 Tbsp. butter	1 1/2 tsp. active dry yeast
1 egg, beaten	

Mix in order in bread baking machine.

Marijean's English Muffin Loaf

5 1/2 - 6 cups flour	1/4 tsp. baking soda
2 pkg. dry yeast	2 cups milk
1 Tbsp. sugar	1/2 cup water
2 tsp. salt	small amount of cornmeal

Combine 3 cups flour, yeast, sugar, salt and soda. Heat liquids until very warm (130 degrees). Add to dry mixture; beat well. Stir in more flour to make a stiff batter. Spoon into two loaf pans that have been greased and sprinkled with cornmeal. Sprinkle tops with cornmeal. Cover and let rise in warm place for 45 minutes. Bake at 400 degrees for 25 minutes. Remove from pans immediately and cool.

Parmesan Pullaparts

1/4 cup butter
parsley flakes
onion flakes
oregano powder

garlic powder
parmesan cheese
1 pkg. refrigerated biscuits

Melt butter in 8 x 8 or 6 x 10 glass dish. Sprinkle to taste the flakes, oregano powder, garlic powder and cheese all over butter and mix together. Cut biscuits into quarters and dip and cover in butter mixture. Leave in pan and bake at 425 degrees for 10 - 12 minutes.

Cheesy Parmesan Loaves

3/4 cup grated parmesan cheese
1/3 cup finely chopped walnuts
3 oz. cream cheese, softened
1 1/2 Tbsp. finely chopped fresh basil

1 garlic clove, minced
1 can refrigerated biscuits
1/4 cup butter, melted

Combine parmesan cheese and walnuts. In separate bowl, combine cream cheese, basil and garlic. Separate dough into 8 biscuits. Spoon 1 tsp. cream cheese mixture on half of each biscuit. Fold biscuit over cream cheese; press edges to seal. Dip each biscuit in melted butter and coat with cheese-walnut mixture. Arrange biscuits in 2 greased loaf pans. Drizzle any remaining butter over biscuits and sprinkle with any remaining cheese mixture. Bake at 350 degrees for 25 - 35 minutes or until golden brown. Immediately remove from pan and serve warm.

Lefse

5 large potatoes
1 tsp. salt

3 tsp. butter
flour to roll thin

Boil potatoes, put through ricer. Add butter and salt. Let cool. Add flour. Take a piece of dough and roll as for pie crust. Roll as thin as possible, using a wedged rolling pin if you have one. Bake on a pancake griddle until a light brown, turning frequently to prevent scorching. Use moderate heat. When they are baked, cover with clean cloths to keep from becoming dry.

Julekage

2 cakes compressed yeast	2 eggs
1/2 cup lukewarm water	1/2 cup currants
3 cups milk, scalded	1/2 cup chopped citron
1/2 cup butter	3/4 cup chopped raisins
3/4 cup sugar	1/2 cup candied cherries
10 to 12 cups flour	1/2 tsp. cardamom, if desired
2 tsp. salt	

Dissolve yeast in water. Pour scalded milk over butter. When lukewarm, add yeast, sugar, half of flour and salt. Beat well for 10 minutes. Add eggs, one at a time, beating thoroughly after each addition. Add fruit and remaining flour. Knead and place in a greased bowl to rise. Cover and set in warm place. When dough has risen to double in bulk, knead again. Let rise until light, shape into loaves and place in greased pans. Brush tops of loaves with egg whites. When double in bulk, bake at 350 degrees for 35 to 40 minutes. After removing from oven, brush crusts with melted butter and sprinkle with sugar and cinnamon.

MARK AND MARY BETH

We celebrated our thirteenth wedding anniversary this year and are still very happily married! There's no doubt life is very busy these days, between work and family, but we always try to have fun along the way!

I continue to work full-time selling all kinds of products on TV, and I still enjoy it just as much as I did ten years ago. Of course, my passions are collectible dolls and teddy bears, 14K gold jewelry, kitchen items, fashions, cosmetics, etc. I always appreciate all the support and kind comments I receive from those who enjoy watching! I try to keep my business travels to a minimum because of my family. When I'm not at work, I'm home with the children spending time with them and trying to keep the house running smoothly. We have a wonderful lady named Paula who comes two days a week to help with the boys and the laundry. We couldn't do it without her, and to us, she's just part of the family! She raised three boys of her own, so she understand my boys real well!

Mark continues to repair brass and woodwind band instruments part-time in his own shop in our basement. However, he also is a "Mr. Mom", because he spends the rest of his time taking care of the boys while I'm at work. This system wouldn't work for everyone, but it works for us, and that's all that matters. I'm so grateful that if I can't be home all the time with the boys, then the boys are with Daddy! He does a lot of things with them like play baseball and basketball, rollerblading, mini-golf, bowling, going to the park, fishing, bike riding, hiking in the woods, etc. What more could a kid ask for?

Mark also loves to play golf, and he's very good at it, too. Now that we have three boys, Mark looks forward to the day when he has a golf foursome all the time!

Both Mark and I are still active in the music program at our church. Marks plays his trombone in the church orchestra, and I sing on the Worship team leading music in the service and singing solos from time to time. Even though I took a year and a half off from being in the choir while I was having Ryan, I have now rejoined the choir as a singer instead of director. Our church is a very important part of our family life and always will be! We are grateful for the many blessings God has given us through the years, and we thank you for being a part of our lives as well! Enjoy the cookbook, and God bless you!!

ERIC

Eric has changed so much in the last couple of years. He has gone from a little boy to a young boy who is discovering who he is and asserting some independence! Eric is nine years old and in the third grade. His interests have changed from dinosaurs and trains to baseball games, baseball players and baseball collectibles. Eric had always said he wasn't interested in sports until he joined Little League this last summer. Suddenly, his whole focus changed. He enjoys playing in the outfield and, of course, being up to bat. The first time I saw him out on the field in his baseball uniform, tears welled up in my eyes. He looked so handsome, and yet I was thinking, "That's my baby out there!" We were so proud of him!

Eric is still very much into his pets! We have Lacey, our two year old Dalmatian, who is very much a part of the family! We also have Prince, the California King snake, Mr. Lazy, the blue-spotted lizard, a tank full of tropical fish, a tank full of goldfish, and a few frogs and turtles found in the yard from time to time! Eric says he wants to grow up to be a pet store owner, although recently he has been asking Mark if he should play for the Philadelphia Phillies or the Minnesota Twins when he grows up!

Eric also loves being in AWANA, a children's program at our church where they learn Bible stories, memorize Bible verses, and play a lot of fun games with the other kids. Eric is a smart boy, and he has a very good heart! He is concerned about others and is eager to please others. He is a true blessing to our family and a big help to Mark and me when it comes to helping out with his two younger brothers! We thank God for him everyday!

Eric and Ryan

Eric

...on the air

...at bat

...down on
the farm!

CORY

Cory is five years old now and really showing his personality. He tries to be a bit of a tough guy on the outside, but he's really a marshmallow on the inside. He has a soft, loving heart and a real sweet spirit about him! He is also the entertainer in the family. He keeps us laughing with all the comical comments he makes totally off the cuff!

Cory loves to ride his bike and also play baseball. With all the practice Eric has had hitting baseballs and catching them in our backyard, Cory has had ample opportunity to practice playing ball, too. He seems to have quite a bit of innate athletic ability already! Since Mark has always been athletic, he thoroughly enjoys playing ball with both boys, and they thoroughly enjoy playing with him!

Cory finished his first year of preschool and will go to preschool one more year before attending kindergarten. Since he turned five shortly before school started, we decided to give him one more year of social and emotional maturity as well as one more year of growth, since he's just a bit on the shorter side. Intellectually, he's ready for school, but I think sometimes it's best to let them wait one extra year, especially with boys.

Cory loves to follow Eric around everywhere, do what Eric does, eat what Eric eats . . . . . he is basically Eric's shadow. Eric is not always pleased about it, but it is sure cute to see the two of them together so much. Cory also plays so well with Ryan! Even though Ryan is still a baby, Cory makes sure Ryan has toys to play with and loves to crawl on the floor with him.

The thing I enjoy most about Cory is that he still likes to cuddle with me. He is very affectionate and loves to sit on my lap and have me read him a book or just hold him. My favorite place to have my children is in my arms! Cory is also such a blessing to our family, and we thank God for him every day!

Mother's Tea
at preschool

Like father,
like son!

King for a day
...I turned 5!

RYAN

"Hello, Ryan! It's your Mommy!" As I said this to my newborn baby who had just been handed to me only a half a minute old, he opened his eyes and turned his face towards mine as if to say, "Hello, Mommy! I know that voice! I've listened to it for the last nine months!" I'll never forget that moment as long as I live! We had found out the baby was going to be a boy about three months ahead of time, so it made it easier for me to get the nursery ready by getting out all the little boy things leftover from Eric and Cory. We also had decided what we were going to name him ahead of time. As a family, we talked about different things we would do after Ryan arrived, so we could hardly wait for him to come! As it turned out, he started to come too soon . . . . . about seven weeks too early. I hung in there at work until after the big all-day gold show, and then I went on bed rest for three weeks. He ended up coming on September 12th, almost three weeks early. This was not really any surprise since the other two boys both came four weeks early! Ryan was 7 pounds, 7 ounces, and 20 inches long. The labor and delivery was not easy (it never is), but it was short - - less than two hours!

Ryan has been an excellent baby! He has a beautiful smile, and he loves watching Eric and Cory, whatever they are doing! He started crawling at nine months old and kept us all busy making sure he didn't put anything in his mouth that he shouldn't! One of his favorite things was to find the dog's water dish and splash his hands in it! He's a typical curious baby, so we have to keep one eyeball on him at all times! Ryan loves to jabber, mostly saying "Da-Da-Da-Da," although the kids are trying to teach him to say "ball, car, doggy, bottle," and of course, I'm trying to get him to say, "Ma-Ma!" That will melt my heart!

We're so glad we have Ryan in our family! He brings us so much joy and laughter, and I can never get enough of cuddling and holding my baby! We now have three precious blessings in our family, and we thank God for each one of them every day!

My girlfriends,
twins Stephanie & Katie

Grandpa & Grandma Larson

Grandma &
Grandpa Roe

What we did on
our summer vacation!

Kenny Rogers

Virginia Olson

Marie Osmond
and the Children's Miracle
Network Telethon

Bette Ball

Annette Funicello

Meats & Main Dishes

Raspberry Chicken

2 tsp. oil
4 boneless, skinless chicken breast halves

1/4 cup seedless raspberry jam
2 Tbsp. orange juice

Heat oil in large nonstick skillet over medium heat until hot. If desired, season chicken with salt and pepper; add to skillet. Cook 10 to 12 minutes or until chicken is fork tender and juices run clear, turning once. Add raspberry jam and orange juice. Stir until melted. Bring to a boil. Boil 1 to 2 minutes or until slightly thickened. Serve sauce over chicken.

Santa Fe Chicken

1 Tbsp. oil
4 boneless, skinless chicken breast halves,
    cut into thin strips
11 oz. can corn, drained

1 cup salsa
2 Tbsp. sliced ripe olives
1 cup broken tortilla chips
1/2 cup shredded cheddar cheese

Heat oil in large skillet over medium-high heat until hot. Add chicken and cook and stir 3 to 5 minutes or until chicken is no longer pink. Stir in corn, salsa and olives. Simmer 3 to 5 minutes or until thoroughly heated, stirring occasionally. Stir in chips; sprinkle with cheese. Serve immediately.

Honey Lemon Chicken with Asparagus

1 Tbsp. olive oil
4 boneless, skinless chicken breasts
1 lb. fresh asparagus, cut into pieces

1/2 tsp. minced garlic
2 Tbsp. honey
1 tsp. finely grated lemon peel

Heat oil in large skillet over medium heat until hot. Add chicken breasts, cook 5 minutes. Turn chicken; add asparagus and garlic. Cook 1 minute, stirring occasionally. Add honey. Increase heat to medium-high; cover and cook 3 to 4 minutes or until chicken is fork tender and juices run clear, and asparagus is crisp-tender. Stir in lemon peel.

Scalloped Chicken

1/2 loaf white bread, cubed
1 1/2 cups cracker crumbs
3 cups chicken broth
3 eggs, lightly beaten
1 tsp. salt

3/4 cup diced celery
2 Tbsp. chopped onion
3 cups cubed cooked chicken
1 can (8 oz.) sliced mushrooms, drained
1 Tbsp. butter

Combine bread cubes and 1 cup cracker crumbs. Stir in broth, eggs, salt, celery, onion, chicken and mushrooms. Spoon into a greased 2 qt. casserole. Melt butter in a saucepan and brown remaining cracker crumbs. Sprinkle over casserole. Bake at 350 degrees for 1 hour. Serves 6 to 8.

Hot Chicken Salad

4 cups chicken, cooked and cubed
2 cups dry bread cubes
1 can mushroom soup
1 soup can water
4 cups celery, diced
4 Tbsp. onion juice or chopped onion

2 cups Miracle Whip
1 Tbsp. lemon juice
2 pkg. slivered almonds
2 cups crushed soda crackers
    or bread crumbs
1/4 cup corn oil

Mix bread cubes with mushroom soup. Cook celery and onion about ten minutes with a can of water. Mix all ingredients together except the bread crumbs (soda crackers) and corn oil, and put in 9 x 13 pan. Mix bread crumbs and corn oil, and sprinkle on top of casserole. Bake for 30 - 45 minutes at 425 degrees.

Wild Rice Chicken Casserole

1 1/2 cups wild rice
3 cups boiling water
1 cup celery, chopped
3 Tbsp. butter
1 chicken, cooked and diced

1 cup diced onions
2 cans mushroom soup
1 can water
mushrooms, optional

Pour boiling water over wild rice, and cook fifteen minutes in the microwave. Add remaining ingredients and bake at 350 degrees for one hour.

Cranberry Chicken

5 chicken breasts (or thighs)
1 can whole cranberry sauce

1 pkg. onion soup mix
8 oz. bottle french dressing

Place chicken in baking dish. Mix remaining ingredients and pour over chicken. Bake at 350 degrees for 1 hour.

Chicken Stroganoff

1/2 cup chopped onion
2 cloves garlic, pressed
1/4 cup margarine
1/4 cup Bisquick baking mix
1/2 tsp. salt
1/4 tsp. pepper

2 cups milk
4 cups bite size pieces cooked chicken
1 cup sour cream
1 can (8 oz.) mushrooms, drained
paprika to taste
parsley to taste

Cook and stir onions and garlic in margarine in 10-inch skillet over low heat until onion is transparent, 2-3 minutes. Stir in baking mix, salt and pepper. Cook over low heat, stirring constantly until bubbly; remove from heat. Gradually stir in milk. Heat to boiling, stirring constantly; boil and stir 1 minute. Stir in chicken, sour cream and mushrooms; heat through. Sprinkle with paprika and parsley and serve over hot cooked plain or spinach noodles.

Chicken Salad Casserole

3 cups cooked chicken, chopped
1 cup rice, cooked
3 hard boiled eggs, chopped
1 Tbsp. chopped onion
1 Tbsp. lemon juice

1 can cream of chicken or celery soup
3/4 cup mayonnaise
salt and pepper to taste
parsley
grated cheese

Mix together chicken, rice, eggs, and onion. Add lemon juice, soup, mayonnaise, salt, pepper and parsley. Put in casserole and add grated cheese on top. Bake at 350 degrees for 50 minutes.

Chicken Casserole

6 to 8 chicken breasts
1/2 cup chicken broth
1 can cream of chicken soup
1 can cream of mushroom soup
1 cup sour cream

1 can sliced water chestnuts
1 stick butter, melted
1 box Town House or Escort crackers
salt and pepper to taste

Cook and debone chicken, cut in bite-size pieces. Finely crush 1/2 box crackers in bottom of 9 x 13 casserole. Pour 1/2 melted butter on top of crumbs. Place chicken on top. Add sliced water chestnuts on top of chicken and sprinkle lightly with salt and pepper. Stir together the broth, soups and sour cream. Spoon on top of chicken. Crumble other 1/2 box crackers on top. Pour the other 1/2 melted butter on top. Bake at 350 degrees for 30 - 40 minutes uncovered.

Chicken Pot Pie

1 cup chicken broth
3 carrots, cut into chunks
1 potato, peeled and diced
1/2 tsp. salt
1 cup frozen pearl onions
1 cup frozen peas

1 lb. skinless boneless chicken thighs, cut
   into pieces
1/2 cup evaporated skim milk
1/4 cup flour
1/2 tsp. dried sage
1/4 tsp. pepper
2 - 17" x 11" sheets filo dough

In saucepan, combine broth, carrots, potato and 1/4 tsp. salt. Bring to a boil, reduce to a simmer, cover and cook until the potato is almost tender, about 5 minutes. Stir in pearl onions, peas and chicken, return to a boil, reduce to a simmer, cover and cook until the chicken is cooked through, about 5 minutes. In another saucepan, combine the evaporated skim milk, flour, sage, 1/4 tsp. salt and pepper. Bring to a boil, reduce to a simmer and cook until the sauce has thickened to the consistency of heavy cream, about 2 minutes. Stir in the chicken mixture and cook for 1 minute longer. Spoon the chicken mixture into a 9-inch deep-dish pie pan. Cut the filo sheets crosswise in half (making 11" x 8 1/2" sheets), and layer on top of the chicken mixture, overlapping the sheets at right angles, tucking in the edges all around the pan of each layer and lightly spraying each layer with nonstick cooking spray. Cut a 3 inch X in the center of the pie, pull back the inside corners of the X (to make a big opening), and lightly spray the corners with nonstick cooking spray. Bake the pot pie at 375 degrees for 10 to 15 minutes, or until the filling is heated through and the filo is crisp and lightly golden.

Barbecued Chicken

Cut up chicken
1 cup water
1 cup ketchup
1 tsp. vinegar

1 Tbsp. brown sugar
1 tsp. pepper
1 bay leaf
1/4 tsp. celery seed

Brown chicken in fry pan and put in layers in baking pan. Combine water, ketchup, vinegar, brown sugar, pepper, bay leaf and celery seed. Pour over meat and bake at 350 degrees for 1 hour or until done.

Herb and Lime Chicken

8 boneless, skinless chicken pieces
1 tsp. salt
1/2 tsp. pepper
1 Tbsp. butter or margarine
3 Tbsp. lime juice

1/2 cup water
1/4 tsp. basil
1/4 tsp. oregano
1 bay leaf

Brown the chicken pieces on both sides in a frying pan for about ten minutes over medium heat. In small container, mix together the remaining ingredients and then pour over the chicken. Reduce heat and cover; simmer for 20 - 30 minutes. Serve with rice or noodles.

Red Chicken Parmesan

4 boneless, skinless chicken breasts
1 egg, slightly beaten
1/2 cup seasoned bread crumbs
2 Tbsp. margarine or butter

1 3/4 cups spaghetti sauce
1/2 cup shredded mozzarella cheese
1 Tbsp. grated parmesan cheese
1/4 cup chopped fresh parsley

Dip chicken breasts into egg then into crumbs to coat. In skillet over medium heat, in hot margarine, brown chicken on both sides. Add spaghetti sauce. Reduce heat, cover, and simmer ten minutes. Sprinkle with cheeses and parsley. Cover, simmer 5 minutes or until cheese melts. Makes 4 servings.

Citrus Ginger Chicken

1/4 cup low-sugar orange marmalade
1 Tbsp. mustard
3/4 tsp. ginger
1/8 tsp. red pepper
4 skinned chicken breast halves

3 Tbsp. reduced calorie margarine
1/2 tsp. grated orange rind
1/4 tsp. ginger
orange rind curls, optional

Combine marmalade, mustard, ginger and red pepper in small bowl, stirring well. Brush half of marmalade mixture evenly over chicken breast halves. Place chicken on grill rack and cook 10 minutes on each side or until chicken is done, brushing frequently with remaining marmalade mixture. Combine margarine, orange rind and ginger in small bowl, stirring to blend. Spoon 1 Tbsp. margarine mixture over each chicken breast. Garnish with orange rind curls, if desired.

Chicken Vegetable Tetrazzini

9 oz. refrigerated linguine
2 Tbsp. olive oil
1 lb. boneless skinless chicken breasts,
    diced
2 Tbsp. butter
2 garlic cloves, minced
1 1/2 cups frozen broccoli, thawed

1 can sliced carrots
1 can sliced mushrooms
2/3 cup milk
1 can cream of chicken soup
1/3 cup grated parmesan cheese
salt and pepper
chopped fresh parsley

Cook linguine according to package directions. Heat oil in large skillet over medium-high heat until hot. Add chicken; cook and stir 4 - 5 minutes. Remove chicken and cover to keep warm. In same skillet, melt margarine over medium heat. Add garlic, broccoli, carrots and mushrooms; cook 4 - 5 minutes or until vegetables are tender. Stir in milk, soup, cheese and chicken; cook 1 - 2 minutes or until thoroughly heated. Stir in linguine; cook 2 minutes or until thoroughly heated, stirring occasionally. Add salt and pepper to taste; sprinkle with parsley.

Bonnie Blair's Championship Chicken

2 boneless, skinless chicken breasts
1/4 cup mayonnaise
1 Tbsp. Dijon mustard

1/2 Tbsp. honey
1/8 tsp. dried tarragon

Place chicken breasts on rack of broiler pan. Mix remaining ingredients together. Brush chicken with half of dressing mixture. Broil for 8 minutes. Turn over and brush with rest of mixture. Broil 8-10 minutes more.

Golden Lemon Chicken

3 boneless, skinless chicken breasts
1 egg, beaten
3 Tbsp. butter or margarine

1 Recipe Golden Herb & Lemon soup mix
1 cup water
4 lemon slices, optional

Dip chicken breasts into beaten egg and then into all-purpose flour. Brown chicken in butter. Blend soup mix and water together and bring to boil. Pour over chicken. Place 4 lemon slices on chicken. Simmer, covered, 10 minutes or until chicken is done. Serve over rice.

Festive Chicken

2 chicken breasts/thighs
2 bacon strips
1/2 cup soy sauce
1/4 cup sugar

2 garlic cloves, minced
1 1/2 tsp. ground ginger
1/8 tsp. paprika
2 - 3 drops hot pepper sauce

Remove skin from breasts or thighs. Wrap each with bacon strips. Place in a shallow glass baking dish. Set aside. In a small mixing bowl combine soy sauce, sugar, garlic, ginger, paprika, and hot pepper sauce. Pour over chicken, turning to coat evenly. Cover with plastic wrap & refrigerate several hours or overnight. Drain and reserve marinade. Bake for 50-60 minutes at 325 degrees. Baste occasionally with marinade.

Chicken and Dumpling Casserole

1/2 cup chopped onion
1/2 cup chopped celery
2 garlic cloves, minced
1/4 cup butter or margarine
1/2 cup flour
2 tsp. sugar
1 tsp. salt
1 tsp. dried basil

1/4 tsp. pepper
4 cups chicken broth
10 oz. frozen green peas
4 cups cubed cooked chicken
Dumplings:
2 cups buttermilk biscuit mix
2 tsp. dried basil
2/3 cup milk

In a large saucepan, saute onion, celery and garlic in butter until tender. Add flour, sugar, salt, basil, pepper and broth; bring to a boil. Cook and stir for 1 minute; reduce heat. Add peas and cook for 5 minutes, stirring constantly. Stir in chicken. Pour into a greased 13 x 9 inch baking dish. For dumplings, combine biscuit mix and basil in a bowl. Stir in milk with a fork until moistened. Drop by tablespoonfuls onto casserole (12 dumplings). Bake, uncovered, at 350 degrees for 30 minutes. Cover and bake 10 minutes more or until dumplings are done. Serves 6 to 8 people.

Chicken Curry

3 Tbsp. butter
1/4 cup minced onion
3 Tbsp. flour
3/4 tsp. salt
3/4 tsp. sugar
1 1/2 tsp. curry powder

1/8 tsp. ground ginger
1 cup chicken broth
1 cup milk
1/2 tsp. lemon juice
2 cups cooked chicken, diced

Melt butter over low heat. Saute minced onion. Blend in curry powder, flour, salt, sugar, and ground ginger. Cook over low heat until mixture is smooth and bubbly. Remove from heat. Stir in chicken broth and milk. Bring to a boil, stirring constantly. Boil one minute. Add lemon juice and diced chicken. Heat and serve over rice.

Chicken Divan

2 cups cooked chicken or turkey
2 cups cooked broccoli
1 can broccoli cheese soup
1/3 cup milk

1/2 cup shredded cheddar cheese
1 Tbsp. margarine
2 Tbsp. dry bread crumbs

Preheat oven to 450 degrees. In 2 quart casserole arrange cooked chicken and cooked broccoli. Combine soup and milk. Pour over chicken and broccoli. Sprinkle cheese over soup layer. Melt margarine and mix in bread crumbs. Sprinkle crumbs over shredded cheese. Bake at 450 degrees for 20 minutes.

Baked Chicken Breasts Supreme

1 1/2 cups plain yogurt or sour cream
1/4 cup lemon juice
1/2 tsp. worcestershire sauce
1/2 tsp. celery seed
1/2 tsp. paprika

1 garlic clove, minced
1/2 tsp. salt, optional
1/4 tsp. pepper
8 boneless skinless chicken breasts
2 cups fine dry bread crumbs

In a large bowl, combine first eight ingredients (all except chicken and bread crumbs). Place chicken in mixture and turn to coat. Cover and marinate overnight in the refrigerator. Remove chicken from marinade; coat each piece with crumbs. Arrange on a shallow baking pan. Bake, uncovered, at 350 degrees for 45 minutes or until juices run clear. Yield 8 servings.

Lemon Chicken

2 Tbsp. butter
1 lb. boneless, skinless chicken breast
1 medium onion, chopped
1 large carrot, thinly sliced
1 garlic clove, minced
1 Tbsp. cornstarch
14 oz. can chicken broth

2-3 Tbsp. lemon juice
1 tsp. grated lemon peel
1/2 tsp. salt
1 1/2 cups uncooked instant rice
1 cup frozen chopped broccoli, thawed
1/4 minced fresh parsley

Cut chicken breasts into strips. Brown chicken strips, onion, carrot, and garlic in butter for five minutes. In a bowl combine cornstarch and chicken broth. Stir in lemon juice, lemon peel, salt and rice. Add to skillet, bring to boil. Reduce heat. Add thawed broccoli and minced fresh parsley. Cover and simmer 5-10 minutes until rice is tender.

Chicken Crunch

1 can cream of chicken soup
1/2 cup of milk
4 boneless, skinless chicken breasts
2-3 Tbsp. flour

1 1/2 cups stuffing mix
1 tsp. parsley flakes
1/2 tsp. lemon juice

In pie plate combine 1/3 cup soup and 1/4 cup milk. Lightly coat chicken breasts with flour. Dip into soup mixture then into finely crushed stuffing mix. Arrange chicken pieces in baking pan. Bake at 400 degrees for 20 minutes or until chicken is tender and no longer pink. In small sauce pan combine remaining soup with 1/4 cup milk, parsley flakes, and lemon juice. Heat through, stirring occasionally. Serve chicken pieces with a little sauce spooned over each piece.

London Chicken

1 chicken
1 can cream of celery soup
1 can cream of mushroom soup

1/2 pkg. onion soup mix
3/4 cup rice
1/2 cup water

Cut chicken into pieces and remove skin. Mix the three soups and water. Blend well. Pour over rice. Put chicken on bottom of casserole. Pour rice and soup mixture over chicken. Bake 1 hour covered at 350 degrees. Uncover and bake 1/2 hour.

Chicken Honey Nut Stir Fry

1 lb. boneless chicken breasts	1 Tbsp. oil
3/4 cup orange juice	2 large carrots
1/3 cup honey	2 stalks celery
3 Tbsp. soy sauce	1 Tbsp. oil
2 Tbsp. cornstarch	1/2 cup cashews or peanuts
1/4 tsp. ground ginger	

Cut chicken breasts into thin strips. In small bowl mix orange juice, honey, soy sauce, cornstarch and ground ginger. Heat oil in skillet over medium heat. Add carrots and celery diagonally cut. Stir-fry 3 minutes. Remove vegetables from skillet. Pour off oil. Add chicken. Stir fry 3 minutes. Return vegetables to skillet. Add sauce mixture and cashews. Cook and stir over medium high heat until sauce is thickened. Serve over hot rice.

Curried Chicken

3 boneless chicken breasts	1 Tbsp. salad oil
1 Tbsp. hot curry powder	1/3 cup golden raisins
1 tsp. chicken bouillon	3/4 cup water
1/2 tsp. sugar	8 oz. plain yogurt
1/4 tsp. salt	2 Tbsp. flour
1 medium onion	1 diced apple

Cut each chicken breast into eight pieces. Mix curry powder, bouillon, sugar and salt. Cook diced onion in salad oil until golden brown. Add chicken and curry powder mixture. Cook 3 to 5 minutes until chicken loses its pink color. Stir in raisins and water. Heat to boiling. Reduce to low heat. In small bowl mix yogurt with flour until well blended. Slowly stir yogurt mixture into liquid in skillet, stirring constantly until heated through. Do not boil. Spoon chicken mixture over rice on a large platter. Sprinkle with diced apple. Makes 4 servings.

Baked Chicken

8 skinless, boneless chicken breasts	1 cup sour cream
8 strips bacon	1 can cream of mushroom soup

Wrap each chicken breast in a slice of bacon. Mix sour cream and cream of mushroom soup; pour over chcken. Bake in greased 9 x 13 pan at 275 degrees for 3 hours. Bake uncovered.

Chicken Wings with Mustard

20 chicken wings (tips removed,
    with remaining piece cut in half)
2/3 cup butter

1/4 cup Dijon mustard
1 1/4 cups seasoned bread crumbs
1/4 cup parmesan cheese

Melt butter and stir in mustard until well blended. Place bread crumbs in flat dish. Roll each piece of chicken in butter mixture then coat with bread crumbs. Arrange on a rack in a roasting pan or on a cookie sheet. Sprinkle with parmesan cheese. Bake in 400 degree oven for 15 minutes. Turn and bake 15 minutes longer or until crispy.

Maple Glazed Chicken and Sweet Potatoes

1 chicken
3 or 4 sweet potatoes
1 Tbsp. salad oil
1/2 tsp. salt
salt and pepper to taste

1/2 Tbsp. butter
1/8 cup maple syrup
1 Tbsp. brown sugar
1/4 cup boiling water

Preheat oven to 450 degrees. Peel and cut sweet potatoes into 2 inch chunks. In large bowl mix sweet potatoes with salad oil and salt. Place sweet potatoes in 9 x 13 pan; set aside. Rub chicken pieces with salt and pepper. Arrange skin side up over sweet potatoes in cake pan. Bake 25 minutes. In small sauce pan melt butter over low heat. Stir in maple syrup and brown sugar. Brush on chicken. Bake 20 minutes longer. Remove chicken and sweet potatoes from pan. Spoon off fat, stir in boiling water and mix well with pan drippings. Spoon juices over chicken and sweet potatoes.

Chicken with Bernaise Sauce

6 boneless, skinless chicken breasts, diced
salt and white pepper
butter
Bernaise Sauce:
1 clove garlic, pressed
1 can cream of chicken soup

1/4 cup butter
2 to 3 tsp. lemon juice
2 to 3 tsp. vinegar
1/2 to 3/4 tsp. tarragon leaves
1/4 cup finely chopped fresh parsley
salt and white pepper to taste

Saute chicken in butter until lightly browned. Season with salt and white pepper. Top with Bernaise sauce: combine all ingredients in saucepan and heat until hot. Do not boil. Use over chicken, vegetables, beef or veal. May be made in advance and refrigerated for several days.

Country Chicken Casserole

2 cups cooked chicken
2 cans cream of chicken soup
2 tsp. poultry seasoning
1 cup sour cream
1/3 tsp. pepper
1 Tbsp. parsley
1 1/2 cups milk
1/2 to 1 cup chicken broth

Ingredients for topping:
1 cup Bisquick
1 tsp. salt
2 tsp. baking powder
1/2 cup milk
1 Tbsp. parsley
2 well beaten eggs
1 cup shredded cheddar cheese

Cook soup, seasoning, pepper, parsley, milk, broth and sour cream to blend ingredients. Add chicken, place in a casserole dish. Combine the Bisquick, salt, baking powder, milk, parsley and eggs. Mix until moistened. Place on top of chicken, top with cheese and bake 40-45 minutes at 350 degrees.

Quick Chicken Casserole

3/4 cup cooked chicken, cut up
1 cup sliced celery
2 tsp. chopped onion
1/2 cup chopped walnuts
1 1/2 cups cooked rice
1 can cream of chicken soup
1/2 tsp. salt

1/4 tsp. pepper
1 Tbsp. lemon juice
3/4 cup mayonnaise
1/4 cup water
3 hard cooked eggs, sliced
2 cups crushed potato chips

In a large bowl, combine diced chicken, celery, onion, nuts, rice, chicken soup, salt, pepper and lemon juice. Mix mayonnaise with water and add to chicken mixture. Gently stir in hard cooked egg slices. Turn mixture into a greased 9-inch square pan, top with crushed potato chips. Bake in a very hot oven (450 degrees) for 15 minutes, or until mixture is bubbly. Serves 6.

Italian Style Chicken

1/2 cup magarine
1/4 cup lemon juice
1 cup lite Italian dressing

1/4 cup worcestershire sauce
2 cloves garlic, crushed
2 whole chicken breasts, split

Combine first 5 ingredients. Cook over medium heat until margarine melts. Place chicken breasts in baking dish. Sprinkle with a little salt and pepper. Pour sauce evenly over chicken. Bake uncovered, in 325 degree oven for 1 hour or until tender.

Baked Chicken Breasts

boneless, skinless chicken breasts
1 pkg. dry onion soup mix

16 oz. bottle Kraft Catalina salad dressing

Place washed boneless, skinless chicken breasts in a 9 x 13 pan. Sprinkle with dry onion soup. Add Kraft Catalina salad dressing. Cover with aluminum foil. Bake 1 1/2 hours at 350 degrees.

Baked Chicken Reuben

8 small boneless chicken breasts
16 oz. can sauerkraut
4 slices swiss cheese

8 oz. thousand island salad dressing
1 Tbsp. chopped parsley

Preheat oven to 375 degrees. In 9 x 13 baking dish arrange chicken breasts in 1 layer. Rinse sauerkraut, press out water. Cut cheese slices. Sprinkle sauerkraut on chicken breasts. Top with dressing and cheese. Bake 40 minutes covered, or until tender. Garnish with parsley.

Turkey Meatballs Tetrazzini

1 slice whole wheat bread
3/4 lb. uncooked ground turkey
1 clove garlic, pressed
1/2 tsp. dried basil leaves
1/2 tsp. salt
pepper
1 tsp. butter

1 onion peeled and diced (small)
1/4 lb. fresh mushrooms, cleaned and quartered
1 1/2 cups milk
2 Tbsp. flour
1/4 cup parmesan cheese
Chopped fresh parsley
Angel hair pasta (fettuccini is good)

Crumble the bread into a medium bowl. Blend in ground turkey, garlic, basil, salt and pepper. Form turkey mixture into one-inch meatballs. Melt butter in large skillet. Saute meatballs on all sides, loosening them carefully before turning. Stir in onion and mushrooms; saute until golden. Whisk flour into milk, whipping until smooth; add to skillet. Cook, stirring constantly, until thickened. Fold in the cheese. Place cooked, drained pasta on serving plate. Spoon tetrazzini into center. Sprinkle with parsley and additional cheese, if desired.

Cheese Turkey Bake

1 1/2 cups small bread cubes
2 Tbsp. butter, melted
1/8 tsp. oregano
2 Tbsp. grated parmesan cheese
1 can cream of mushroom soup
1 1/4 cups evaporated milk

1/4 tsp. onion powder
1 tsp. dried parsley flakes
1/8 tsp. oregano
3 cups chopped cooked turkey
5 oz. lasagna noodles, cooked
2/3 cup shredded mozzarella cheese

Combine bread cubes, butter, 1/8 tsp. oregano and parmesan cheese. Set aside. Combine soup, milk, onion powder, parsley flakes and 1/8 tsp. oregano. Stir in turkey. In a 2 quart oblong baking dish, layer in order, one-half the noodles, soup mixture and cheese. Repeat. Top with bread crumbs. Bake at 375 degrees for 30 - 35 minutes or until bubbly around the edges. Let stand 10 minutes before cutting into squares. Makes 6 large servings.

Turkey Wild Rice Bake

1 - 6 oz. box wild rice mix
1/4 cup melted butter
1/2 cup chopped onion
1 cup cream or part milk
1 cup broth or turkey gravy
1/4 cup chopped parsley

4 Tbsp. chopped almonds
1 small jar pimento
chicken or turkey, diced
1 tsp. salt
pepper
1/3 cup flour

Cook rice as directed. Saute onion in butter; add salt, pepper and flour; add cream and broth. When thick, add remaining ingredients. Bake in a casserole 40 minutes at 400 degrees.

Easy Turkey Lasagna

8 oz. carton lasagna noodles
1 lb. ground turkey
32 oz. jar spaghetti sauce
1/2 cup water
1 tsp. salt

1/8 cup sugar
1 tsp. Italian seasoning
15 oz. carton Ricotta cheese (low fat)
3 cups shredded mozzarella cheese
1/2 cup grated parmesan cheese

Brown ground turkey. Pour off fat, if any. Add spaghetti sauce, water and seasonings. Simmer 7 minutes. In a 13 x 9 inch pan, layer 1/3 of the sauce, 1/2 of the uncooked lasagna noodles, 1/2 of Ricotta cheese and 1/3 of the mozzarella cheese. Repeat layers, ending with sauce, mozzarella and parmesan cheeses. Cover tightly with foil. Bake at 350 degrees about 55 minutes. Note: Lasagna noodles get tender with sauce below and above them.

Scalloped Turkey

1 cup regular rice
2 cups water
2 bouillon cubes
1/4 cup butter
1 cup fresh sliced mushrooms
1 Tbsp. chopped onion
3 Tbsp. flour
2 cups chopped cooked turkey

1/2 tsp. salt
1/4 tsp. marjoram
1/8 tsp. pepper
2 cups milk
2 cups shredded cheddar cheese
1 1/4 oz. pimento
3 slices white bread
2 Tbsp. butter

Cook rice in water, bouillon cubes, and a little oil. Melt 1/4 cup butter in 2 quart saucepan. Saute mushrooms and chopped onion. Stir in flour, salt, marjoram, and pepper. Gradually stir in milk. Bring to a boil, stirring constantly. Boil and stir one minute. Add 1 1/2 cups shredded cheese and pimento. Stir until cheese melts. Add turkey and cooked rice. Spoon into buttered 2 quart casserole. Sprinkle 1/2 cup shredded cheese on top. Remove crust from bread and cube. Toss bread cubes in 2 Tbsp. melted butter. Arrange around edge of casserole. Bake 20 minutes at 350 degrees.

Easy Casserole

2 cups uncooked macaroni
1 can celery soup
1 can mushroom soup
1 small jar pimento
2 cups milk

4 oz. mushroom pieces
1/2 lb. Velveeta cheese
1/4 cup diced green pepper
2 cups diced, cooked chicken, turkey ham, or chipped beef

Combine all ingredients in 9 x 13 pan or 3 quart casserole. Bake at 350 degrees for 1 hour.

Crockpot Dilled Pot Roast

3 - 3 1/2 lbs. beef pot roast
1 tsp. salt
1/4 tsp. pepper
1 tsp. dill weed
1/4 cup water

1 Tbsp. vinegar
3 Tbsp. flour
1 tsp. dill
1 cup sour cream

Sprinkle meat with salt, pepper and dill weed. Place in crockpot. Add water and vinegar. Cook slowly 7 - 9 hours. Remove meat. Turn crockpot to high. Dissolve flour in a small amount of water and stir into the meat juice. Add dill and cook on high 10 minutes. Add sour cream and cook a little longer to heat. Serve meat with meat sauce.

Oriental Pot Roast

1 (2-3 lbs.) beef chuck pot roast
1/3 cup cooking oil
1/3 cup soy sauce
2 Tbsp. lemon juice
2 Tbsp. honey
1 clove garlic, minced

1 1/4 Tbsp. ground ginger
1/4 cup cold water
1 Tbsp. cornstarch
1 1/2 cups sliced celery
1 1/2 cups sliced carrots

Trim excess fat from meat. Place meat in a casserole or 4 qt. Nesco roaster.
Marinade: Combine cooking oil, soy sauce, lemon juice, honey, garlic and ginger. Pour over meat, cover. Marinate overnight in refrigerator. Turn meat occasionally to distribute marinade.
Next day cook in 325 degree oven for 5-6 hours or until meat is tender.
Gravy: For gravy, skim excess fat from pan juices. Pour juices into a 2 cup measure. Add water to juices if necessary to yield 1 1/4 cup liquid. Using a small saucepan, combine 1 1/4 cup liquid, mixture of 1/4 cup water and cornstarch. Cook and stir until thickened and bubbly. Serve gravy over meat.
Optional: If you would like vegetables to be cooked along with meat, add 2 medium onions prior to placing into casserole. Add vegetables listed below the last 3 1/2 hours of cooking time: 1 1/2 cups celery (bias sliced into 1/2-inch pieces), 4 medium carrots (bias sliced into 1/2-inch pieces equal to 1 1/2 cups). Vegetables will become dark in coloration due to soy sauce.

Chinese Pepper Steak

1 Tbsp. soy sauce
1 clove garlic
1/4 cup salad oil
1 lb. round steak, cut in strips or cubed
2 green peppers, sliced
1 large onion, coarsely chopped

1/2 cup diced celery
1 tsp. cornstarch
1/4 cup water
2 tomatoes, cut into eighths
mushrooms, optional

Mix soy sauce, garlic, and salad oil together, and pour over steak that has been cut into strips or 1 inch cubes. Let stand for one hour. Pour mixture into fry pan, and allow meat to brown thoroughly on all sides. Add peppers, onion, celery, and cover and cook 5 to 10 minutes over low heat, or until vegetables are tender. Stir in cornstarch dissolved in water. Stir until thickened. Add tomatoes and mushrooms, cover and cook 5 to10 minutes longer, until meat is tender. Serve over rice.

Beef Roast Supreme

4 lb. beef roast
1 can mushroom soup

1 envelope onion soup mix
salt and pepper to taste

Place roast in foil. Cover with mushroom soup and sprinkle dry onion soup mix over soup. Season with salt and pepper. Seal tight in foil and place in pan or roaster. Do not peek or open foil until ready to serve. There will be juice for gravy. Oven temperature: 350 degrees. Baking time: 3 1/2 to 4 hours.

Easy Broiled Sirloin

2 Tbsp. lemon juice
2 Tbsp. Dijon mustard
1 tsp. dried basil leaves

1/2 tsp. salt
1 boneless beef top sirloin steak,
    1"-1 1/2 " thick (2 1/2 lb.)

Mix lemon juice, mustard, basil and salt. Trim fat from steak; put steak on broiler pan. Spread half of mustard mix on steak. Broil 7 minutes. Turn steak and spread with rest of mixture. Broil 5 minutes longer or until done. Thin-slice the steak and serve.

Peppered Rib Eye Steaks

4 beef rib eye steaks
1 Tbsp. olive oil
1 Tbsp. garlic powder
1 Tbsp. paprika
2 tsp. thyme
2 tsp. oregano

1 1/2 tsp. pepper
1 tsp. salt
1 tsp. lemon pepper
1 tsp. ground red pepper
orange slices, optional
parsley sprig, optional

Brush steaks lightly with olive oil. In a small bowl, combine all seasonings. Sprinkle seasonings over steaks and press into both sides. Cover and chill for 1 hour. Grill steaks, turning once, over medium-hot coals 14-18 minutes for rare; 18-22 minutes for medium; 24-28 minutes for well-done. Place on a warm serving platter; cut across the grain into thick slices. Garnish with orange slices and parsley if desired. Yield: 8 servings.

Salisbury Steak

1 can condensed onion soup
1 1/2 lb. ground beef
1/4 tsp. salt
1/2 cup bread crumbs
dash pepper
1 egg, slightly beaten

1/4 cup ketchup
1 tsp. worcestershire
1/2 tsp. mustard
1/4 cup water
1 Tbsp. flour

Mix 1/3 cup soup, beef, bread crumbs, egg, salt and pepper. Shape into 6 oval patties. Brown patties in skillet, pour off fat. Add remaining soup, ketchup, worcestershire sauce and mustard. Gradually blend water into flour until smooth. Stir into soup mixture. Cover; cook over low heat 20 minutes or until done. Stir occasionally. Serves 6.

Rosy Meatballs

1 lb. ground beef
1/2 cup cracker or bread crumbs
1 egg, beaten
1 tsp. instant minced onion, rehydrated

1/4 tsp. dry mustard
16 oz. whole-berry cranberry sauce
8 oz. tomato sauce

Combine all ingredients except cranberry sauce and tomato sauce. Shape into bite-sized meatballs and brown in skillet. Mix cranberry sauce and tomato sauce in bowl and pour over meatballs. Simmer covered 30 minutes.

Porcupine Balls

1 lb. ground beef
1/2 lb. ground pork
1/2 green pepper
1/2 onion, cut fine
1 cup raw rice

2 slices bread soaked in milk and mashed
1 egg, beaten
1 Tbsp. salt
1 tsp. pepper
1 can tomato soup

Mix all ingredients together except soup. Form into balls (20 or 30). Place in baking dish, or roaster, and pour soup and 2 cans water over the meat balls. Bake at 325 degrees for two hours.

Norsk Meatballs

1 lb. ground beef
1/3 lb. ground pork
1/2 cup bread crumbs
1/2 cup milk
1 egg
1 tsp. salt
Fresh ground pepper
small amount of flour

Gravy:
Drippings
4 cups water
6 Tbsp. flour
Salt to taste and a little sugar

Have meat ground as fine as possible. Blend other ingredients in blender and combine with meat. Add a little flour to make meat mixture easy to handle and shape into walnut-sized balls. Place on broiler rack and bake at 350 degrees until brown - 30 to 45 minutes. From drippings, make gravy; add to meat balls and simmer one hour.

Barbecued Meatballs

2 lb. hamburger
1 egg
1 cup milk
2 cups cubed, soft bread
Salt and pepper

1 cup ketchup
4 Tbsp. vinegar
4 Tbsp. worcestershire sauce
2 Tbsp. brown sugar

Mix first column of ingredients together, make into balls and brown. Put all the other ingredients in a sauce pan. Boil over low heat, stir and pour over browned meatballs which have been placed in baking dish. Cover and bake slowly for 2 hours at 325 degrees. The sauce is delicious on other meats also.

Meatballs with Mushroom Soup

1 lb. ground beef
1/2 lb. ground pork
2 eggs well beaten
2/3 cup parmesan cheese
1/2 tsp. oregano

1/4 tsp. thyme
Dash of pepper
1 can cream of mushroom soup
2/3 cup water

Mix the beef, pork, eggs, cheese, oregano, thyme and pepper. Make into balls about one inch in diameter. Brown in skillet. Drain off fat. Combine soup and water and pour over meatballs. Simmer for about 25 minutes or put in casserole in oven for about one hour at 325 degrees.

Champion Meat Loaf

1 1/2 lbs. ground beef
2 eggs, slightly beaten
1 envelope onion soup mix

1 cup sour cream
1 cup decrusted soft bread crumbs
2 strips bacon

Mix together beef, eggs, soup mix, sour cream and bread crumbs. Shape in a loaf pan and top with two strips of bacon. Put in oven preheated to 500 degrees. Turn down heat to 375 degrees and bake for one hour.

Barbecued Meat Loaf

1 1/2 lbs. ground beef
1/2 lb. ground pork
2 Tbsp. chopped onion
1/2 cup dry bread crumbs
3/4 cup milk
2 eggs, beaten

2 tsp. salt
1/8 tsp. pepper
1/2 dill pickle, chopped
3 Tbsp. brown sugar
1/2 cup ketchup
1 tsp. Kitchen Bouquet

Mix all ingredients together and put in loaf pan. Bake 1 1/2 hours at 350 degrees.

Glorified Meat Loaf

1 1/2 lbs. ground beef
2 cups cereal flakes
2 eggs
1 cup milk
3 Tbsp. minced green onion
2 tsp. salt
Pepper

1/8 tsp. dry mustard
1/8 tsp. sage
3 Tbsp. brown sugar
1/4 cup ketchup
1 tsp. dry mustard
1/4 tsp. nutmeg

Put flakes, eggs, milk, onion, salt, pepper, dry mustard and sage in bowl and mix thoroughly. Add ground meat and mix. Put in greased loaf pan. Bake at 350 degrees for 1 1/2 hours. After loaf is in oven mix the brown sugar, ketchup, 1 tsp. dry mustard and nutmeg. One half hour before meat loaf is done put sauce mixture on top of loaf.

10 Minute Meat Loaf

1 lb. ground beef
1/2 cup bread crumbs
2 Tbsp. onion soup mix (dry)
2 Tbsp. ketchup

1/2 cup shredded swiss cheese
1 egg
1/4 cup milk
2 Tbsp. soy sauce

Combine all ingredients and shape into a round or oval loaf. Place in a microwave-safe dish, cover with waxed paper and microwave on High for 10 minutes, turning dish after 5 minutes of cooking. Drain and cover with foil. Let stand 10 minutes before slicing.

Beef and Broccoli

1 lb. lean beef
2 Tbsp. soy sauce
1/4 tsp. garlic powder
1/4 tsp. powdered garlic
1 tsp. worcestershire sauce
1/2 cup + 2 Tbsp. water

2 Tbsp. oil
1 medium onion, sliced
1 cup cauliflower
3 cups broccoli
1 cup fresh mushrooms
1 Tbsp. cornstarch

Cut beef across grain into strips. Combine soy sauce, garlic powder, powdered garlic, worcestershire sauce and 1/2 cup water, and pour over meat. Marinate while preparing vegetables. Heat oil in wok or fry pan. Add onion, cauliflower and broccoli, plus 2 Tbsp. water. Cover and cook for 2 minutes. Meanwhile, drain beef, reserving marinade. Add mushrooms to other vegetables and cook 1 minute. Remove vegetables from pan. Stir fry beef until just the color changes. Add vegetables and stir until heated. Combine reserved marinade with cornstarch; add to meat mixture. Stir until thickened. Serves 5.

Beef Stroganoff

1 lb. beef tenderloin or sirloin
1/2 tsp. salt
1/4 tsp. pepper
1/4 cup flour
2 Tbsp. shortening
2 Tbsp. flour

1 medium onion, chopped
8 oz. can mushrooms, drained
1/2 cup beef bouillon
3/4 cup water
1/2 tsp. salt
1/2 cup sour cream

Cut meat into one inch strips. Shake strips in paper sack with salt, pepper, and 1/4 cup flour until evenly coated. Brown in hot shortening. Remove meat from skillet and brown 2 Tbsp. flour. Add onion and mushrooms; cook for 5 minutes. Add meat, bouillon, water and salt. Simmer covered, for 30 to 45 minutes, adding more water if necessary. Stir in sour cream and heat through. Serve immediately over hot rice or noodles. 4 servings.

Lite Beef Stroganoff

3/4 lb. lean round steak,
   boneless and trimmed
1 cup sliced fresh mushrooms
1/2 cup thinly sliced white onion
1/2 cup beef broth
1/2 cup water

1 tsp. ketchup
pepper to taste
2 Tbsp. flour
1 cup buttermilk
2 cups egg noodles, cooked

Slice steak across the grain into thin strips about 1/8 inch wide and 3 inches long. You'll find it easier to thinly slice the meat if it is slightly frozen. In a large nonstick frying pan, place the beef strips, mushrooms and onion. Cook, stirring often, over medium-high heat, until the meat is well browned. Add the broth, water, ketchup and pepper. Reduce heat, cover and simmer about 45 minutes, stirring occasionally. In a small bowl, mix the flour with 1/4 cup of the buttermilk until smooth. Add the remaining buttermilk, mix well. Stir into the hot beef mixture. Cook, stirring constantly, until thickened. Serve immediately over the hot egg noodles. Serves 4 people.

Stuffed Burger Bundles

1/3 cup evaporated milk
1 lb. hamburger
1 can cream of mushroom soup
2 tsp. worcestershire sauce
1 tsp. ketchup

Dressing:
3 cups dry bread cubes
1 1/2 Tbsp. shortening
1/4 cup chopped onion
1/3 tsp. salt
1 1/2 cups milk (or more)
pinch of celery salt
1 1/2 tsp. sage

Melt the shortening, add onions, and cook for a few minutes. Add to the bread cubes, and add seasonings and milk. Combine the evaporated milk and meat, and divide into six patties. Pat into 6 inch circles. Put 1/4 cup dressing mixture in center of each pattie. Pull sides of meat up to cover dressing and seal. Place in baking pan. Combine soup, sauce and ketchup, pour over meat. Bake uncovered at 350 degrees for 1 1/2 hours or until done. Makes 6 servings.

Easy Goulash

1 lb. lean beef cubes (don't brown)
1 can (16 oz.) stewed tomatoes
1 envelope onion soup mix
1 Tbsp. flour
1 Tbsp. paprika
1 tsp. salt

1/4 tsp. pepper
1/4 tsp. thyme
1 tsp. sugar
dash of allspice
1/3 cup water (or red wine)
1/2 cup sour cream

Place beef cubes in 2 qt. casserole. Combine remaining ingredients in blender. Mix with beef. Cover and bake at 350 degrees for 1 1/2 hours. Stir in sour cream. Serve over rice or noodles. Casserole can be prepared a day before being baked, or can be frozen for later use.

Spaghetti Sauce

1 lb. hamburger
2 Tbsp. vegetable oil
1 large onion, diced
1 lb. sweet sausage, optional
pork or chicken pieces, optional
1/4 cup green pepper, diced
1 can mushrooms
1 large can tomato sauce
1 large can tomato paste

1 large can Italian tomatoes
1/2 tsp. black pepper
1/2 tsp. allspice
1/2 tsp. oregano
1/8 tsp. cayenne pepper
1 tsp. basil
1 tsp. sugar
1/4 tsp. fennel seed

Brown meat in oil. Add remaining ingredients and simmer.

Zucchini Lasagna

1/2 to 1 lb. lean ground beef
1/2 cup chopped onion
15 oz. can tomato sauce
1/2 tsp. salt
1/4 tsp. basil
1/2 tsp. oregano

1/8 tsp. pepper
4 medium zucchini
8 oz. cottage cheese
1 egg
1/4 lb. mozzarella cheese, shredded
2 Tbsp. flour

Brown beef and onion. Drain and add sauce and spices. Bring to boil and simmer 5 minutes. Slice zucchini lengthwise in 1/4 inch slices. Mix cottage cheese and egg. In 9 x 13 pan, layer half of zucchini, 1 Tbsp. flour, half of the cottage cheese, meat and mozzarella cheese. Repeat layers. Bake in 375 degrees for 40 minutes. Let stand 10 minutes before serving.

Pizza Casserole

16 oz. rotini pasta, cooked
2 1/2 lb. hamburger
1 medium onion, chopped
salt and pepper to taste
dash of garlic powder
3 - 15 oz. cans pizza sauce
6 oz. can tomato paste

8 oz. can tomato sauce
1/2 tsp. sugar
dash of onion salt
dash of oregano
1/4 lb. pepperoni, sliced thin
4 cups grated mozzarella cheese
Romano cheese, grated

Grease casserole. Brown hamburger with onion, salt and pepper, and garlic. Drain and then add cooked rotini. Mix together pizza sauce, tomato paste, tomato sauce, sugar, onion salt and oregano. Layer in casserole the sauce, hamburger mixture, pepperoni and mozzarella cheese, using one-fourth of the amounts at a time. End layers with sauce. Sprinkle with grated romano cheese. Bake at 350 degrees for 45 minutes or until cheese is melted and bubbling. This dish can be made in advance and kept in refrigerator or freezer.

Chow Mein Hotdish for 80

12 lbs. hamburger
8 cups diced celery
8 onions, chopped
16 cans cream of mushroom soup
8 cans chicken with rice soup

8 small cans mushrooms with juice
64 oz. frozen mixed vegetables
4 cups water
16 Tbsp. soy sauce
16 cups chow mein noodles

Brown hamburger, celery and onion. Mix all ingredients except chow mein noodles in 18 quart roaster and cook at 350 degrees until heated through. Add the chow mein noodles and cook for one more hour.

Baked Luncheon Dish

1 1/2 lbs. ground beef, browned
1/2 lb. ground pork, browned
2 pkgs. Chinese noodles
1 can whole kernel corn
1 cup grated cheese

1 green pepper, chopped
1 egg, beaten
1 can tomato soup
1 small onion, cut fine

Cook noodles 1 minute, then mix all together. Bake 1 hour at 350 degrees. Serves 12 people. If desired, serve with mushroom sauce.

French Green Beans and Tator Tot Hot Dish

2 lb. ground beef - browned
1 can french cut green beans
1 pkg. dry onion soup mix

1 can cream of mushroom soup
1 can cream of chicken soup
1 bag tater tots

Pour mixture of beef, beans and onion soup in a casserole. Pour over it cream of mushroom soup and cream of chicken soup. Bake 30 minutes at 350 degrees. The last 15 minutes of baking put tator tots on top.

Rice Hot Dish

2 lb. hamburger
onions to taste
1/2 cup raw rice
1/2 cup celery
2 cans cream of chicken soup

2 cans cream of mushroom soup
1 can water
3 Tbsp. soy sauce
salt and pepper to taste
Chow mein noodles if desired

Brown hamburger and onions. Add other ingredients. Top with chow mein noodles if desired. Bake at 350 degrees for 45 to 60 minutes.

Johnny Mozette

2 cups chopped green pepper
1 cup chopped celery
2 cups chopped onion
1 lb. ground beef
1 lb. ground pork
1 cup butter or margarine
2 tsp. salt

1/3 cup chopped stuffed olives
4 oz. can sliced mushrooms with liquid
1 can tomato soup
8 oz. can tomato sauce
8 oz. can tomato mushroom soup
1 lb. broad noodles
2 cups grated American cheese

Saute pepper, celery, onion and ground meat in hot butter. Add salt, reduce heat, cook 5 minutes. Stir in olives and liquid of mushroom, soups and sauces. Cook 5 minutes. Cook noodles and drain. Turn noodles into 14x10 roasting pan. Add other ingredients and mix. Sprinkle cheese on top. Bake at 350 degrees for 35 minutes.

Barbecued Hamburger

2 lb. ground beef, browned
3/4 cup chili sauce
1 tsp. salt
pepper

1 tsp. chili powder
1 Tbsp. prepared mustard
1/2 cup chopped onion

Brown ground beef, and add remaining ingredients. Simmer 45 minutes.

Macaroni and Hamburger Hot Dish

2 cups macaroni
1 lb. hamburger
1 small onion
1 large can tomatoes
1 can tomato soup

1 can cream of mushroom soup
1/2 tsp. salt
1/2 tsp. pepper
1/2 tsp. celery salt

Cook the macaroni. Brown the hamburger and onion. Add the rest of the ingredients to the browned hamburger and add this to the cooked macaroni. Place in casserole dish. Bake at 350 degrees for 1/2 to 1 hour.

Hamburger Vegetable Fry

1 lb. hamburger
1 chopped onion
1 cup orzo or tiny shells

1 pkg. frozen vegetables,
        Japanese or Hawaiian style

Brown hamburger and onion. Cook frozen vegetables according to package directions. Cook macaroni, drain. Mix together all ingredients and serve. Makes 4 servings.

Plantation Supper

1 lb. hamburger
1/2 cup chopped onion
3/4 cup milk
1 can cream of mushroom soup
8 oz. cream cheese

1 1/2 cups (1 can) whole kernel corn
1/4 cup chopped pimento
8 oz. noodles, cooked
1 1/2 tsp. salt
dash of pepper

Brown hamburger, add onions and cook until tender. Stir in milk, soup and cheese until well blended. Add remaining ingredients and heat.

Taco Casserole

16 oz. medium taco sauce
1 can refrigerated buttermilk biscuits
1 1/2 cups shredded cheddar cheese
1 1/2 cups shredded mozzarella cheese
1 can sliced ripe olives, drained

1/2 lb. lean ground beef
1/4 cup chopped red bell pepper
1/4 cup chopped green bell pepper
1 can mushrooms, drained

Spread taco sauce evenly over bottom of greased 9 x 13 pan. Separate dough into 10 biscuits and cut each biscuit into 4 pieces. Place biscuit pieces in taco sauce, turning to coat. Sprinkle biscuits with 1 cup of cheddar cheese, 1 cup of mozzarella cheese and the olives. Mix gently. Bake at 400 degrees for 15 - 18 minutes or until bubbly. Meanwhile, combine ground beef, peppers and mushrooms in large skillet and cook until beef is browned; drain. Sprinkle remaining 1/2 cup cheddar cheese and 1/2 cup mozzarella cheese over mixture in casserole. Top with ground beef mixture. Bake an additional 5 - 7 minutes or until mixture bubbles vigorously around edges.

Squash Spaghetti

2 lb. ground beef
1 onion, diced
1 bell pepper, diced
1 cup diced celery
1 cup chopped mushrooms
3 diced garlic cloves
1/2 tsp. basil

1/2 tsp. oregano
1/2 tsp. salt
1/8 tsp. pepper
3 cups peeled, diced summer squash
1 large can chopped tomatoes
1 large can spaghetti sauce

Saute the ground beef, onion, pepper, celery, mushrooms, garlic and spices. Add squash. Cover and simmer 5 minutes on low to medium heat. Add chopped tomatoes and spaghetti sauce. Simmer 30 minutes. Serves 8. Squash doesn't alter taste much; but merely extends recipe to serve more.

Sauerkraut and Spareribs

2 lbs. spareribs
salt
1 qt. sauerkraut

1 onion
1/2 cup water

Season spareribs with salt. Add sauerkraut, onion and water. Cook 1 hour on top of stove, then put in a baking dish and place spareribs on top. Bake at 350 degrees for 1 to 1 1/2 hours.

Greek Pizza

Boboli bread shell
1 pkg. frozen spinach,
    thawed and squeezed
1/2 cup crumbled feta cheese
1/2 cup grated mozzarella cheese

1/4 cup sliced black olives
1 tomato, chopped
1/4 lb. cooked shrimp
some chopped red onion

Layer all ingredients on the Boboli bread shell. Bake at 450 degrees for ten minutes.

Upside Down Pizza

1 1/2 lbs. ground beef
1 medium onion, chopped
1 can (15 oz.) pizza sauce
1/2 tsp. garlic salt
1/4 tsp. dried oregano leaves
8 oz. mozzarella cheese, grated

2 eggs
1 cup milk
1 Tbsp. oil
1/2 tsp. salt
1 cup flour
1/2 cup grated parmesan cheese

Brown ground beef and onion, pour off fat. Blend in pizza sauce, garlic salt and oregano. Put mixture in greased 9x13 pan and sprinkle with mozzarella. In small bowl mix eggs, milk, oil, salt and flour; pour over meat mixture and sprinkle with parmesan cheese. Bake 30 minutes at 350 degrees. Makes 12 servings. Note: mushrooms, bell pepper strips, Italian sausage or Canadian bacon may be added if desired.

New Italian Swiss Twist Pizza Bianca

1 1/2 cups shredded swiss cheese
1/2 cup shredded parmesan cheese
1/2 cup diced cooked turkey sausage
1/4 cup chopped pickle

1/2 cup mayonnaise
1 Tbsp. prepared mustard
1/4 tsp. white pepper
4 prepared Italian bread shells

Combine the cheeses, sausage, pickle, mayonnaise, mustard and pepper. Mix well. Spread mixture evenly over bread shells. Place on large baking sheet. Bake at 450 degrees for 10 minutes or until cheese is melted and crust is browned and crisp.

Saucy Ham Balls

2 1/2 lbs. ground ham loaf mix
2 cups bread crumbs (fine)
2 eggs
1 cup milk

Sauce:
1 cup brown sugar
1/2 cup vinegar
1/2 cup water
1 tsp. dry mustard

Combine ham ball ingredients, mix and shape into 1-1/2 inch balls. Put in 9 x 13 pan. Mix sauce and pour over balls. Bake at 325 degrees for 1 hour. Turn balls and bake for 30 minutes more.

Ham and Broccoli Bake

2 - 20 oz. pkg. frozen broccoli
1 onion, chopped
2 cans cream of mushroom soup
1 can cream of celery soup
1 can cream of chicken soup

2 soup cans of milk
2 cups shredded cheese
6 cups cooked ham or chicken
4 cups Minute Rice, uncooked
1 Tbsp. worcestershire sauce

Cook broccoli and drain. Saute onion. Mix in soups, milk and cheese, then add drained broccoli, ham and uncooked rice and worcestershire sauce. Mix well. Divide between two 2 1/2 quart casseroles. Bake at 350 degrees for 45-50 minutes. Serves 20.

Ham Bake

16 oz. bag frozen broccoli/
   cauliflower/carrots
1 can corn, drained
8 oz. box of shell macaroni
2 cups chopped ham
3 Tbsp. flour

2 Tbsp. melted butter
1 1/2 cups milk
1/2 cup grated American cheese
Topping:
1/4 cup bread crumbs
1 Tbsp. melted butter

Boil frozen vegetables and macaroni shells in big pot. Drain. Put in a separate big bowl. Sauce: Melt butter. Add flour and milk in at one time. Stir until thick, then add cheese until melted. Toss all ingredients in a big bowl and mix. Place in 9 x 13 pan. Mix bread crumbs and butter. Sprinkle over top. Brown under broiler and serve. Note: If you are making this to serve later, cook at 325 degrees for 30 minutes instead of placing under the broiler.

Barbecued Pork Chops

1/2 cup ketchup
1/2 cup hot water
1 tsp. dry mustard
1/2 tsp. cloves
1 Tbsp. flour

2 Tbsp. brown sugar
Salt and pepper to taste
6 pork chops
1 onion, chopped (optional)

Put 6 chops in a baking dish, cover with chopped onions if desired. Mix remaining ingredients and pour sauce over chops. Bake about 35 minutes or until tender.

Pork Chop Casserole

6 pork chops
3/4 cup raw rice
1 large onion
2 cups tomatoes

1 green pepper
3 cups beef bouillon or tomato juice
1/8 tsp. marjoram (if desired)

Brown pork chops in skillet. Place chops on top of rice in bottom of fairly deep casserole or pan and add pork chop drippings. Put a thick slice of onion, tomato and a ring of green pepper on each chop. Salt and pepper to taste. Pour in beef bouillon or tomato juice and sprinkle with marjoram. Cover and bake in a moderate oven at 350 degrees for at least one hour. Serves 6.

Pork with Mushroom Sauce

5 tsp. butter
1 shallot, finely chopped
1 can sliced mushrooms, drained
1 tsp. oil
3/4 lb. pork tenderloin, cut into slices

1/8 tsp. salt
1/8 tsp. pepper
1 Tbsp. apple juice
1 Tbsp. Dijon mustard
1/2 cup whipping cream

Cook shallot and mushrooms in 2 tsp. butter. Remove from skillet. Add remaining butter and oil to skillet. Add pork and cook 8 - 10 minutes or until browned and no longer pink. Sprinkle with salt and pepper. Remove from skillet, cover to keep warm. Gradually add apple juice to skillet; stir in mustard and cream. Bring to a boil for 1 - 2 minutes, or until slightly thickened, stirring constantly. Add mushroom mixture; cook 1 minute or until thoroughly heated. Serve pork with sauce poured over it. Great with rice.

San Francisco Chops

1 Tbsp. oil
4 pork chops or spare ribs
1 clove garlic
2 tsp. oil
4 Tbsp. dry sherry or broth

4 Tbsp. soy sauce
2 Tbsp. brown sugar
1/4 tsp. crushed red pepper
2 tsp. cornstarch
2 Tbsp. water

Trim fat from chops or ribs. Heat l Tbsp. oil in skillet. Brown meat on both sides. Mix garlic, oil, sherry, soy sauce, brown sugar and red pepper. Pour over meat and cover tightly. Simmer 30-35 minutes. Add 1-2 Tbsp. water if needed. Dissolve cornstarch in water. Add to pan and cook until thickened. Serve over parsley buttered noodles.

Orange Pork Chops

4 pork chops
1 Tbsp. oil
1/2 cup orange juice
5 Tbsp. sugar

1/4 tsp. cinnamon
1/4 tsp. cloves
1/2 Tbsp. cornstarch

Trim fat from pork chops. Brown in oil. Sprinkle with salt, pepper, and paprika. Add orange juice, sugar, cinnamon and cloves. Cover and simmer 45 minutes. Add cornstarch dissolved in a little orange juice. Heat until bubbling and clear.

Pork Chops A La Dixie

6 fresh loin or rib chops
salt and pepper
Creole Sauce:
2 cups tomato sauce
1 1/2 Tbsp. worcestershire sauce

1/2 tsp. pepper
dash tabasco sauce
1 tsp. lemon juice
1/4 cup chopped green pepper
1 tsp. salt

In hot frying pan, brown chops slowly and thoroughly on both sides. Season chops with salt and pepper. Make Creole Sauce by heating together remaining ingredients. Pour over browned pork chops. Cover and cook slowly for l hour or until very tender. Serve chops on platter with fluffy rice and creole sauce. 6 servings.

Polynesian Pork

3 lb. pork, cut in bite-size pieces
3 Tbsp. soy sauce
1/4 tsp. ginger
1/3 cup brown sugar

24 oz. tomato sauce
1 clove garlic, minced
1/3 cup vinegar
3/4 cup pineapple tidbits and juice

Trim fat off meat, cut in bite-size pieces, and lightly brown pork in large skillet. Add remaining ingredients, cover and simmer 45 minutes or longer. Skim fat off top.

Reuben Sausage Casserole

3 medium potatoes, peeled & cubed
1 lb. ground sausage
2 cups drained sauerkraut

1/2 cup thousand island dressing
3 Tbsp. shredded fresh parsley
3 oz. shredded swiss cheese

Partially boil potatoes. In skillet, brown the sausage. Combine all ingredients in a baking dish, putting the cheese on the top. Bake at 350 degrees for 30 minutes.

Italian Sausage Florentine

2 - 10 oz. pkg. frozen spinach, thawed
18 oz. medium wide noodles, cooked
3/4 lb. Italian sausage, cooked & sliced
3/4 lb. lean ground beef, browned
15 oz. can tomato sauce
1/2 tsp. salt
1/2 tsp. pepper

1/2 tsp. garlic powder
16 oz. cream cheese, softened
1/3 cup milk
8 oz. sour cream
1/2 cup chopped onion
6 oz. grated cheddar cheese

Mix sausage and beef well. Mix in cooked noodles. Add tomato sauce, salt, garlic powder, and pepper. Mix together cream cheese, sour cream and milk, and add onions. Mix well. In 9 x 13 pan layer half of the noodles, then half of the cream cheese mixture. Cover using all of the spinach. Then layer the remaining noodles and cream cheese mixture. Bake at 350 degrees for 40 minutes. Remove from oven and sprinkle cheddar cheese over the top, return to the oven or place under the broiler until the cheese melts.

Apricot Sausage on Rice

1 lb. smoked sausage,
    cut in 1/2 inch slices
10 oz. jar apricot preserves (or any flavor)

1 Tbsp. prepared mustard
2 cups rice

Cook rice according to package directions. Brown sausage in frying pan. Add preserves and cook over low heat until preserves melt. Add mustard. Serve sausage and sauce over rice.

Spanish Rice With Little Pig Sausages

1 cup raw rice, cooked
1 1/2 lb. sausage, little pig or pork
1 can tomato soup
1 can water

1 No. 2 can tomatoes
1/2 cup sugar, or to taste
Salt and pepper

Mix all ingredients except sausages. Pour into a buttered casserole and arrange little pig sausages over top. Bake at 350 degrees, for about 1 hour. If pig sausage cannot be obtained, any pork sausage can be used. This is very good served with cabbage salad.

Oven Barbecued Frankfurters

1 lb. frankfurters
1/2 cup ketchup
1/4 cup minced onion
1 Tbsp. flour
1 Tbsp. brown sugar
1 1/2 Tbsp. worcestershire sauce

2 Tbsp. vinegar
2 Tbsp. water
2 tsp. salt
1/4 tsp. pepper
1 tsp. paprika
1 tsp. chili powder

Heat oven to 350 degrees. Pierce each frankfurter several times with fork. Place in baking dish. Blend together all other ingredients and pour over franks - cover and bake 1 hour. Serve between toasted buns or as a meat course.

Gremolata Grilled Veal Chops

4 well-trimmed veal rib or loin chops
2 medium red bell peppers,
    cut lengthwise in half
2 tsp. olive oil
salt and pepper

Gremolata:
3 Tbsp. finely chopped fresh basil
3 Tbsp. finely chopped fresh parsley
1 tsp. grated lemon peel
1 clove garlic, crushed

Combine gremolata ingredients; mix well. Brush peppers with oil. Reserve 1 Tbsp. gremolata, and press remaining into both sides of veal chops and peppers. Place chops and peppers on grill for 12 - 14 minutes until veal is medium doneness and peppers are tender, turning occasionally. Sprinkle reserved gremolata on chops. Season with salt and pepper as desired.

Chinese One-Dish Meal

1 lb. veal or beef, cut in cubes
2 medium onions, finely chopped
1 cup chopped celery
2 Tbsp. shortening
1/2 cup uncooked rice
1 can cream of chicken soup

1 can cream of mushroom soup
4 Tbsp. soy sauce
1 tsp. salt
1/4 tsp. pepper
1 cup canned peas
2 cups water

Brown meat, onions and celery in shortening. Add other ingredients, mixing well. Place in large greased casserole. Bake 1 1/2 hours at 325 degrees. Serves 10. (A can of mixed vegetables may be added for a larger quantity.)

Baked Dish

1 lb. veal, cubed
2 large onions, chopped
2 cups celery, diced large
2 cans mushroom soup

2 cans water
1 small can mushrooms
2 cubes chicken bouillon
1 cup raw rice

Brown veal with onions. Mix all ingredients together and bake 1 hour.

Savory Veal Stew

2 1/2 lbs. veal, cut in pieces
1/3 cup flour
1/2 tsp. salt
1/2 tsp. pepper
3 Tbsp. olive oil
1 large onion, coarsely chopped

3 large cloves garlic, crushed
1 can chicken broth
2 tsp. dried thyme leaves
1 lb. baby carrots
1 lb. small new red potatoes, cut in half
1 cup frozen peas

Combine flour, salt and pepper. Add veal and toss to coat. Heat 1/2 the oil until hot. Add 1/2 the veal and brown evenly, stirring occasionally. Remove veal. Repeat with remaining veal and oil. In same pan, add onion and garlic. Cook and stir 1 minute. Gradually stir in broth and thyme. Return veal to pan. Bring to a boil; reduce heat to low. Cover tightly and simmer 45 minutes. Stir in carrots and potatoes. Cover and continue cooking 30 minutes or until tender. Skim fat from cooking liquid. Stir in peas; heat through. Makes 8 servings.

Breaded Lamb Chops

1/3 cup bread crumbs
1/4 cup finely minced parsley,
    fresh or dried
1 large garlic clove, minced
1 large shallot, minced

3 Tbsp. butter, melted
1 tsp. dry mustard
salt and pepper
4 lamb chops (about 4 oz. each)

Combine breadcrumbs, parsley, garlic, and shallot in one shallow dish. Mix melted butter and dry mustard in another shallow dish. Dip each lamb chop into the butter mixture first, then into the bread crumb mixture. Season each chop with salt and pepper. Place a rack in a pan, and the lamb chops on the rack. Roast at 450 degrees until coating is golden brown and lamb is cooked to desired doneness, about 20 - 25 minutes for medium rare to medium.

Corned Beef Macaroni Loaf

8 oz. macaroni
12 oz. can corned beef
1/4 lb. cheese
bread crumbs

1/4 cup chopped onion
1 can cream of chicken soup
1 cup milk

Cook macaroni and drain. Chop corned beef. Add corned beef, cheese, onion, soup and milk. Mix together; put bread crumbs on top. Bake at 350 degrees for 45 minutes.

Corned Beef Casserole

8 oz. box macaroni, uncooked
1/2 lb. American cheese, diced
1 medium onion, chopped
1 small green pepper, chopped

1 can corned beef, broken up
2 cans cream of chicken soup
2 cups milk
10 oz. box frozen peas

Mix all together and put in buttered 9 x 13 inch baking dish. Let stand overnight. Bake 1 hour at 375 degrees.

Mashed Potatoes with Corned Beef

corned beef slices
mashed potatoes

sliced cheese

Put corned beef in bottom of baking dish. Spread on a layer of mashed potatoes, then on top put slices of cheese. Bake until heated through and cheese is brown at 350 degrees for about 30 minutes.

Individual Newburg Casseroles

1/4 cup butter
1/4 cup flour
1 1/2 cups milk
1 1/2 cups light cream
4 beaten egg yolks
1 pkg. lobster or crabmeat, (5 oz.) drained,
broken & cartilage removed

1 can shrimp (4 1/2 oz.)
1/4 cup dry sherry (optional)
3/4 cup bread crumbs
1 Tbsp. parmesan cheese
1/2 tsp. paprika
2 Tbsp. butter
salt & pepper to taste

Melt butter. Stir in flour, salt and pepper. Add milk and cream at once. Cook and stir until thick and bubbly, then cook and stir one minute more. Gradually stir 1 cup of hot mixture into yolks, and then return all to pan. Cook until bubbly. Remove from heat, and add lobster, shrimp and sherry. Put in the individual casserole dishes. Stir together the bread crumbs, parmesan cheese and paprika. Add melted butter and mix. Sprinkle on top of casseroles. Bake for 10 minutes at 400 degrees. Serves six.

Salmon Scallop

8 medium potatoes
1 large can salmon
4 slices bacon
1 tsp. salt

1/2 tsp. pepper
3/4 cup milk
1 egg
1/4 cup bread crumbs

Peel and slice potatoes. Put layer of potatoes in greased baking dish, then layer of salmon, sliced bacon, salt and pepper. Continue layers until pan is full. Mix milk and egg. Pour over all. Sprinkle bread crumbs on top and bake in moderate oven until potatoes are done. Serves 6.

Baked Salmon Loaf

1 large can red salmon
6 eggs, well beaten
6 Tbsp. melted butter

7 soda crackers rolled fine
1/2 tsp. salt

Remove oil, skin and bones from salmon. Flake fine. Add rest of ingredients and stir until very smooth. Pour into buttered deep dish or mold. If dish is also lined with a fine cloth or cheese cloth, it will greatly facilitate handling. Bake for 1 hour at 350 degrees. Serve with Lemon Sauce.

Salmon Crown

1 large can salmon (15 oz.)
1/2 cup finely chopped celery
1/4 cup finely chopped green pepper
1/2 cup grated cheddar cheese
1 tsp. dill weed

1/2 tsp. tarragon
dash of pepper
3 Tbsp. mayonnaise
pastry for a double crust
salmon juice or milk

Drain salmon and mix with remaining ingredients, except pastry. Roll out pastry in a long rectangle about 5 x 18 inches. Spread with salmon mixture to within 1/2 inch of one long end. Roll starting from wider side and seal seam with water. Form a ring and place on a cookie sheet seam side down. Slit pastry and brush with salmon juice or milk. Bake at 375 degrees 30 - 40 minutes or until pastry is golden brown and flaky. Let stand 5 minutes before serving.

Shrimp Dish

1/2 cup ketchup
1/4 cup sugar
1 tsp. salt
2 tsp. worchestershire sauce
1/4 cup sherry

2 Tbsp. olive oil
1 clove garlic, chopped
1 tsp. ginger
1 lb. shrimp, peeled and deveined

Mix ketchup, sugar, salt, worchestershire sauce and sherry in bowl. Saute shrimp in olive oil, garlic and ginger for 2 - 3 minutes, and then add the sauce. Simmer for 5 - 10 minutes. Serve with rice. Low fat and low calories.

Shrimp Scampi

1 1/2 lbs. raw shrimp
1/4 cup olive oil
2 small cloves garlic, minced
2 small red peppers, cut in strips
1 cup onion, thinly sliced

2 small green peppers, cut in strips
1/2 cup tomato sauce
1/4 cup fresh parsley, chopped
salt and pepper

Peel and devein shrimp. Heat oil in large skillet. Add garlic and cook, stirring constantly for 30 seconds. Add shrimp and saute for about four minutes, tossing shrimp occasionally. Shrimp are done when they turn pink. Do not overcook. With a slotted spoon, remove shrimp to plate and set aside. Add peppers and onion to skillet. Saute six to eight minutes or until onion is translucent and peppers are tender. Stir in tomato sauce and parsley. Return shrimp to pan. Cover and simmer two to three minutes or until heated through. Sprinkle with salt and pepper to taste. Makes four servings.

Imperial Shrimp

3 eggs
juice of 1/4 lemon
1/2 cup mayonnaise
1 tsp. mustard
salt and pepper to taste
1/2 green pepper, finely diced

1 pimento diced fine
1 lb. cooked shrimp, small pieces
2 slices bread, diced and crust removed
4 large portabella mushrooms
4 slices of your favorite cheese

Whip eggs and lemon juice; add mayonnaise, mustard, salt and pepper. While continuing to whip, fold in green pepper, pimento, cooked shrimp and bread. Remove stems from mushrooms and roast stem side down for 15 minutes at 375 degrees or saute in frying pan for 10 minutes. Place mushrooms on baking sheet, stem side up, and fill with shrimp mixture. Place piece of cheese on top and bake for 15 minutes at 375 degrees.

Lutefisk

Select firm, fresh lutefisk in amount desired. Place on a rack in a large roasting pan, with enough water in the bottom of the pan to form steam, but not touching the fish. Cover tightly. Steam about 20 minutes or until lutefisk is tender. Cooked this way, it will be tender and flaky and not waterlogged. Serve with white sauce or butter.

Fresh Fish with Tomatoes and Fennel

1 Tbsp. olive oil
4 fresh fish fillets
4 plum tomatoes, diced

1 1/2 tsp. minced garlic
1/2 to 1 tsp. finely grated orange peel
1/2 tsp. fennel seed, crushed

Heat oil in large skillet over medium-high heat until hot. Add fish fillets, cook 2 minutes. Turn fish. Add remaining ingredients. Cover, cook 5 to 6 minutes until fish flakes easily with fork. If desired, season with salt and pepper.

Tuna Noodle Casserole

8 oz. egg noodles, wide
2 cans tuna, well drained
1 1/2 cups sour cream
3/4 cup milk
1 can (3.5 oz.) sliced mushrooms, drained
1 1/2 tsp. salt

1/4 tsp. pepper
1 Tbsp. garlic powder
1/4 cup dry bread crumbs
8 oz. cheddar cheese, grated
1/4 cup grated parmesan cheese
2 Tbsp. butter, melted

Cook noodles as directed on pkg. Return drained noodles to kettle. Stir in tuna, sour cream, milk, mushrooms, salt, pepper and garlic. Pour into ungreased 2 qt. casserole. Mix breadcrumbs, cheeses and butter. Sprinkle over casserole. Bake uncovered at 350 degrees for 35 - 40 minutes or until bubbly. Serves 6 - 8.

Tuna Luncheon Casserole

4 oz. pkg. potato chips
7 oz. can tuna fish
1 cup peas

1 can mushroom soup
potato chips or rice cereal
grated cheese

Beginning with potato chips make alternate layers in a buttered casserole of potato chips, tuna fish and peas. When the casserole is filled, pour over all the contents of 1 can mushroom soup which has first been diluted with 1 1/2 cups water. For topping, crush potato chips with grated cheese and spread over, or 1/4 cup rice cereal. Bake at 350 degrees for 45 minutes.

Tuna Cashew Casserole

6 oz. can tuna
1 can mushroom soup
1 can cream of chicken soup
1/4 soup can of water

1 cup chopped celery
1/4 cup chopped onion
1/4 lb. cashew nuts
3 oz. can chow mein noodles

Combine all ingredients except the noodles. Put half of chow mein noodles in the bottom of a casserole. Add the combined ingredients. Place the remaining noodles on top. Bake 1 hour at 300 degrees. Serves 6.

Overnight Tuna Casserole

1 can cream of celery soup
1 cup milk
1 can tuna, drained
1 cup uncooked elbow macaroni

1 cup frozen green peas
1/2 cup chopped onion
1 cup shredded cheddar cheese

Whisk soup and milk in microwave-safe bowl until well blended. Stir in remaining ingredients except reserved 1/4 cup cheese. Cover and refrigerate at least 12 hours or overnight. Cover with lid or vented plastic wrap. Microwave on high 15 to 17 minutes until bubbly. Sprinkle with reserved cheese. Let stand uncovered 5 to 7 minutes until cheese melts. Makes 4 servings.

Seafood Bake

1 can cream of mushroom soup
1/3 cup salad dressing
1/3 cup milk
6 oz. can shrimp, drained
7 oz. can tuna, drained and flaked
5 oz. can water chestnuts, drained, sliced

1 cup finely diced celery
2 Tbsp. chopped parsley
2 tsp. grated onion
2 cups cooked macaroni
paprika

In a 1 1/2 qt. casserole blend soup, salad dressing and milk. Mix in all other ingredients except paprika; sprinkle it on top. Bake at 350 degrees for 30 minutes.

Seashore Fettuccine

1 lb. fettuccine noodles
1/2 cup butter or margarine
1 small onion, diced
12 oz. fresh or frozen shrimp, thawed
1/4 tsp. dried basil
1/8 tsp. crushed red pepper

1/2 tsp. salt
pinch black pepper
8 oz. tomato sauce
8 oz. heavy cream
1/2 cup grated parmesan cheese

Cook pasta until tender; drain, place in a large bowl and set aside. In large skillet, melt butter, add onion, shrimp, basil, red pepper, salt and pepper. Saute for about 2 minutes, then add the tomato sauce and heavy cream. Bring to a boil. Simmer until sauce is creamy, about 3 minutes. Add sauce and parmesan cheese to pasta. Mix and serve. Note: this also tastes great with imitation crabmeat or scallops.

Hearty Fisherman's Lasagna

1 1/2 lb. frozen cod fillets
1/4 cup chopped onion
1/3 cup diced green pepper
2 Tbsp. butter
1 small can tomato paste
1 can (19 oz.) tomatoes

1/2 tsp. salt
dash pepper
1/2 tsp. basil
6 lasagna noodles, cooked
12 oz. sliced mozzarella cheese
1/4 cup grated parmesan cheese

Partially thaw fillets and cut in 1 inch pieces. Saute vegetables in butter until onion is translucent. Stir in tomato paste, tomatoes and seasonings. Simmer 5 minutes. Add fish and simmer 5 minutes. Layer half of the noodles in a greased, shallow baking dish. Cover with half of the fish sauce and the mozzarella cheese. Repeat layers. Sprinkle with parmesan cheese. Bake at 375 degrees for 25 - 30 minutes or until bubbly and lightly brown.

Easy Rice Pilaf

3/4 cup butter
1 to 2 onions
4 1/2 cups long-grain rice

6 cups strong chicken broth
salt and white pepper to taste
sliced almonds or chopped green onions

One hour before serving, melt butter in skillet over medium-high heat. Add onion and saute until transparent. Mix in rice, stirring until sizzling. Add broth and bring to boil. Reduce heat, cover and simmer for 20 minutes. Remove from heat, transfer to chafing dish and keep warm until ready to serve. May be garnished with sliced almonds and/or chopped green onions.

Wild Rice

1 cup wild rice

boiling water

Preheat oven to 500 degrees. Cover wild rice in a casserole with boiling water (or boiling chicken broth) to about 1 1/2 inches over the rice. Cover casserole. Put in the oven. Turn off heat. Rice is popped and ready when the oven is cool so it is an ideal time to do before you go to bed. The "popped" cooked rice can be used in salads, casseroles, soup, etc., and divided in amounts you want to have on hand or freeze.

Cheese Filled Shells

2 lbs. ricotta cheese
1/2 lb. mozzarella cheese, shredded
2 eggs
1 Tbsp. chopped parsley
chopped onions, optional

1 1/2 to 2 qts. tomato sauce
3/4 cup grated parmesan cheese
salt and pepper to taste
jumbo macaroni shells, parboiled

Mix together ricotta, mozzarella, eggs and parsley. Add chopped onions if desired. Season with salt and pepper. Mix until well blended. Fill parboiled shells immediately. Cover with sauce and sprinkle with grated cheese. Cover pan with foil and bake at 450 degrees for 30 minutes.

Meat Filled Shells

1 1/2 lbs. hamburger
1 onion, chopped
1 egg
1/2 lb. mozzarella cheese, shredded
3 slices bread, diced
jumbo macaroni shells, parboiled

1/2 cup milk
1 Tbsp. chopped parsley
salt and pepper
1 1/2 to 2 qts. tomato sauce
grated parmesan cheese

Brown hamburger with onion. Remove from heat and add egg, mozzarella cheese, bread, milk and parsley. Season with salt and pepper. Fill parboiled shells. Cover with sauce, sprinkle with grated parmesan cheese, and cover pan with foil. Bake at 450 degrees for 30 minutes.

One Dish Breakfast

1 pkg. frozen shredded hash browns
diced ham or fried sizzlers
1 1/2 lb. Velveeta cheese

14 eggs
1 cup milk
salt and pepper

Place shredded hash browns in bottom of 9 x 13 pan. Top with ham or sizzlers, and then with slices of Velveeta cheese. Beat together eggs, milk, and salt and pepper. Pour over cheese in pan. Bake for 1 hour at 350 degrees.

Quiche

2 unbaked pie shells
1 1/2 cups grated cheese
broccoli
diced ham or bacon

5 eggs
1/2 cup milk
1 can mushroom soup

Put grated cheese, broccoli, ham, and any other ingredients you would like in your quiche into the bottom of the pie shells. Beat together the eggs, milk, and soup. Pour over cheese in pie shells. Bake for 1 hour at 350 degrees.

Brunch Casserole

1 lb. bacon	16 eggs
1/2 cup butter	3/4 tsp. salt
1/2 cup flour	1/4 tsp. pepper
4 cups milk	1 cup evaporated milk
8 oz. chopped ham	1/4 cup butter
6 oz. sliced mushrooms, drained	8 oz. cheddar cheese

Fry and crumble bacon; set aside. Make white sauce with the 1/2 cup butter, flour, and milk. Add the ham and mushrooms, and season to taste. Beat eggs with butter, salt, pepper, and milk. Scramble eggs, and then put in 9 x 13 buttered casserole. Cover with sauce, and top with bacon and then cheese. Cover and bake at 300 degrees for one hour. Add 15 minutes if casserole is prepared the day ahead and refrigerated overnight.

Ham and Cheese Oven Omelet

4 eggs	1/2 cup chopped ham
1/2 cup rich milk	1/2 cup shredded cheese
1/4 tsp. seasoned salt	1 1/2 Tbsp. finely chopped onion

Mix all ingredients together. Pour into greased 1 quart casserole. Bake 40-45 minutes at 325 degrees until omelet is set and top is golden brown.

Pastries & Desserts

Desserts

Pies

Easy Flaky Pie Crust

1 cup shortening
1/3 cup boiling water

2 cups flour
1 tsp. salt

Put shortening in bowl. Pour boiling water over it. Mix with fork until smooth. Add flour and salt and mix until it will form a ball. Cool. Roll out between waxed paper. Bake at 450 degrees for 15 minutes. Makes 2 shells or one double crust pie.

Key Lime Pie

1 can sweetened condensed milk
1 cup sour cream

1/2 cup lime juice
1 cup Cool Whip
graham cracker pie shell

Beat together milk, sour cream, lime juice and Cool Whip. Pour into pie shell. Refrigerate. Top with more Cool Whip.

White Christmas Pie

1/2 cup sugar
1/4 cup flour
1 envelope or 1 Tbsp. unflavored gelatin
1/2 tsp. salt
1 3/4 cups milk
1/4 tsp. almond flavoring

3 egg whites
1/4 tsp. cream of tartar
1/2 cup sugar
1/2 cup whipping cream, whipped
1 cup moist shredded coconut
1 baked pie shell

Blend sugar, flour, gelatin and salt. Gradually stir in milk. Cook over medium heat until mixture boils, stirring constantly. Boil for 1 minute. Place pan in cold water until mixture mounds slightly when dropped from spoon. Blend in flavoring. Make meringue by beating egg whites and cream of tartar until soft peaks form. Add sugar slowly and beat until stiff. Carefully fold in first mixture into the meringue. Then fold in whipped cream and coconut. Pile into a baked and cooled pie shell. Sprinkle some coconut on top. Chill several hours until set. Serve cold. Delicious topped with crushed strawberries or raspberries.

Chocolate Pie

1/2 cup butter
3/4 cup sugar
2 squares unsweetened chocolate, melted

2 eggs
2 cups Cool Whip
9 inch pie shell, baked

Cream butter and sugar. Stir in cooled melted chocolate. Add eggs, one at a time, beating five minutes after each addition. Fold in Cool Whip. Pour into a cooled baked pie shell. Chill until firm, about 2 hours, or freeze.

Raspberry Angel Pie

3 eggs whites
1 cup sugar
1 tsp. vanilla
1/2 tsp. baking powder
3/4 cup cracker crumbs

3/4 cup chopped nuts
1 cup whipping cream
3 Tbsp. sugar
red food coloring
10 oz. frozen raspberries, thawed, drained

Beat egg whites until soft peaks form. Add sugar slowly, beating until stiff and glossy (ten minutes). Add vanilla and baking powder. Stir in cracker crumbs and nuts. Place meringue in well greased 9 inch pie pan, spreading up sides of pan to the rim. Bake for 45 minutes at 325 degrees. Cool throughly. Whip cream; add sugar and a few drops of red food coloring. Fold in drained raspberries. Fill meringue shell with raspberry mixture. Chill several hours.

Grasshopper Pie

1 cup sugar
1/4 cup butter
3 eggs
1 tsp. vanilla
1/2 tsp. vinegar

1/2 cup pecans
1/2 cup coconut
2 oz. chocolate chips
9 inch pie shell, unbaked

Combine all ingredients in medium mixing bowl. Mix well. Pour filling into pie shell. Bake at 350 degrees for 45 minutes.

Mock Pecan Pie

1/4 cup margarine
1/4 tsp. salt
1/2 cup sugar
3 eggs

1 cup dark corn syrup
1/2 cup coconut
1/2 cup quick cooking oats
9 inch pie shell

Mix together margarine, salt, sugar, eggs and syrup, and beat well. Stir in coconut and oats. Pour in pie shell. Bake at 350 degrees for 50 minutes.

Easy Coconut Pie

2 cups milk
3/4 cup sugar
1/2 cup biscuit mix
1 1/3 cups coconut

4 eggs
1/4 cup margarine or butter
1 tsp. vanilla

Heat oven to 350 degrees. Combine milk, sugar, biscuit mix, eggs, margarine and vanilla in blender; cover. Blend on low speed 3 minutes. Pour into greased 9 - inch pie plate. Let stand 5 minutes. Sprinkle with coconut. Bake 40 minutes. Serve warm, or cool on wire rack. Makes 8 servings.

Jello Strawberry Pie

1/2 cup sugar
1 cup water
2 Tbsp. cornstarch

3 cups strawberries, sliced
3 oz. pkg. strawberry jello
whipped cream

Cook sugar, water, and cornstarch until it boils. Add Jello after removing from heat. Allow to cool. Add berries to Jello mixture and chill until fairly firm. Pour into baked pie shell and chill until firm, for several hours or overnight. Top with whipped cream.

Peach Custard Pie

1 cup sugar
1 Tbsp. flour
Sliced fresh peaches to fill pie crust or 1
large can drained peaches

2 eggs, well beaten
1 Tbsp. butter
1/2 tsp. cinnamon
9 inch unbaked pie shell

Add sugar and flour to well beaten egg. Slice peaches to fill unbaked pie shell and cover with egg mixture. Sprinkle with cinnamon and dot with butter. Bake 10 minutes at 450 degrees and 30 minutes at 350 degrees or until custard is done. (Custard is done when knife inserted around the edges comes out clean.)

Pineapple Cream Pie

3/4 cup sugar
1/4 cup flour
1/2 tsp. salt
1 large can (20 oz.) crushed pineapple
Meringue

1 cup sour creaam
1 Tbsp. lemon juice
2 slightly beaten egg yolks
9 inch baked pastry shell

In saucepan, combine sugar, flour and salt. Stir in undrained pineapple, sour cream and lemon juice until thoroughly blended. Cook and stir until mixture thickens and bubbles. Cook and stir 2 minutes more. Remove from heat. Stir a moderate amount of hot mixture into egg yolks, then return to hot mixture, stirring constantly. Cook and stir 2 minutes more. Spoon hot mixture into cooled pastry shell. Spread meringue on top. Bake at 350 degrees for 12 - 15 minutes. Cool before cutting.

Cherry Cream Cheese Pie

1 graham cracker pie crust
8 oz. cream cheese, softened
14 oz. can sweetened condensed milk

1/3 cup lemon juice
1 tsp. vanilla
21 oz. can cherry pie filling

In medium bowl, beat cream cheese until light and fluffy. Slowly add sweetened condensed milk, beating until smooth. Stir in lemon juice and vanilla until well mixed. Pour into crust. Chill 3 hours, until firm, and then top with cherry pie filling.

Peanut Butter Pie

1 cup confectioners' sugar
1/2 cup peanut butter
2 Tbsp. cornstarch
2/3 cup sugar
dash salt
3 cups milk

3 eggs, separated
1 tsp. vanilla
1/2 cup sugar
1/4 tsp. cream of tartar
9 inch graham cracker or baked pie shell

Mix confectioners' sugar and peanut butter until crumbly and set aside. Put cornstarch, 2/3 cup sugar, salt and milk in double boiler and cook until mixture thickens. Add small amount of hot mixture to slightly beaten egg yolks, then add egg mixture to sauce and add vanilla. Cook until thick again. Place half of peanut butter mixture in bottom of a 9" graham cracker or baked pie crust shell. Pour filling over this. Beat egg whites with 1/2 cup sugar and cream of tartar. Spread over filling and top with remaining peanut butter mixture. Bake at 350 degrees until brown.

Hot Fudge Pie

2 oz. unsweetened chocolate
1/2 cup butter
2 well beaten eggs
1 cup sugar
1/4 cup flour

1/2 tsp. salt
1 tsp. vanilla
1/2 cup pecans
9 inch unbaked pie shell
Cool Whip

Melt chocolate and butter in microwave. Cool mixture; then add beaten eggs. Add sugar, flour, salt, vanilla and pecans. Pour in pie shell and bake 30 - 35 minutes at 350 degrees. Serve warm, and add Cool Whip on top of each serving.

French Strawberry Pie

9 inch baked pie shell
3 oz. cream cheese, softened
1 qt. fresh strawberries

1 cup sugar
3 Tbsp. cornstarch
1 cup whipping cream

Spread softened cream cheese over bottom of pie shell. Drain washed berries. Place half the berries in cheese-coated shell. Mash and strain remaining berries until juice is well extracted. Bring juice to boiling point and slowly stir in sugar and cornstarch. Cook 10 minutes. Cool and pour over berries in pie shell. Place in refrigerator until cold. Decorate with sweetened whipped cream just before serving.

Coffee Banana Pie

1/2 lb. marshmallows (32)
2 Tbsp. instant coffee
1/2 cup hot water

1 cup heavy cream, whipped
2 cups sliced bananas
9 inch baked pie shell

Combine marshmallows, coffee and water. Cook over medium heat until marshmallows are dissolved. Cool until slightly thickened. Fold in sliced bananas and sweetened whipped cream. Pour into baked pie shell. Chill.

Rhubarb Cream Pie

9-inch pie shell, unbaked
2 cups diced rhubarb
3 eggs, separated
1/2 cup cream
1/2 tsp. salt

1 1/4 cups sugar
2 Tbsp. flour
nutmeg
6 Tbsp. sugar

Put rhubarb in pie shell. Beat egg yolks. Add cream. Mix salt, sugar and flour together. Add to egg mixture and pour over rhubarb. Pour into unbaked pie crust and sprinkle with a little nutmeg. Bake at 400 degrees for 10 minutes, then 350 degrees for about 40 minutes. Beat egg whites until stiff, add 6 Tbsp. sugar and spread on pie. Bake at 300 degrees until brown.

Custard Meringue Pie

Crust:
14 graham crackers, crushed
1/2 cup melted butter
2 Tbsp. sugar
1 tsp. cinnamon
Meringue:
3 egg whites
3 Tbsp. sugar

Custard:
2 cups milk
1/2 cup sugar
2 Tbsp. cornstarch
3 egg yolks
1 tsp. vanilla

Reserve 1/2 cup of cracker crumbs for top of the pie. Mix all ingredients for crust and pat into pie pan. Mix all ingredients for custard and cook in double boiler until thick. Pour into pie pan on top of crust. Make meringue by beating egg whites stiff and adding sugar slowly at the end. Spread meringue over top of custard and sprinkle reserved cracker crumbs on top. Bake in the oven at 300 degrees until lightly browned.

Ritz Cracker Pie

3 egg whites, beaten stiff
1 cup sugar
1 tsp. baking powder
20 Ritz crackers, crushed

3/4 cup chopped walnuts
1 tsp. vanilla
1/2 cup shredded coconut
whipped cream topping

Mix all ingredients and place in greased pie plate. Bake in a 350 degree oven for 20 - 25 minutes. Cool. Top with whipped cream.

Angel Refrigerator Pie

Meringue:
4 egg whites
1 tsp. cream of tartar
1 cup sugar

Filling:
4 egg yolks
juice and rind of 1 1/2 lemons
1/2 cup sugar
2 Tbsp. water
1 tsp. butter
whipped cream

Beat egg whites until foamy, then add cream of tartar and sugar. Beat 8 minutes and pour into greased pie tin. Bake 1 hour at 275 degrees, then remove from oven and cool. Beat egg yolks until lemon colored, add sugar, water and lemon juice. Cook over water until thick. Remove from heat and add butter. Cool. Spread a thin layer of whipped cream over meringue, then spread on lemon filling. Top with another thin layer of whipped cream. Let stand in refrigerator overnight, or at least 8 hours before serving.

Chocolate Chiffon Pie

1 pkg. plain gelatin
1/4 cup water
2 squares unsweetened chocolate
1 cup milk
1 graham cracker or cookie pie shell

3 eggs, separated
1/8 tsp. salt
1/4 cup sugar
1 tsp. vanilla
1/4 cup sugar

Dissolve gelatin in water. Melt chocolate with milk. Add gelatin to chocolate mixture. Whisk egg yolks with salt and add 1/4 cup sugar. Gradually add this mixture to the chocolate mixture, and then chill. Beat the egg whites, then gradually adding 1/4 cup sugar and vanilla to make meringue. Add the meringue to the chocolate mixture. Pour into pie shell. Keep refrigerated.

Pumpkin Impossible Pie

1/2 cup Bisquick mix
4 eggs
15 oz. can pumpkin
1/2 tsp. cinnamon

1 tsp. ginger
1 tsp. nutmeg
2 cups milk
3/4 cup sugar

Combine all ingredients in blender and blend 3 minutes or use electric mixer on high. Pour into greased and floured pie pan and bake one hour at 350 degrees. Cool and refrigerate.

Marshmallow Pumpkin Pie

2 3/4 cups miniature marshmallows
1 cup canned pumpkin
1/2 tsp. cinnamon
1/8 tsp. ginger
1/8 tsp. nutmeg
1/8 tsp. cloves

1/4 tsp. salt
1 cup uncooked rolled oats
3 Tbsp. brown sugar
2/3 cup walnuts, cut fine
1/3 cup butter, melted
1 cup cream, whipped

Cook in double boiler marshmallows, pumpkin, cinnamon, ginger, nutmeg, cloves and salt, stirring until marshmallows are melted. Cool and fold in whipped cream. Combine the brown sugar, walnuts and butter. Preheat oven. Spread oats into shallow pan. Bake 10 minutes. Toss with sugar, nuts and melted butter. Press oats mixture into pie pan. Bake 10 minutes at 350 degrees. Pour marshmallow mixture into oatmeal shell.

Makes Its Own Crust Pie

1 cup flour
1 tsp. baking powder
1/2 tsp. salt
1 Tbsp. sugar

1 egg
2/3 cup shortening
1/4 cup water
1 can pie filling

Combine flour, baking powder, salt, sugar, egg, shortening and water. Blend well. Pour batter into greased pie pan. Pour pie filling into center of batter. Do not stir. Bake at 425 degrees for 45 to 50 minutes. Serve with whipped topping, if desired.

Fudge Brownie Pie

9 inch unbaked pastry shell
1 cup chocolate chips
1/4 cup butter or margarine
14 oz. can sweetened condensed milk

1/2 cup biscuit baking mix
2 eggs
1 tsp. vanilla
1 cup chopped nuts

Bake pastry shell for ten minutes at 350 degrees. Remove from oven. Reduce oven temperature to 325 degrees. Over very low heat, melt chips with butter. In large mixer bowl, beat chocolate mixture with remaining ingredients except nuts until smooth. Stir in nuts and pour into prepared pastry shell. Bake 35 to 45 minutes or until center is set. Cool. Serve warm or at room temperature with ice cream, if desired.

Chocolate Mint Pie

1 cup crushed chocolate mint cookies
3 Tbsp. hot water
1 graham cracker pie crust
4 oz. cream cheese, softened
1/3 cup sugar
maraschino cherries

2 Tbsp. milk
1/4 tsp. peppermint extract
3 1/2 cups whipped topping
8 - 10 drops food coloring
additional whipped topping

Mix cookies and hot water in small bowl. Spread evenly in bottom of pie crust. Beat cream cheese and sugar until smooth. Add milk and peppermint extract, beating until smooth. Gently stir in whipped topping and food coloring. Spoon mixture into pie crust. Refrigerate until set, at least 3 hours. Garnish each piece with additional whipped topping and a cherry.

Frozen Lemonade Pie

1 graham cracker crust
1 can sweetened condensed milk

1 small can frozen lemonade
9 oz. cool whip

Chill milk. Beat well. Add frozen lemonade right from freezer. Beat until real thick. Fold in Cool Whip. Pour into crust and refrigerate about 1 hour. Will keep for a week. If using store bought crusts, recipe makes 2 small pies.

Double Layer Pumpkin Pie

4 oz. cream cheese, softened
1 Tbsp. milk
1 Tbsp. sugar
1 1/2 cups whipped topping
1 graham cracker pie crust
additional whipped topping
chopped nuts

1 cup cold milk
2 pkg. vanilla instant pudding
1 can pumpkin
1 tsp. cinnamon
1/2 tsp. ginger
1/4 tsp. cloves

Mix cream cheese, 1 Tbsp. milk and sugar in large bowl until smooth. Gently stir in whipped topping. Spread on bottom of crust. Pour milk into bowl and add pudding mix. Beat until well blended, about 2 minutes. Stir in pumpkin and spices, mix well, and spread over cream cheese layer. Refrigerate at least 3 hours. Garnish with additional whipped topping and nuts.

Cranberry Cherry Pie

pie crusts for 2-crust pie
2 cups fresh or frozen cranberries
3/4 cup sugar

2 Tbsp. cornstarch
1 can cherry pie filling
1 Tbsp. sugar

Combine cranberries, 3/4 cup sugar, cornstarch and pie filling, and mix lightly. Spoon into crust-lined pan. Place top crust over filling and fold edge of top crust under bottom crust; flute. Sprinkle with 1 Tbsp. sugar. Bake at 425 degrees for 35 - 45 minutes or until golden brown and filling is bubbly. Cover edge of crust with strips of foil after 15 - 20 minutes of baking to prevent excessive browning.

Peach Cream Pie

3 medium peaches
3/4 cup sugar
3 Tbsp. flour

3/4 cup cream
1/2 tsp. cinnamon
1 pie crust, unbaked

Peel peaches, cut in half and put in pie crust. Mix sugar and flour together and sprinkle over peaches. Pour on cream, sprinkle cinnamon on top. Bake 40 minutes at 450 degrees.

Rhubarb Pudding

1 heaping cup flour
1/2 tsp. salt
1 tsp. baking soda
1 cup sugar
3 Tbsp. soft butter
1/2 cup sour milk

1 egg
2 1/2 cups cut up rhubarb
butter
nutmeg
1 cup sugar
1 cup boiling water

Mix together flour, salt, soda and 1 cup sugar. Add soft butter, sour milk and egg. Beat until smooth. Add rhubarb and put in large pan. Dot with butter and sprinkle with nutmeg. Dissolve 1 cup sugar in boiling water. Pour over mixture. Bake for 45 minutes at 350 degrees. (You can use fresh cherries, drain juice and add enough water to have 1 cup liquid, add sugar and pour over mixture.)

Bread and Butter Pudding

1/2 cup golden raisins
5 slices day-old white bread
3 Tbsp. butter or margarine, softened
2 cups milk or half & half

1/2 cup sugar
1 tsp. vanilla
3 eggs

Soak raisins in 1 cup hot water for 5 minutes. Trim crust from bread, spread one side of each slice with butter, and cut slices in half. Place bread buttered side up in greased 8 inch square baking dish. Drain raisins, and sprinkle over bread. Heat milk and sugar until steaming. Remove from heat, stir in vanilla. In mixing bowl, beat eggs lightly, then gradually stir in hot milk. Pour mixture over bread. Bake uncovered for 30 minutes in 300 degree oven until golden brown or until knife inserted in center comes out clean. Serves 4.

Chocolate Bread Pudding with Vanilla Sauce

2 cups dry bread, crumbled
3 cups milk
1 1/2 squares chocolate, melted
1 tsp. vanilla
1/4 tsp. salt
1/2 cup sugar
3 eggs, beaten

Vanilla Sauce:
2/3 cup sugar
2 Tbsp. flour
1/8 tsp. salt
1 1/2 cups water
2 Tbsp. butter
1 1/2 tsp. vanilla

Mix bread and milk, let stand 5 minutes. Add rest of ingredients. Pour into a buttered baking dish, set in a pan of hot water. Bake 50 minutes at 350 degrees. To make sauce, blend sugar, flour and salt. Add water and boil gently until creamy sauce forms, stirring constantly. Add butter and vanilla and serve warm over Chocolate Bread Pudding.

Cracker Pudding

1 quart milk
2 eggs, separated
2/3 cup sugar

2 cups broken saltine crackers
1 cup coconut
1 tsp. vanilla

Warm the milk. Beat egg yolks and sugar until frothy. Add to hot milk and stir in crackers and coconut. Cook until thick. Remove from heat and add stiffly beaten egg whites and vanilla. Cool. Serves 8.

Brownie Pudding Dessert

1 cup flour
2 tsp. baking powder
1/4 tsp. salt
3/4 cup sugar
1 1/2 Tbsp. cocoa
1/2 cup milk
2 Tbsp. melted butter

1 tsp. vanilla
1 cup chopped nuts

Sauce:
1 cup brown sugar
4 Tbsp. cocoa
1 3/4 cups hot water

Sift flour, baking powder, salt, sugar and cocoa in mixing bowl. Stir in milk, butter and vanilla and mix until smooth. Blend in nuts. Put in well greased 8-inch pan. Mix together the brown sugar and cocoa for the sauce and sprinkle over the batter in the pan. Pour the hot water over all. Bake at 350 degrees for 45 minutes. Serve hot or cold.

Christmas Pudding

1 pkg. pistachio pudding
2 cups milk
maraschino cherries

1 can cherry pie filling
Cool Whip

Prepare pistachio pudding with milk according to package directions. In parfait glasses or small glass bowls, layer pistachio pudding and cherry pie filling, beginning with pistachio pudding and ending with cherry pie filling. Top with Cool Whip and a cherry.

Paula's Banana Pudding

8 oz. cream cheese, softened
2 1/4 cups milk
1 pkg. vanilla instant pudding

24 vanilla wafers
2 cups banana slices

Combine cream cheese and 1/2 cup milk, mixing at medium speed until well blended. Add remaining milk and pudding mix. Beat at low speed one minute. Layer 1/3 of pudding mixture, half of wafers and half of bananas in 1 1/2 quart serving bowl. Repeat layers and top with remaining pudding. Cover surface with wax paper or plastic wrap; chill. Garnish with additional banana slices and wafers. Makes 8 - 10 servings.

Date Nut Pudding

1 cup sugar
1 tsp. butter
1/2 cup milk
1 cup flour
1 tsp. baking powder
1 cup dates, chopped
1 cup nuts, chopped

Sauce:
4 cups water
3/4 cup white sugar
1/4 cup brown sugar
1 Tbsp. butter
1/2 tsp. vanilla
whipped topping

Mix together sugar, butter, milk, flour, baking powder, dates and nuts. Set aside. Put ingredients for sauce together in saucepan and bring to boil. Put boiling sauce into baking dish and add pudding mixture. Bake in 300 degree oven 1 hour uncovered. Garnish with whipped topping and nuts.

Snicker Cheesecake

8 oz. cream cheese
1 cup sugar
juice of 2 lemons

1 cup whipping cream, whipped
6 snicker bars
graham cracker pie shell

Beat together cream cheese, sugar and lemon juice. Fold in whipped cream and chopped snicker bars. Put in graham cracker pie shell. Refrigerate overnight.

New York Cheese Cake

1 lb. ricotta cheese
16 oz. cream cheese
4 eggs
juice of 1/2 lemon
1 tsp. vanilla
1 pint sour cream

4 eggs
3 Tbsp. cornstarch
3 Tbsp. flour
1 stick butter or margarine, melted
1 1/2 cups sugar
1 can pie filling

Cream ricotta and cream cheese until smooth. Gradually add eggs, beating smooth after each egg. Add the remaining ingredients, except the sour cream. Continue beating until well blended. Fold in sour cream. Pour in a springform pan and bake at 325 degrees for one hour and ten minutes. Turn oven off and leave cake in oven for two hours longer. When cooled, top with pie filling if desired.

Mini Cheese Cakes

12 vanilla wafers
16 oz. cream cheese, softened
1/2 cup sugar

1 tsp. vanilla
2 eggs
fruit, preserves, or choc. curls to garnish

Line muffin tin with foil cups. Place one vanilla wafer in each liner. Mix cream cheese, vanilla and sugar until well blended. Add eggs. Mix well. Pour over wafers, filling 3/4 full. Bake at 325 degrees for 25 minutes. Remove from pan when cool. Chill. If desired, top with fruit, preserves or chocolate curls.

Pumpkin Cheesecake

1/3 cup margarine	16 oz. can pumpkin
1/3 cup sugar	1 tsp. cinnamon
1 egg	1/4 tsp. ginger
1 1/4 cups flour	1/4 tsp. nutmeg
16 oz. cream cheese, softened	dash of salt
3/4 cup sugar	2 eggs

Cream margarine and sugar until light and fluffy; blend in egg. Add flour and mix well. Press dough on bottom and 2 inches high around sides of a 9" springform pan. Bake crust at 400 degrees for 5 minutes. Remove crust from oven and reduce oven temperature to 350 degrees. Combine cream cheese and sugar, mixing until well blended. Blend in pumpkin, spices and salt. Add eggs, one at a time, mixing well after each addition. Pour mixture into pastry lined pan; smooth surface to edge of crust. Bake at 350 degrees for 50 minutes. Loosen cake from rim of pan. Cool before removing rim of pan. Chill. Garnish with whipped cream just before serving, if desired.

Chocolate Amaretto Cheesecake

6 chocolate wafers, finely crushed	1/4 cup amaretto
1 1/2 cups cream cheese	1 tsp. vanilla extract
1 cup sugar	1/4 tsp. salt
1 cup low-fat cottage cheese	1 egg
1/4 cup plus 2 Tbsp. unsweetened cocoa	2 Tbsp. chocolate chips
1/4 cup flour	chocolate curls, optional

Sprinkle chocolate wafer crumbs in bottom of a 7 or 8 inch springform pan. Set aside. Beat cream cheese and then next 7 ingredients, until smooth. Add egg and mix just until blended. Fold in chocolate chips. Slowly pour mixture over crumbs in pan. Bake at 300 degrees for 65 - 70 minutes for 7" pan or 45 - 50 minutes for 8" pan, or until cheesecake is set. Let cool, then cover and chill at least 8 hours. Remove from pan and garnish with chocolate curls, if desired.

Easy Sour Cream Cheesecake

1 graham cracker pie crust
8 oz. cream cheese, softened
1/3 cup sugar
2 tsp. vanilla

1 cup sour cream
8 oz. whipped topping
fresh strawberries to garnish

Beat cream cheese until smooth, gradually beat in sugar. Blend in sour cream and vanilla. Fold in whipped topping, blending well. Spoon into crust. Chill until set, at least 4 hours. Garnish with fresh strawberries, if desired.

Chocolate Cream Cheese Crescents

1/4 cup powdered sugar
4 oz. cream cheese, softened
1 1/2 tsp. cooled strong coffee
1/2 tsp. vanilla

1/4 cup finely chopped macadamia nuts
1 can crescent rolls
1/4 cup chocolate chips
1/2 tsp. shortening

Combine powdered sugar, cream cheese, coffee and vanilla. Blend well. Stir in macadamia nuts. Separate dough into 8 triangles. Spoon 1 Tbsp. cream cheese mixture onto shortest side of each triangle. Loosely roll up, starting at shortest side and rolling to opposite point. Place point side down on greased cookie sheet. Curve into crescent shape. Bake at 350 degrees for 12 - 15 minutes or until golden brown. Cool 5 minutes. Melt chocolate chips and shortening over low heat. Stir until smooth. Drizzle over warm rolls. Serve warm or cool.

Strawberry Popover Dessert

3 eggs
1/2 cup milk
1/2 cup flour
pinch of salt
1 Tbsp. butter

powdered sugar
sweetened whole strawberries
1 cup sour cream
1/4 cup brown sugar

Mix together eggs, milk, flour, and salt. Melt butter in pie plate in oven at 450 degrees. Add batter to the hot pie plate. Bake in the oven at 450 degrees for ten minutes. Sprinkle with powdered sugar. Add strawberries, and top with sour cream and brown sugar mixture. Sprinkle brown sugar on top.

Peppermint Dessert

1 pt. whipping cream
40 miniature marshmallows
1/2 cup peppermint stick candy, ground

1/2 cup chopped nuts
1/2 lb. crushed vanilla wafers

Whip whipping cream until stiff. Add marshmallows, peppermint candy, and nuts. Use 1/2 of crushed vanilla wafers as crust in 9 x 13 pan, add peppermint mixture, and other half of vanilla wafers on top. Chill.

Chocolate Cup Dessert

4 cups miniature marshmallows
1/4 tsp. salt
1/4 cup milk
1 pkg. (6 oz.) chocolate chips
2 tsp. instant coffee

1/4 tsp. cinnamon
1 cup cream, whipped
8 individual sponge cake dessert shells
1 cup finely chopped nuts

Combine marshmallows, salt and milk in saucepan. Cook, stirring occasionally, over low heat until marshmallows melt. Remove from heat, and stir in chocolate pieces, instant coffee and cinnamon. Cool slightly. Fold 1/2 cup chocolate mixture into whipped cream. Cover and chill. Frost sides and top edges of sponge cake dessert cups with remaining chocolate mixture. Roll in chopped nuts. Place cups on cookie sheet; spoon chocolate whipped cream mixture in center of cups. Chill several hours. Serves 8.

Fat Free Dessert

1 angel food cake, prepared and baked
Mrs. Richardson's fat free caramel topping
Cool Whip
pineapple

Jello custard, prepared according to box
bananas
kiwi

Make each serving individually. Break angel food cake up into small pieces. Put some pieces in small dish or on dessert plate. Drizzle over cake some of Mrs. Richardson's fat free caramel topping. Pour over this some Jello custard, made according to the box directions. Add sliced fruit: bananas, kiwi, pineapple. Top with Cool Whip. This is a delicious guilt-free dessert! Great for a diabetic diet also.

Chocolate Raspberry Tart

1 baked pie crust
10 oz. frozen raspberries, thawed
1 Tbsp. cornstarch
1 Tbsp. sugar
1 cup fresh raspberries, if desired
1/2 cup butter, softened

1/3 cup sugar
4 oz. white chocolate, melted
2 eggs
2 oz. (2 squares) semi-sweet chocolate
2 Tbsp. butter

Bake pie crust. Puree frozen (thawed) raspberries in blender. In small saucepan, combine cornstarch and sugar; blend well. Gradually add raspberry puree. Cook over low heat until thickened, stirring constantly. Cool. Spread over pie crust. Arrange fresh raspberries over raspberry layer. Refrigerate. In small bowl, beat 1/2 cup butter and 1/3 cup sugar until light and fluffy. Gradually add melted white chocolate, beating constantly. Add eggs one at a time, beating at highest speed three minutes after each addition. Pour over raspberries; refrigerate until set. In small saucepan over low heat, melt chocolate and 2 Tbsp. butter. Carefully pour and spread over white chocolate layer. Refrigerate at least 2 hours or until set. To serve, let stand at room temperature about 30 minutes to soften chocolate layers.

Raspberry Delight

20 graham crackers, crushed
1/4 cup melted butter
2 Tbsp. sugar
2 beaten eggs
2 cups powdered sugar

3/4 cup butter
3 oz. pkg. raspberry jello
1 1/4 cups hot water
2 - 10 oz. pkg. frozen raspberries

Combine crushed graham crackers, melted butter and sugar, and press into 9 x 9 pan for crust. Mix together eggs, powdered sugar and butter, and spread over cracker crust. Dissolve jello in hot water, and add frozen raspberries. When thickened, pour over mixture in pan. Chill.

Cherry Dessert (or Blueberry)

2 cans cherry pie filling (or blueberry)   1 stick butter, melted
1 white cake mix   Cool Whip or ice cream
1 pkg. slivered almonds

Place pie filling in bottom of 9 x 13 pan. Sprinkle cake mix evenly over pie filling. Scatter almonds over cake mix. Drizzle melted butter over the top of all other ingredients. Bake for 35 - 45 minutes in 350 degrees until nicely brown, but not too dark. Serve with Cool Whip or ice cream.

Easy Elegant Dessert

1 egg   1/4 cup brown sugar
3//4 cup sugar   1/2 cup chopped walnuts
1 cup fruit cocktail   3/4 cup sugar
1/4 cup cocktail syrup   1/2 cup evaporated milk
1 cup flour   1/3 cup butter
1 tsp. soda   1 tsp. vanilla
whipped cream

Beat egg and sugar. Mix in fruit cocktail and syrup. Stir in flour and soda. Pour in a 9 inch pan. Combine nuts and brown sugar, and sprinkle on top. Bake at 325 degrees for 35 minutes. Combine sugar, evaporated milk, butter, and bring to a boil. Add vanilla. When cake comes out of oven, pour hot icing over cake. Serve with whipped cream.

Easy Lemon Dessert

1 angel food cake   4 cups milk
2 small boxes lemon pudding   8 oz. Cool Whip

Break angel food cake into bite size pieces and put into a 9 x 13 pan. Cook pudding according to directions on box. While hot, pour over cake. Let set until cool, then refrigerate. When ready to serve, spread with Cool Whip.

Twinkie Dessert

1 small box instant vanilla pudding
2 cups milk
1 box (10) twinkies

6 chocolate Heath bars, crushed
18 oz. Cool Whip

Prepare pudding as directed on box. Set aside. Slice twinkies in half lengthwise. Line bottom of 9 x 13 pan with bottom twinkie halves, creme filling side up. Sprinkle half of crushed candy on top. Pour pudding over candy. Arrange other twinkie half on top, creme side down. Spread with Cool Whip. Top with remaining half of candy. Cover and refrigerate.

Peach Dessert

3/4 cup butter
2 egg yolks or 1 beaten egg
1 1/4 cups flour
1 tsp. sugar
1/4 tsp. salt
1 Tbsp. vanilla

6 cups peaches, sliced
2 1/4 cups sugar
9 Tbsp. flour
2 eggs
1/2 cup cream
2 Tbsp. sugar

Combine butter, eggs, flour, sugar, salt and vanilla. Press mixture into 9x13 pan, extending l inch on sides of pan. Mix together peaches, sugar and flour. Place on top of crust mixture. Dot with butter. Combine 2 eggs, cream and 2 Tbsp. sugar. Pour over peaches. Bake at 375 degrees for one hour. Serve with ice cream or whipped cream.

A Sweet Tooth's Delight

1 brownie mix
1 cup chopped walnuts
4 cups cold milk
2 small boxes instant chocolate pudding
16 oz. Cool Whip

2 pints fresh strawberries, sliced
  (or substitute 2 pt. raspberries
  or 4 bananas)
6 chocolate-toffee candy bars, broken into
  small pieces

Prepare brownie mix as directed and bake according to package directions. When cool, cut in 1/2 inch squares. While brownies are baking, prepare the pudding according to package directions. Let stand for 5 minutes. Stir 4 cups Cool Whip into pudding and refrigerate one hour. In large 5-quart serving bowl, layer 1/2 of the brownie pieces, 1/2 of the fruit, 1/2 of the candy pieces, 1/2 of the chopped walnuts and 1/2 of the pudding. Repeat the layers. Top with remaining Cool Whip. Refrigerate one hour. Serve in bowls. Makes 12 - 16 servings.

Macadamia Fudge Torte

1/3 cup sweetened condensed milk
1/2 cup chocolate chips
1 box devil's food cake mix
1 1/2 tsp. cinnamon
1/3 cup oil
1 can sliced pears, drained

2 eggs
1/3 cup chopped macadamia nuts or pecans
2 tsp. water
17 oz. butterscotch caramel fudge ice cream
   topping
1/3 cup milk

Spray springform pan with nonstick cooking spray. Combine sweetened condensed milk and chocolate chips, and cook over medium-low heat until chocolate is melted to make filling. Combine cake mix, cinnamon and oil. Blend at low speed for 20 - 30 seconds or until crumbly. Mixture will be dry. Place pears in blender and blend until smooth. In large bowl, combine 2 1/2 cups of cake mixture, pears and eggs, and beat at low speed until moistened. Beat 2 minutes at medium speed. Spread batter evenly in pan. Drop filling by spoonfuls over batter. Stir nuts and water into remaining cake mix mixture. Sprinkle over filling. Bake at 350 degrees for 45 - 50 minutes or until top springs back when touched lightly in center. Cool 10 minutes. Remove sides of pan. Cool completely. Combine butterscotch topping and milk, cooking over low heat until well blended. To serve, spoon 2 Tbsp. warm sauce onto each serving plate. Place wedge of torte on top of sauce. If desired, serve with vanilla ice cream and garnish with chocolate curls.

Strawberry Tapioca Dessert

2 - 3 oz. pkg. tapioca pudding mix
3 cups boiling water
3 oz. pkg. strawberry jello

8 oz. Cool Whip
1 qt. strawberries
angel food cake

Boil water. Stir in tapioca to a rolling boil. Remove and add strawberry jello. Mix and cool. Add Cool Whip and strawberries. Pour into individual dessert cups, or layer in parfait glasses with broken up pieces of angel food cake.

Dessert Pizza

1 pkg. (20 oz.) refrigerated cookie dough,
any flavor
3 cups Cool Whip

2 cups sliced fruit, such as bananas, kiwi,
strawberries, grapes, peach slices or
crushed pineapple

Press dough evenly into 12-inch pizza pan. Bake 15 - 20 minutes at 350 degrees or until golden brown. Place cookie crust on serving plate. Spread Cool Whip on cookie crust. Top with fruit of your choice. Serve immediately or refrigerate until ready to serve. Makes 12 servings.

Lemon Bisque

20 graham crackers, crushed
3 oz. pkg. lemon jello
1 1/4 cups boiling water
1/3 cup sugar

1/8 tsp. salt
3 Tbsp. lemon juice
1 lemon rind grated
1 cup evaporated milk, whipped

Put crushed graham crackers in bottom of pan. Mix jello, boiling water, sugar, salt, lemon juice and lemon rind. Let mixture set to syrupy stage. Stir mixture into whipped evaporated milk. Put jello and whipped milk mixture in pan and sprinkle some crushed crackers on top. Refrigerate overnight.

Peppermint Dazzler

2 graham cracker pie crusts
2/3 cup butter
2 cups powdered sugar
4 eggs

4 squares chocolate
2 cups whipping cream
6 cups mini marshmallows
1/3 cup crushed peppermint candy

Combine butter, powdered sugar and eggs. Whip with mixer. Melt chocolate and add to butter mixture. Pour into crusts. Whip cream and add marshmallows. Spread over chocolate mixture. Sprinkle with crushed peppermint candy. Chill well.

Grasshopper Crepes

2 cups miniature marshmallows
1/3 cup milk
2 Tbsp. white cream de cacao
3 Tbsp. green creme de menthe
green food color (optional)
1 cup heavy cream
whipped cream (optional)
1/2 oz. semi-sweet chocolate

Chocolate Crepes:
3 eggs
1 cup flour
2 Tbsp. sugar
2 Tbsp. cocoa
1 1/4 cups buttermilk
2 Tbsp. melted butter

Heat marshmallows and milk in saucepan over low heat, stirring constantly, until marshmallows just melt. Refrigerate, stirring occasionally, until mixture mounds slightly when dropped from spoon. Stir creme de cacao, creme de menthe and several drops of coloring into marshmallow mixture. Beat heavy cream until stiff. Fold green mixture into whipped cream. Fill cooked crepes; fold over. Chill until firm. Top with extra whipped cream, if desired. Grate chocolate over top. Crepes: Beat eggs. Add flour, sugar and cocoa alternately with buttermilk, beating until smooth. Beat in butter. Refrigerate batter about 1 hour. Cook in crepe pan or in small skillet. Makes 18 to 22 crepes.

Prairie Apple Crunch

6 lg. apples, peeled and sliced
1/2 cup sugar
1/2 tsp. cinnamon
1/2 tsp. nutmeg

dash salt
1 cup packed brown sugar
1 cup flour
1/2 cup butter, melted

Place apples in ungreased 12 x 7 baking dish. Sprinkle with the sugar, cinnamon, nutmeg and salt. Combine brown sugar, flour and butter. Sprinkle over apple mixture. Bake at 350 degrees for 40 - 45 minutes. Serve warm with whipped cream. Serves 10 - 12.

Rhubarb Crisp

1 cup flour
3/4 cup oatmeal
1 cup brown sugar
1 tsp. cinnamon
1/2 cup melted butter

4 cups diced rhubarb
1 cup water
1 tsp. vanilla
1 cup sugar
2 Tbsp. cornstarch

Mix flour, oatmeal, brown sugar, cinnamon and melted butter. Place half of crumb mixture in 9x9 pan. Cover with rhubarb. Combine and cook until thick the water, vanilla, sugar and cornstarch. Pour over rhubarb and top with crumbs. Bake at 350 degrees for 1 hour. Serve warm wiith milk, cream or ice cream.

Nutty Peach Crisp

1 large can peaches
1 butter pecan cake mix
1/2 cup butter

1 cup pecans
1 cup coconut

Pour large can of peaches with juice into cake pan. Sprinkle cake mix over it. Melt butter and pour over cake mix. Sprinkle pecans and coconut over. Bake at 325 degrees for 55 to 60 minutes. Serve warm with ice cream.

Peach Crisp

29 oz. can sliced peaches, undrained
1/2 cup butter, melted
18 oz. pkg. yellow cake mix

1 cup chopped nuts
1 cup shredded coconut

Heat oven to 350 degrees. Put peaches and juice in the bottom of a 9 x 13 pan. Sprinkle the cake mix over the peaches. Pour melted butter over the cake mix. Sprinkle the coconut and nuts over the top. Bake for 50 - 60 minutes. Serve with vanilla ice cream. Serves 12.

Cherry Crisp

1 cup cooking oats
1 cup brown sugar, packed
1 cup flour

1/2 cup butter, softened
2 - 16 oz. cans of cherry pie filling
1/2 cup chopped walnuts (or pecans)

Heat oven to 375 degrees. Combine oats, flour and brown sugar, and mix in softened butter with a fork until crumbly. Put half of the mixture into a 9 x 13 pan and pat into the bottom. Spread the cherry pie filling over the bottom. Sprinkle the remaining mixture over the top, and bake about 45 - 50 minutes. Serves 12.

Never Fail Meringue

1 Tbsp. cornstarch
2 Tbsp. cold water
1/2 cup boiling water
3 egg whites

6 Tbsp. sugar
1 tsp. vanilla
pinch of salt

Blend cornstarch and cold water in saucepan. Add boiling water and cook, stirring until clear and thickened. Let stand until cold. With electric beater at high speed, beat egg whites until foamy. Gradually add sugar and beat until stiff and dry. Turn mixer to low speed; add salt and vanilla. Gradually beat in cornstarch mixture. Spread meringue over cooled pie filling. Bake about 10 minutes at 350 degrees.

Cakes & Frostings

Cakes

Frostings

Lemon Pudding Chiffon Cake

1 pkg. yellow cake mix
1 pkg. lemon instant pudding
1/2 cup cooking oil

6 eggs
1/2 cup milk
1/2 cup water

Put all together and beat at medium high speed 5 minutes. Bake in ungreased angel food pan 50 minutes at 350 degrees. Invert to cool. Frost with Butter Cream Frosting or powdered sugar.

Hot Milk Cake

2 cups flour
2 tsp. baking powder
1/2 tsp. salt
4 eggs

2 cups sugar
2 tsp. vanilla
1 cup milk
2 Tbsp. butter

Beat eggs until thick and light colored. Add sugar gradually, and add vanilla. Heat milk and butter until hot and melted, and beat into mixture quickly. Add dry ingredients a little at a time, mixing well. Pour into well greased 9 x 13 pan. Bake at 350 degrees for 35 - 40 minutes. Spread hot cake with Broiled Nut Topping.

Cherry Ripple Rave Cake

1 can cherry pie filling
1/2 cup chopped almonds
1/2 tsp. almond extract
3 cups flour
3 tsp. baking powder

1 tsp. salt
3/4 cup butter
1 1/4 cups sugar
3 eggs
1 1/4 cups milk

Cream butter, sugar and eggs thoroughly. Add dry ingredients to creamed mixture alternately with milk. Blend well. Spread half of batter into greased 9 x 13 pan. Combine pie filling, almonds and almond extract. Spoon cherry mixture on batter, spreading evenly. Spoon remaining batter over cherries. Spread evenly to cover. Bake at 350 degrees for 45 - 55 minutes until cake tester inserted in center comes out clean. Cool. Frost with Creamy Butter Frosting.

Fresh Banana Cake

1 cup butter, softened
1 cup sugar
2 large eggs (at room temp.)
1 cup mashed ripe bananas
1 3/4 cups flour

1/4 tsp. salt
1 tsp. baking soda
1/3 cup buttermilk
1 tsp. vanilla

Preheat oven to 350 degrees. Grease bottom and sides of two round cake pans. Dust with flour and shake out excess. Set aside. Beat together butter and sugar in large bowl until light and fluffy. Add eggs, one at a time, beating well after each addition. Add banana, mixing until incorporated. Stir together the flour, salt, and soda in a small bowl. With mixer on low speed, alternately mix flour in fourths and buttermilk in thirds into batter, beginning and ending with the flour. Add vanilla and beat 1 minute on medium speed. Divide batter equally into prepared pans. Bake in 350 degrees until cake is golden and springs back when lightly touched, 30 - 35 minutes. Cool completely before frosting with Banana Frosting.

Blackberry Cake

2 cups buttermilk
2 tsp. baking soda
2 cups dark brown sugar
3 cups sifted flour
1 tsp. ground cloves
1 tsp. allspice
1 tsp. cinnamon

1 tsp. cocoa
1/2 cup solid shortening
2 eggs
1 cup blackberry preserves
1/2 cup to 1 cup raisins, optional
1/2 cup chopped English walnuts

Mix baking soda into buttermilk. Mix dry ingredients together, add shortening, eggs (one at a time) and buttermilk. Mix well with mixer. Fold in blackberry preserves and nuts by hand. Pour into 3 well-greased and floured round cake pans. Bake at 350 degrees for 40 - 45 minutes. Frost with Caramel Icing. A blue ribbon winner at the county fair!

Swedish Apple Cake

1 cup butter
3 cups dry bread crumbs
3 Tbsp. sugar
2 tsp. cinnamon

2 tsp. soft butter
3 cups applesauce
2 Tbsp. butter

In a 10-inch skillet, melt butter over medium heat. Add crumbs, sugar and cinnamon; stir until lightly browned. Spread 2 qt. mold or pan with 2 tsp. soft butter. Cover with 1/2 inch of crumbs, thick layer of applesauce, and alternate layers, ending with crumbs. Dot with bits of butter. Bake 25 minutes at 350 degrees. Serve with cold vanilla sauce.

Apple Spice Custard Cake

1 box spice cake mix
2 medium apples, pared, cored and finely chopped (about 2 cups)
14 oz. can sweetened condensed milk

1 cup sour cream, room temperature
1/4 cup lemon juice
Ground cinnamon for garnish

Preheat oven to 350 degrees. Prepare cake mix according to package directions; stir in apples. Pour batter into a well-greased and floured 9 x 13-inch baking dish. Bake for 30 minutes or until wooden toothpick inserted in center comes out clean. Meanwhile, in a medium-sized bowl, combine sweetened condensed milk, sour cream and lemon juice. Remove cake from oven and spread cream mixture over top. Return cake to oven and bake for 10 minutes more or until set (like custard). Sprinkle with cinnamon. Cool completely. Keep refrigerated.

Nobby Apple Cake

3 Tbsp. butter or margarine
1 cup sugar
2 eggs, beaten
1/2 tsp. cinnamon
1/2 tsp. nutmeg
1/2 tsp. salt

1 tsp. baking soda
1 cup sifted flour
3 cups diced apples
1/2 cup chopped walnuts
1 tsp. vanilla

Cream butter and sugar, add eggs and mix well. Sift dry ingredients together and add to creamed mixture. Stir in diced apples, nuts and vanilla. Pour into greased 8x8x2 pan. Bake at 350 degrees for 40 to 45 minutes. Serve hot or cold, with whipped or ice cream.

Lemon Cake

1 1/2 cups flour
1/4 tsp. baking powder
1/8 tsp. baking soda
1 cup sugar
1/2 cup butter, softened
3 large eggs

1/2 cup sour cream
grated peel of 1 lemon

Glaze:
1/3 cup lemon juice
1/3 cup sugar

Beat sugar and butter at high speed until light and fluffy, about 5 minutes. Reduce speed to low, beat in eggs, 1 at a time, until blended. Add flour, baking powder and baking soda alternately with sour cream, beating until well mixed. Stir in lemon peel by hand. Pour batter into greased and floured 9 x 5 loaf pan. Bake 1 to 1 1/4 hours at 325 degrees until toothpick inserted in center comes out clean.

Prepare glaze: mix lemon juice and sugar. Spoon lemon-juice mixture evenly over hot cake in pan. Cool in pan.

Peach Upside Down Cake

1/2 cup butter or margarine
1 cup light brown sugar, packed

29 oz. can sliced peaches, drained
1 pkg. yellow cake mix for 2-layer cake
    made according to pkg. directions

In each of two round cake pans melt 1/4 cup butter. Sprinkle each pan with 1/2 cup sugar and add half of the peaches, then the batter. Bake at 350 degrees for the same time as the cake mix box directions.

Marlene's White Fruit Cake

3/4 lb. butter
2 cups sugar
4 beaten eggs
1 cup milk
3 cups flour
1 tsp. baking powder
1 lb. white raisins
1 lb. nuts

1/4 lb. candied peel
1 can moist coconut
1 bottle maraschino cherries, drained
Candied pineapple
1 tsp. vanilla
1 tsp. almond extract
1 tsp. lemon extract

Cream together butter and sugar. Add the rest of the ingredients. Bake in 2 round cake pans. Preheat oven to 200 degrees. Turn oven up to 325 degrees when you put cakes in the oven. Bake at 325 degrees for 1 hour and 15 minutes.

Hawaiian Dream Cake

1 box yellow cake mix
juice from 20 oz. can crushed pineapple
eggs - per pkg. directions
oil - per pkg. directions
2 cups milk

20 oz. can crushed pineapple, drained
8 oz. cream cheese, softened
1 pkg. vanilla instant pudding
8 oz. Cool Whip

To make cake, mix cake according to package directions, substituting pineapple juice for water. If not enough juice, add water to make up difference. Pour into greased and floured tube pan. Bake at 350 degrees for 40 - 45 minutes. Cool. Cut into two layers. For topping, beat cream cheese, pudding and milk until well blended. Fold in Cool Whip and pineapple. Frost cooled cake with mixture. Refrigerate several hours.

Orange Coconut Cake

1 box lemon cake mix
3 eggs
1/4 cup oil
orange juice
Grated rind of one orange
1/2 tsp. orange extract
Few drops of almond extract
Filling:
1 1/4 cups powdered sugar
1 orange, grated rind and juice

2 egg yolks
1 cup coconut
1/2 tsp. orange extract
Frosting:
4 Tbsp. butter
1 large egg yolk
3 cups powdered sugar
3 Tbsp. orange or lemon juice
1 tsp. grated orange rind

Combine cake mix, eggs and oil. Substitute orange juice for amount of water called for on cake mix box. Add orange rind, orange extract and almond extract. Follow beating and baking directions on box and put in two 9" layer pans. Bake at 350 degrees for 40 to 45 minutes. Mix rind, juice and sugar. Add beaten yolks and cook in double boiler 10 minutes. Add coconut and extract. Cool and spread between layers. Blend together the butter, l egg yolk, powdered sugar, orange or lemon juice and grated orange rind. Frost cake.

Strawberry Cake

1 box white cake mix
3 Tbsp. sifted flour
1 tsp. baking powder
3 oz. box strawberry jello
3/4 cup oil
1/2 cup water

4 eggs
1/2 pkg. frozen strawberries, thawed
1/2 cup margarine
4 3/4 cups powdered sugar
1/2 pkg. frozen strawberries, thawed

Mix together cake mix, flour and baking powder. Then add strawberry jello, oil, water, eggs and 1/2 box strawberries. Bake in a 9x13 pan or two 8" round pans at 350 degrees for 35 minutes. Mix together margarine, powdered sugar and 1/2 box frozen strawberries. Put between layers and on top. For 9 x13 pan use just half of icing recipe.

Cranberry Cake with Butter Sauce

3 Tbsp. butter
1 cup sugar
2 cups flour
1 cup milk
3 tsp. baking powder
1/4 tsp. salt
3 cups cut-up cranberries

1 cup sugar
1 Tbsp. flour
1/2 cup butter
1/2 cup cream
1/2 Tbsp. vinegar
1 tsp. vanilla

Combine butter, sugar, flour, millk, baking powder, salt and cranberries. Bake in a 9x9 pan at 350 degrees for 35-40 minutes. Serve with Butter Sauce. Combine sugar, flour, butter, cream, vinegar and vanilla. Cook over medium heat until blended and comes to boil. Serve warm.

Frosted Sunshine Cake

1 box pudding recipe yellow cake mix
4 eggs
1/2 cup vegetable oil
1 large can mandarin oranges with liquid

Topping:
3 oz. pkg. vanilla instant pudding
1 large can crushed pineapple with liquid
8 oz. Cool Whip

Mix cake mix with eggs, oil, and oranges for 2 minutes. Spread batter in three 9 inch greased and floured cake pans. Bake for 20 - 25 minutes at 350 degrees. Cool in pans for 10 minutes, then remove. Combine instant pudding mix with pineapple and let set 5 minutes. Add thawed Cool Whip and blend. Frost cake and refrigerate.

Banana Crunch Cake

5 Tbsp. butter
1 pkg. coconut pecan or
  coconut almond frosting mix
1 cup oatmeal

1 cup sour cream
4 eggs
2 large ripe bananas
1 pkg. yellow cake mix

Preheat oven to 350 degrees. Grease and flour 10 inch tube pan. In a saucepan melt butter, stir in frosting and oatmeal until crumbly. Set aside. In a large bowl blend sour cream, eggs and bananas until smooth. Blend in cake mix for 2 minutes, then pour 1/3 batter into tube pan, and sprinkle 1/3 crumb mixture into pan on top of batter. Repeat twice with batter and crumb mixture, ending with crumb mixture on the top. Bake for 50 to 60 minutes. Remove from oven when toothpick inserted comes out clean. Cool.

Bavarian Peach Cheese Cake

First Layer:
2 cups butter
4 cups flour
1 cup sugar
1 cup chopped walnuts
Second Layer:
24 oz. cream cheese
8 oz. Cool Whip

1 1/2 cups sugar
2 - 3 oz. pkg. lemon jello
2 cups hot water
Third Layer:
2 1 lb. cans peaches
3 - 3 oz. pkg. instant vanilla pudding
8 oz. Cool Whip
1/2 cup chopped nuts

Grease and flour 2 9 x 13 cake pans. Combine ingredients for first layer and bake at 350 degrees for 10 minutes. Let cool. Add jello to hot water and let cool. When jello is cool add to cream cheese, Cool Whip and sugar. Chill in refrigerator. When cool pour over first layer. Drain peaches and chop to medium size. MIx peaches and instant pudding together. Stir Cool Whip into peach mixture. Put over second layer. Sprinkle with chopped nuts. This recipe makes two 9 x 13 cakes.

Orange Chiffon Cake

2 1/4 cups cake flour
1 1/2 cups sugar
3 tsp. baking powder
1 tsp. salt
1/2 cup cooking oil
5 unbeaten egg yolks

juice of 2 oranges plus water
  to make 3/4 cup
3 Tbsp. grated orange rind
1 cup egg whites
1/2 tsp. cream of tartar

Heat oven to 325 degrees. Sift flour, sugar, baking powder and salt into bowl. Make a well and add oil, egg yolks, orange juice and rind. Beat with spoon until smooth. Beat egg whites and cream of tartar in a large bowl until whites form very stiff peaks for 3 to 5 minutes with electric mixer on high speed. Do not underbeat. Pour egg yolk mixture slowly over beaten egg whites folding just until blended. Do not stir. Pour into ungreased 10 inch tube pan. Bake 55 minutes, then increase to 350 degrees and bake 10 to 15 minutes longer or until top springs back when lightly touched. Turn upside down over neck of funnel or bottle. Hang until cold. Loosen from sides with spatula. Hit edge sharply on table to loosen. Frost.

Cream Cheese Cake

3 cups graham cracker crumbs
3/4 cup butter
9 Tbsp. powdered sugar
3/4 tsp. Knox unflavored gelatin
3 cups sour cream
1/2 cup sugar

3 - 3 oz. pkgs. cream cheese
1 cup sugar
5 eggs, separated
2 tsp. vanilla
1 tsp. vanilla
frozen strawberries, thawed

For the crust, combine graham cracker crumbs, butter, powdered sugar and gelatin. Spread evenly in 9 x 13 pan and chill for 15 minutes. For the filling, beat cream cheese and sugar until thick and smooth, then add egg yolks one at a time and 2 tsp. vanilla. In separate bowl, beat egg whites until stiff. Fold this into the cheese mixture. Pour over the crust. Bake at 350 degrees for 1 hour. Meanwhile beat together the sour cream, sugar and 1 tsp. vanilla. At the end of 1 hour, pour this mixture over the hot cake without removing it from the oven rack. Return it to bake for another 5 minutes. Cool and chill before serving it. This may be topped with strawberries.

Light as a Cloud Coconut Cake

Cake:
4 egg yolks
2 whole eggs
1 1/2 cups sugar
1/2 cup butter, cut up
1 cup hot milk
2 1/2 cups all-purpose flour
1 Tbsp. baking powder
1 tsp. vanilla
1/2 cup toasted pecans or walnuts

Frosting:
1 3/4 cups sugar
1/2 cup water
3 egg whites
1/2 tsp. cream of tartar
1 tsp. vanilla
2 cups shredded fresh coconut

Preheat oven to 350 degrees. Grease and flour three 9-inch round cake pans.
To make the cake: In a large mixing bowl, beat the egg yolks, whole eggs and sugar with an electric mixer for at least 5 minutes or until light and fluffy. Stir the butter pieces into the hot milk until the butter has melted. Combine the flour with the baking powder. Add 1/2 cup of the flour mixture into the egg mixture, beating slowly. Add half the hot mixture, l cup of the flour mixture then the remaining hot milk, beating after each addition. Add the remaining flour mixture and the vanilla. Beat well. Fold in the nuts. Bake layers in the oven for 12 to 15 minutes or until a wooden toothpick inserted in the centers comes out clean. Cool for 5 minutes in the pans. Remove the cakes from the pans and cool completely on wire racks.
To make the frosting: In a medium saucepan, combine the sugar with the water. Bring the mixture to boiling and boil for 2 minutes or until it is syrupy and the sugar dissolves. In a large mixing bowl, beat the egg whites with the cream of tartar with an electric mixer until foamy. Slowly pour the hot sugar syrup into the egg whites, beating constantly for 4 to 6 minutes or until the frosting is stiff enough to spread. Beat in the vanilla. Place a cake layer on a cake plate; spread with about l cup of frosting and sprinkle with 1/3 cup of coconut. Repeat with the remaining layers. Frost the sides of the cake and sprinkle with the remaining coconut. Store the cake in the refrigerator up to 24 hours.

Pina Colada Cake

1 box yellow cake mix
1 can sweetened condensed milk
1 (8 or 10 oz.) Pina Colada mix
1 (8 or 10 oz.) Cool Whip

1 small can coconut
chopped pecans (as many as desired)
1 large can crushed pineapple

Mix cake mix by directions. Pour in sheet cake pan and bake until done. Mix milk and pina colada mix. Punch holes in cake while hot. Pour milk mix over holes and then spread pineapple on top. Refrigerate overnight. Spread Cool Whip on top. Sprinkle coconut and pecans on top.

Peanut Butter Meltaway Cake

1/4 cup buttermilk
1/4 cup cocoa
2 eggs, (beaten)
1 cup water
1 cup margarine
2 cups sugar
2 cups flour
1 tsp. baking soda

1 tsp. vanilla
1 cup peanut butter
1 Tbsp. salad oil
1/2 cup margarine
1/4 cup cocoa
1 lb. powdered sugar
6 Tbsp. buttermilk
1 tsp. vanilla

Mix together 1/4 cup buttermilk, 1/4 cup cocoa, eggs, water and 1 cup margarine. Add in sugar, flour, baking soda and vanilla. Beat until smooth. Grease and flour a 9 x 13 baking pan. Bake at 350 degrees for 25 minutes. Let cool. Mix together the peanut butter and salad oil. Spread over cooled cake. Refrigerate for 20 minutes. Heat 1/4 cup cocoa and 1/2 cup margarine. Stir until it bubbles. Add powdered sugar, 6 Tbsp. buttermilk and vanilla. Beat until smooth and spread over cake.

Poppy Seed Cake

1/4 cup poppy seed
1 cup boiling water
1 yellow or lemon cake mix
4 eggs
1/2 cup vegetable oil
3 oz. pkg. instant coconut cream
    or lemon pudding mix

Frosting:
3 oz. cream cheese
1/4 cup butter
1 tsp. vanilla or lemon flavoring
powdered sugar
chopped nuts

Mix cake ingredients together. Bake 45 minutes at 350 degrees in 2 greased and floured bread pans. Mix frosting ingredients and add powdered sugar until thick enough to spread. Frost cakes and pour chopped nuts over top.

George Washington Fun Cake

1 can apple or blueberry pie filling
1 lg. can crushed pineapple
1 box yellow cake mix - dry

1 stick butter or margarine, cut in pieces
1/2 cup chopped nuts, optional
Cool Whip topping

Place ingredients in buttered cake pan in the following order: pie filling, pineapple, yellow cake mix, butter, and nuts. Bake for one hour in a 350 degree oven. Serve with Cool Whip or whipped cream, if desired.

Pumpkin Cake

1 pkg. spice cake mix
2 eggs
1 tsp. vanilla
2 tsp. soda

15 oz. can pumpkin
3 cups powdered sugar
1 egg yolk
1/3 cup butter

Beat together the cake mix, eggs, vanilla, soda and pumpkin. Bake in a well greased and floured 9x13 cake pan for 45 minutes at 350 degrees. Blend together the powdered sugar, egg yolk and butter. After the cake has cooled, spread on frosting.

Vanilla Wafer Cake

12 oz. box vanilla wafers
3 1/2 oz. flaked coconut
3/4 cup butter or margarine
1 1/2 cups sugar

6 eggs
1/2 cup milk
1/2 cup chopped nuts

Crush vanilla wafers. Add coconut and mix well. Set aside. Blend together butter and sugar. Add eggs, beating until light and fluffy. Add vanilla wafer mixture and milk. Beat until well blended. Add chopped nuts. Turn into greased and floured tube pan. Bake at 325 degrees for 90 minutes or until done. Allow cake to cool thoroughly before removing from pan.

Banana Split Cake

2 graham cracker crusts
2 sticks butter
2 eggs
2 cups powdered sugar
2 - 3 bananas

20 oz. can crushed pineapple
9 oz. Cool Whip
1/2 cup chopped nuts
strawberries for garnish

Cream together butter, eggs, and powdered sugar, beating for 15 minutes. Spread over crusts. Slice bananas over mixture. Spread pineapple over bananas, and then spread Cool Whip over top. Sprinkle nuts on top and garnish with strawberries, if desired. Refrigerate 4 - 6 hours. This can also be made in a 9x13 pan with 2 cups graham cracker crumbs and 1 stick melted butter for crust.

Gingerbread Cake

2 1/2 cups flour
1 Tbsp. instant coffee
1 1/2 tsp. cinnamon
2 tsp. ginger
1/2 tsp. cloves
1 tsp. baking soda
1/2 tsp. salt

1/2 cup unsalted butter
3/4 cup dark brown sugar, packed
2 eggs
1 cup molasses
1 cup buttermilk
1/2 tsp. nutmeg

Preheat oven to 375 degrees. Grease and flour a 9-inch square baking pan. Sift together flour, coffee powder, spices, baking soda and salt. Set aside. Cream butter and brown sugar with electric mixer until light and fluffy. Add eggs one at a time, beating well after each addition. Add molasses and beat about 2 minutes, scraping bowl often. With mixer on lowest speed, add sifted dry ingredients in thirds alternately with buttermilk, beginning and ending with dry ingredients. Scrape sides of bowl frequently and do not overbeat. Turn into baking pan and bake until gingerbread tests done with toothpick, about 50-55 minutes. Serve warm or at room temperature. Top with applesauce, lemon sauce, caramel or other favorite topping.

Butterfinger Cake

6 Butterfinger candy bars
1 angel food cake
4 egg yolks

1 tsp. almond flavor
2 cups powdered sugar
12 oz. Cool Whip

Crush candy bars. Break cake into bite size pieces. Mix together egg yolks, almond flavor, powdered sugar and Cool Whip. Layer in a 9 x 13 pan, 1/2 of cake, 1/2 of Cool Whip mixture and 1/2 of candy bars. Repeat layers. Refrigerate 2-3 hours or overnight.

Heath Bar Cake

2 cups flour
2 cups brown sugar
1/2 cup butter
1 tsp. baking soda
1/2 tsp. salt

1 egg
1 cup milk
1 tsp. vanilla
1/2 cup nuts
8 Heath candy bars, cut up

Mix brown sugar, flour, soda, salt and butter. Cut butter in like pie crust. Put 1 cup aside, then add egg, milk and vanilla to mixture. Pour into greased pan. Sprinkle with remaining mixture, the nuts and cut up candy bars and put in oven at 350 degrees for 35 minutes.

Heavenly Chocolate Spice Cake

1 cup butter or shortening
2 1/2 cups sugar
2 eggs, beaten
8 Tbsp. cocoa
2 tsp. baking soda
1 tsp. ground cloves

1 tsp. cinnamon
1 tsp. vanilla
1 tsp. salt
2 cups buttermilk
3 cups cake flour

Cream shortening and 1 1/2 cups sugar in mixing bowl. Add eggs, one at a time, beating well after each addition. Mix remaining sugar with cocoa and spices and add to first mixture. Add alternately the buttermilk and flour sifted with soda and salt. Add vanilla. Bake in a moderate oven (375 degrees) for about 30 minutes. This makes a very large cake if baked in a pan 16 x 11 inches or two smaller pans. It is almost too soft and fluffy for layers. Half of the recipe makes a good sized cake. The flavor is unusually delicious.

Lemon Jelly Roll

Cake:
4 eggs
3/4 tsp. baking powder
1/4 tsp. salt
3/4 cup sugar
3/4 cup sifted cake flour
3/4 tsp. vanilla

Filling:
3 oz. pkg. lemon pudding
1 Tbsp. butter
1/4 cup sugar
1 Tbsp. lemon juice

Beat eggs, baking powder and salt until foamy. Add sugar gradually and beat until thick and lemon colored. Add vanilla. Fold in cake flour by hand. Spread in a jelly roll pan that has been greased and lined with wax paper and greased. Bake 10 minutes in 400 degree oven. Put on towel dusted generously with powdered sugar. Roll up with towel and let cool. Unroll and spread filling, and roll up. Filling: Make lemon pudding, following directions, but add butter, sugar and lemon juice. Cool.

Burnt Sugar Cake

1 1/2 cups sugar
1/2 cup butter
3 eggs
1 cup cold water
3 cups cake flour

1 tsp. salt
2 heaping tsp. baking powder
5 Tbsp. burnt sugar
1 tsp. vanilla

To make burnt sugar, carmelize 1 cup sugar, remove from stove and add 1/2 cup boiling water. Cool before using in cake. Cream sugar and shortening. Add the 3 egg yolks, burnt sugar and vanilla. Sift flour, baking powder and salt and add alternately with the water. Beat 2 egg whites and fold in last. Pour into 9 x 13 pan and bake in 350 degree oven until done.

Whipped Cream Pound Cake

1 cup butter
3 cups sugar
6 eggs

1 tsp. vanilla or almond flavoring
1 cup whipping cream
3 cups cake flour + 3 tsp.

Cream butter and sugar. Add eggs, one at a time, beating well after each. Add flavoring. Alternately add whipping cream and flour, beating well until mixed. Use tube pan, lightly oiled and waxed paper on bottom. Cake is placed in a cold oven. Then set the temperature and time to bake. Bake at 300 degrees for 1 1/2 hours. Let cake cool about 15 minutes before removing from pan.

Coconut Pound Cake

3 cups sugar
1 cup margarine
1 cup crisco
6 eggs
3 cups plain flour

1 cup milk
1 can angel flake coconut
1 tsp. coconut flavor
1 tsp. almond flavor
1 cup chopped nuts

Mix sugar, margarine, crisco well. Add flour and milk alternately, starting with the flour. Add eggs one at a time and beat well after each addition. Add flavoring, coconut and nuts, mix well. Bake in greased tube pan at 350 degrees for 1 1/2 hours.

Sour Cream Pound Cake

1 cup butter, softened
3 cups sugar
6 eggs
3 cups flour

1/4 tsp. baking soda
1 cup (8 oz.) sour cream
2 tsp. almond extract
1 tsp. vanilla extract

Cream butter and sugar. Add egg yolks. Sift flour three times and set aside. Combine baking soda and sour cream; add alternately with flour to creamed mixture. Add extracts and mix well. Beat the egg whites until soft peaks form, and fold into batter. Pour into a greased and floured 10-inch tube pan. Bake at 300 degrees for 1 1/2 hours or until the cake tests done.

Bunny Pound Cake

3 cups flour
2 tsp. baking powder
1 cup butter, softened
1 lb. powdered sugar

5 eggs
1 cup milk
1 Tbsp. grated lemon peel
2 tsp. vanilla

Stir together flour and baking powder. Cream butter and sugar until light and fluffy. Beat in eggs, one at a time. Combine milk, lemon peel and vanilla. Thoroughly blend in flour mixture alternately with milk, beginning and ending with flour. Pour into two greased and paper-lined 9" round pans. Bake in 325 degree oven 55 to 60 minutes or until golden brown. Cool ten minutes before removing from pans. Cut one layer in half for ears; use second layer for head. Position cake on large tray to form bunny face and ears. Cool completely before frosting. Frost with Lemony Frosting and decorate face with candy: jelly beans and licorice for eyes, nose, mouth and whiskers.

Chocolate Wet Cake

2 cups sugar
2 cups flour
1 cup margarine
3 Tbsp. cocoa
1 cup water

1 cup buttermilk
1 tsp. baking soda
1 tsp. vanilla
4 tsp. cinnamon
2 eggs slightly beaten

Combine in large mixing bowl sugar and flour. Bring to a boil the margarine, cocoa and water. Pour over sugar and flour. Add buttermilk, soda, vanilla, cinnamon and eggs. Mix well. Pour into 9 x 13 greased and floured pan. Bake 35 - 45 minutes at 350 degrees. Leave in pan and ice while hot with Chocolate Wet Icing.

Moist Chocolate Cake

1 box chocolate fudge cake mix   3 eggs
9 oz. Cool Whip   1 1/4 cups water

Mix all ingredients together, using 3 cups of the Cool Whip. Pour into greased and floured bundt or tube pan. Bake at 350 degrees for 45 to 50 minutes. Cool and remove from pan. Frost with remaining Cool Whip.

Chocolate Chip Cake

1 3/4 cups boiling water   1 3/4 cups flour
1 cup uncooked oats   1 tsp. soda
1 cup brown sugar   1/2 tsp. salt
1 cup sugar   1 Tbsp. cocoa
1/2 cup margarine   12 oz. chocolate chips
2 eggs   3/4 cup walnuts, chopped

Mix boiling water and oats, and let stand 10 minutes. Add sugars, margarine and eggs and mix well. Then add flour, soda, salt and cocoa and mix well. Add half of the chocolate chips and nuts. Pour batter in 9 x 13 pan, and then sprinkle rest of nuts and chocolate chips on top. Bake at 350 degrees for 40 minutes. This is a great picnic cake!

Quick Devil's Food

1 cup flour   3 Tbsp. melted shortening
1 cup sugar   1 tsp. soda dissolved in a little cold water
3 Tbsp. cocoa   1 cup sour milk
Pinch of salt   1 tsp. vanilla
1 egg

Sift flour, sugar, cocoa and salt into mixing bowl. Make a hole in middle and put in egg, shortening, soda, milk, and vanilla. Beat until well mixed. Bake at 375 degrees. Use 8x8 greased pan.

Chocolate Cake Supreme

2 eggs
1 1/2 cups milk
2 cups sugar
2 cups flour
2 tsp. baking powder

1 cup nuts
1/2 cup butter
4 oz. bitter chocolate
2 tsp. vanilla

Cream butter and sugar. Melt chocolate. Beat eggs and add to creamed mixture. Add melted chocolate. Mix nuts with dry ingredients and add alternately with vanilla and milk. Bake in loaf pan at 350 degrees for 45 minutes. After loaf has cooked, cover with Uncooked Frosting.

Texas Cake

2 cups flour
2 cups sugar
1/2 tsp. salt
1 tsp. baking soda
2 sticks margarine
4 Tbsp. cocoa
1 cup water
1/2 cup sour cream

2 eggs
Icing:
1 stick margarine
6 Tbsp. milk
4 Tbsp. cocoa
1 box powdered sugar
1 Tbsp. vanilla
1 cup chopped nuts

Mix together dry ingredients. Set aside. Mix together margarine, cocoa and water. Bring to a boil. Add to flour mixture. Mix well and add sour cream and eggs. Bake in a sheet cake pan for 20 to 25 minutes at 350 degrees. Icing: Boil together margarine, milk and cocoa. Add powdered sugar and vanilla. Ice cake while hot. Sprinkle nuts over cake while icing is hot.

Dark Chocolate Cake

2 cups sugar
1 3/4 cups flour
3/4 cup cocoa
1 1/2 tsp. baking soda
1 1/2 tsp. baking powder
1 cup boiling water

1 tsp. salt
2 eggs
1 cup milk
1/2 cup vegetable oil
2 tsp. vanilla

Mix all ingredients except boiling water. Mix until well blended; add boiling water. Pour into well greased and floured 9 x 13 pan. Bake at 350 degrees for 45 minutes or until toothpick comes out clean.

Special Chocolate Cake

1/2 cup butter
2 cups sugar
1 cup sweet milk
3 cups cake flour
1 tsp. cream of tartar
5 egg whites

1 tsp. baking soda
1/2 tsp. salt
2 sq. chocolate
2/3 cup coffee, cooked
1 tsp. vanilla

First melt chocolate in coffee carefully to make thick custard. Cream butter and sugar. Sift flour, soda and salt. Add alternately with milk. Add melted chocolate. Beat egg whites and cream of tartar and fold carefully into cake batter. Bake in 9 x 13 pan in 350 degree oven for 40 to 45 minutes.

Banana Cupcakes

2 cups flour
1 tsp. baking powder
1 tsp. soda
1/2 cup butter
1 1/2 cups sugar

2 eggs
3 - 4 mashed ripe bananas
3/4 cup sour milk
1 tsp. vanilla

Cream butter and sugar until puffy. Add eggs and beat well. Add bananas and beat well. Add flour and dry ingredients alternately with milk. Add vanilla. Put in muffin cups and bake at 350 degrees for 20 minutes. Makes 24 cupcakes.

Easy Chocolate Cupcakes

1 3/4 cups flour
2 1/2 tsp. baking powder
1/2 cup sugar
3 Tbsp. cocoa
1/2 tsp. cinnamon

3/4 tsp. salt
1 egg, beaten
3/4 cup milk
1/3 cup oil
1/3 cup chopped nuts

Stir together the flour, sugar, cocoa, baking powder, cinnamon and salt. Make a well in the center. Combine egg, milk and oil. Add all at once to dry ingredients, stirring just until moistened. Batter should be lumpy. Fold in nuts. Fill muffin cups. Bake at 400 degrees for 18 to 20 minutes.

Self-Filled Cupcakes

1 pkg. (2 layer) chocolate cake mix
8 oz. pkg. cream cheese, (soft)
1/2 cup sugar

1 egg
dash of salt
1 cup chocolate chips

Preheat oven to 350 degrees. Mix cake mix by directions on box. Fill muffin cups 2/3 full. Beat cream cheese with sugar. Beat in egg and salt. Stir in chocolate chips. Drop 1 tsp. cheese mixture into each cupcake center. Bake until done. Makes 30 cupcakes.

Brownie Frosting

1 stick butter
6 Tbsp. milk
4 Tbsp. cocoa

2 - 3 cups powdered sugar
1 tsp. vanilla

Melt butter, milk and cocoa together. Boil for 1 minute. Add powdered sugar and vanilla, and beat until smooth.

Chocolate Wet Icing

1/2 cup margarine
3 Tbsp. cocoa
6 Tbsp. milk

1/2 tsp. vanilla
1 box confectioner's sugar

Boil margarine, cocoa and milk together. Take off stove and add vanilla and sugar. Pour over cake while hot, punching holes in cake to let frosting through. Cool 2 hours in pan before cutting.

Chocolate Frosting

1 1/2 cups sugar
4 1/2 Tbsp. corn starch
9 Tbsp. cocoa
1/4 tsp. salt

1 1/2 cups boiling water
1 1/2 tsp. vanilla
4 Tbsp. butter

Mix together sugar, corn starch, cocoa, and salt. Add boiling water and boil on stove until thick. Remove from heat and add vanilla and butter. Stir. Good for hot fudge sundaes also.

Quick Chocolate Frosting

2 squares unsweetened chocolate
1 can sweetened condensed milk
1 Tbsp. water

dash of salt
1/2 tsp. vanilla

Melt chocolate in top of double boiler. Add condensed milk gradually, mixing well. Then add water and salt and blend. Cook 5 minutes over rapidly boiling water, stirring constantly. Remove from heat. Add vanilla. Cool. Makes enough frosting to cover tops of two 9-inch layers or two 8-inch layers generously.

Fudge Frosting

2 squares unsweetened chocolate
1 cup milk
2 cups sugar
dash of salt

2 Tbsp. corn syrup
2 Tbsp. butter
1 tsp. vanilla

Add chocolate to milk and place over low heat. Cook until smooth, stirring constantly. Add sugar, salt and syrup, stirring until sugar is dissolved. Continue boiling without stirring until a small amount of mixture forms a very soft ball in cold water. Remove from heat. Add butter and vanilla. Cool to lukewarm (110 degrees). Beat until of right consistency to spread. If necessary, place over hot water to keep soft while spreading.

Uncooked Chocolate Frosting

1 Tbsp. butter
1 cup powdered sugar
1 egg
1/4 cup milk

1/2 tsp. vanilla
pinch of salt
2 squares chocolate, melted

Combine all ingredients in a bowl. Set in a pan of ice cold water and beat until real stiff, or until it stands up in peaks.

Never Fail Frosting

10 marshmallows
1 cup sugar
4 Tbsp. milk
1 Tbsp. butter

powdered sugar
vanilla, lemon, or other flavoring
2 squares chocolate, melted (optional)

Boil together marshmallows, sugar, milk and butter for 1 minute. When cool add powdered sugar until it spreads easily. Add flavoring, or if chocolate frosting is wanted, add 2 squares chocolate, melted.

Chocolate Fluff Frosting

4 Tbsp. butter
3/4 cup powdered sugar
1 tsp. vanilla
3 squares chocolate, melted

1/4 tsp. salt
2 egg whites
3/4 cup powdered sugar

Mix butter and 3/4 cup powdered sugar, then add vanilla, chocolate and salt. In a separate bowl, beat egg whites, adding 3/4 cup powdered sugar two tablespoons at a time. Beat until mixture will stand in peaks. Add to first mixture folding in just enough to blend.

One Minute Frosting

1 cup sugar
1/4 cup cocoa
1/3 cup milk

1/4 cup vegetable shortening
1 tsp. vanilla
Pinch of salt

Mix all ingredients. Bring to a boil. Boil one minute. Let cool until lukewarm - then beat well until thick enough to spread.

Chocolate Glaze

1/2 square chocolate, melted
2 Tbsp. butter
1 cup powdered sugar

1 tsp. hot water
1/2 tsp. vanilla

Melt together the chocolate and butter. Blend in sugar, hot water and vanilla. Stir until smooth.

Mock 7 Minute Icing

8 oz. sour cream
1 cup sugar

2 tsp. vanilla
8 oz. Cool Whip

Beat sour cream and sugar until sugar dissolves. Add vanilla and Cool Whip and mix well. This is really good on chocolate cake.

Creamy Butter Frosting

1 cup sugar
1/3 cup flour
1 cup milk

3/4 cup butter
1/4 tsp. almond extract

Combine sugar and flour in medium saucepan. Stir well to blend. Add milk and blend well. Heat over medium heat until mixture boils for 1 minute and thickens, stirring constantly. Remove from heat. Cool at room temperature several minutes. Refrigerate 1 hour until thoroughly chilled. Cream butter in small mixer bowl until light and fluffy. Add cooled milk mixture gradually, beating constantly, until light and fluffy. Beat in almond extract.

Butter Frosting

1/4 cup butter
2 cups powdered sugar

1/4 cup cream
1 tsp. vanilla

Melt butter over hot water, add sugar and cream. Leave over hot water ten minutes. Remove. You may need to add some more cream to make it spread easily.

Variations:
Chocolate - Melt 2 squares chocolate with butter
Orange - Use 1/4 cup orange juice instead of cream and 1 Tbsp. grated orange rind.

Seven Minute Frosting

2 egg whites
1 1/2 cups sugar
dash salt

1/3 cup water
2 Tbsp. Karo syrup
1 tsp. vanilla

Place egg whites, sugar, salt, water and syrup in double boiler and beat seven minutes.
Add vanilla.

Variations:
1. Add 1 cup diced marshmallows.
2. Add 1 cup shredded coconut.
3. Omit syrup, use 2 Tbsp. lemon juice for the water.
4. Omit syrup, use 3 Tbsp. orange juice.
5. Use 2 Tbsp. caramel syrup instead of vanilla.
6. Omit syrup, use 2 cups brown sugar.
7. Stir 3 squares melted chocolate in just before spreading.

Four Minute Frosting

1 egg white
3/4 cup sugar
1 tsp. corn syrup
    or 1/4 tsp. cream of tartar

1/4 cup (scant) cold water
pinch of salt
vanilla

Mix all ingredients together, except vanilla. Put on very low heat and beat constantly at
high speed for 4 minutes. Add vanilla when done. Double this recipe for large cakes.

Topping for Cake

3 Tbsp. butter
6 Tbsp. brown sugar

2 Tbsp. sweet cream
1/2 cup chopped nuts

Mix all ingredients. Spread over cake, and put under broiler being careful not to burn.
Leave until it bubbles.

Quick White Frosting

1/2 cup white Karo syrup   dash of salt
1 egg white

Beat egg white. Bring Karo just to boiling point. Beat into egg slowly. Add flavoring and beat until it holds up.

Vanilla Glaze (For Angel Food Cake)

2 cups powdered sugar   2 Tbsp. butter
3 Tbsp. milk   1/2 tsp. vanilla

Measure powdered sugar into bowl. Heat milk and butter over low heat, stirring constantly, just until butter melts. Remove from heat. Add sugar, stirring until smooth. Stir in vanilla. Spread hot glaze over top of cake, allowing to drip down sides.

Broiled Nut Topping

1/3 cup soft butter   3 Tbsp. light cream or milk
3/4 cup brown sugar   1 cup nuts or flaked coconut

Mix ingredients and spread on hot cake. Place 6 inches under broiler for 2 - 4 minutes, or until golden brown. Watch this very closely.

Caramel Icing

1/2 cup butter   1/4 cup milk
1 cup dark brown sugar   2 - 3 cups confectioner's sugar

Melt butter, and add brown sugar. Boil over low heat for 2 minutes, stirring constantly. Stir in milk and stir until it comes to a boil. Cool gradually. Add confectioner's sugar. Beat until it spreads. If too stiff, add a little hot water. Tastes great on Blackberry Cake.

Banana Frosting

8 oz. cream cheese, softened
1/3 cup mashed ripe banana
2 cups powdered sugar

1 to 2 firm bananas (for slicing)
1/2 cup coarsely chopped nuts

Beat cream cheese in small bowl on medium speed until smooth. Mix in mashed banana. Beat in sugar until mixture is light and creamy. Add more powdered sugar if consistency is not desirable. Place 1 layer of cake, flat side up, on plate. Spread with a quarter of the frosting. Thinly slice 1 firm banana and arrange a layer of slices over frosting. Top with second layer, flat side down. Frost top and sides of cake. Garnish with 1 inch border of nuts around top of cake. Refrigerate until serving time. Before serving slice banana and arrange slices in a circle around center of cake.

Peanut Crunch Frosting

1/3 cup butter
1/3 cup crunchy peanut butter

2 1/2 or 3 cups powdered sugar
Coffee

Mix butter, peanut butter and powdered sugar. Add coffee to make frosting the right consistency.

Peanut Butter Icing

3/4 cup white sugar
1/4 cup brown sugar

1/2 cup rich milk
1/3 cup smooth peanut butter

Combine ingredients and boil 2 minutes. Remove from heat, stir in peanut butter. Beat to spreading consistency. Thin with cream if necessary.

Quick Butterscotch Frosting

1 cup powdered sugar
3 Tbsp. brown sugar
1 tsp. vanilla

2 Tbsp. butter
2 Tbsp. cream

Combine brown sugar, butter and cream over heat and boil 3 minutes. Add vanilla and powdered sugar. To make chocolate frosting, melt 1 square chocolate in boiling mixture.

Lemony Frosting

1/4 cup butter, softened
1/4 cup shortening
1 egg white
1/2 tsp. salt

1/2 tsp. lemon extract
1 lb. powdered sugar
3 - 4 Tbsp. milk
food coloring

Cream butter, shortening, egg white, salt and lemon extract until smooth. Blend in sugar. Add enough milk to reach spreading consistency. Tint with a few drops of desired food coloring for Bunny Pound Cake.

Lemon Filling

1 cup sugar
2 2/3 Tbsp. cornstarch
1 cup lukewarm water

1 egg yolk
1 Tbsp. butter
1/4 cup lemon juice

Cook sugar, cornstarch, water, egg yolk and butter until thick and transparent. Add lemon juice. Cook 5 more minutes. Cool. Spread between cake layers.

Orange Cream Cheese Frosting

6 oz. cream cheese
1/2 cup softened butter
1 Tbsp. orange juice

4 1/2 cups powdered sugar
1/2 tsp. finely shredded orange peel

Beat together cream cheese, butter and orange juice. Gradually beat in powdered sugar to make frosting spreadable. Stir in finely shredded orange peel. Makes 2 3/4 cups.

Cookies, Bars & Candies

Bars

Candies

Cookies

Melting Moments

1 cup flour   1/2 cup cornstarch
3/4 cup butter   1/2 cup powdered sugar

Beat butter until fluffy. Mix together flour, cornstarch and powdered sugar, and add to butter. Beat until thoroughly combined. Refrigerate for 1 hour. Shape into 1 inch balls and place about 1 - 2 inches apart on ungreased cookie sheets. Flatten with fork. Bake at 300 degrees for 20 minutes or until edges are light brown.

Snicker Cookies

1 cup butter   2 tsp. vanilla
1 cup creamy peanut butter   3 cups flour
1 cup sugar   1 tsp. baking powder
1 cup brown sugar   1 tsp. baking soda
2 eggs   60 Snicker Miniatures (2 bags)

In a large bowl, beat together butter, peanut butter, sugar and brown sugar until fluffy. Add eggs and vanilla. Combine flour, baking powder and baking soda. Add to peanut butter mixture beating until smooth. Shape about 1 Tbsp. of dough around Snicker bar. Bake on ungreased cookie sheet at 350 degrees for 10 - 12 minutes. Kids love these! (Big kids, too!)

Everything Cookies

1 cup salad oil   1 tsp. salt
1 cup butter   1 tsp. baking soda
1 cup brown sugar   1 tsp. cream of tartar
1 cup sugar   1 cup oatmeal
1 egg   1 cup coconut
3 tsp. vanilla   1 cup Rice Krispies
3 1/2 cups flour   1 cup chocolate chips

Mix ingredients in order. Drop by spoonful onto greased cookie sheet. Bake at 350 degrees for 10 - 12 minutes.

Brownie Drops

1/2 cup butter
1 1/2 sq. unsweetened chocolate
1 cup brown sugar
1/2 cup buttermilk
1 egg
1 tsp. vanilla

1 1/2 cup flour
1/2 tsp. baking powder
1/2 tsp. baking soda
1/4 tsp. salt
6 oz. chocolate chips

Melt together butter and chocolate. Add brown sugar, buttermilk, egg and vanilla. Blend well. Add dry ingredients, blend well, and stir in chocolate chips. Drop by spoonful onto ungreased baking sheet. Bake at 375 degrees for 10 - 12 minutes. While warm, spread with Chocolate Glaze.

Christmas Confetti Cookies

1 cup butter
1/2 cup sugar
1/2 cup brown sugar
1 egg
1 tsp. vanilla
2 cups flour

1 tsp. baking soda
1/2 tsp. salt
1 1/2 cups oatmeal
2/3 cup chopped nuts
1/4 cup chopped red maraschino cherries
1/4 cup chopped green maraschino cherries

Beat together butter and sugars until light and fluffy. Blend in egg and vanilla. Add flour, baking soda and salt to butter mixture, mixing well. Stir in oats, nuts and cherries. Shape dough to form 1 inch balls. Place on ungreased cookie sheet. With tines of fork, flatten to make crisscross pattern. Bake at 350 degrees for 12 - 15 minutes or until golden brown.

Oatmeal Crispies

1/2 cup butter
1/2 cup margarine
1/2 cup sugar

1 cup flour
1 1/2 cups oatmeal

Beat sugar and shortening. Add flour and oatmeal. Mix well and chill. Shape into small balls on greased baking sheet. Flatten. Bake at 350 degrees for 12 - 15 minutes. Remove when slightly cool. Dip in powdered sugar. Store in tight container.

California Rangers

1 cup shortening
1 cup sugar
1 cup brown sugar
2 eggs, beaten
1 Tbsp. milk
1 tsp. vanilla
2 cups flour

1/2 tsp. baking powder
1 tsp. baking soda
1/2 tsp. salt
2 cups quick oats
2 cups cornflakes (stale is OK)
1 cup coconut

Cream together shortening and sugars. Add eggs, milk and vanilla. Sift together the flour, baking powder, baking soda and salt, and add to mixture. Add oats, cornflakes and coconut. Mix well and drop by teaspoonful on ungreased cookie sheet. Bake at 350 degrees for 10 - 12 minutes.

Homemade Ginger Snaps

3/4 cup shortening
1 cup sugar
1/4 cup Brer Rabbit light or dark molasses
1 egg
2 cups flour
2 tsp. baking soda

1 tsp. cinnamon
1/2 tsp. ground cloves
1/2 tsp. ginger
1/2 tsp. salt
some granulated sugar

Cream together shortening and sugar. Add molasses and egg, beat well. Sift flour, baking soda, cinnamon, cloves, ginger and salt. Add to first mixture. Mix well. Cover. Chill. Form into 1 inch balls and roll in granulated sugar. Place on greased cookie sheet and bake at 375 degrees for 8 - 10 minutes or until golden brown. Cool on wire rack. Makes 48 cookies.

Peanut Butter Bon-Bons

2 cups peanut butter
1/2 cup margarine
4 1/2 cups sifted powdered sugar

3 cups Rice Krispies
18 oz. butterscotch chips

In double boiler melt peanut butter and margarine. In large bowl combine powdered sugar and Rice Krispies. Pour peanut butter mixture over this. Blend together with hands and form into 1/2 inch balls. Chill until firm. Melt butterscotch and dip balls in, swirling with a spoon. Place on wax paper and let butterscotch firm.

Sandies

1 cup margarine
1/4 cup confectioner's sugar
2 tsp. vanilla

1 tsp. water
2 cups sifted flour
1 cup chopped pecans

Cream margarine and sugar. Add vanilla and water. Add flour, mix well, and add pecans. Form small balls, about 1 inch. Bake on ungreased cookie sheets at 300 degrees for 20 minutes or until delicately browned. While cookies are hot, roll in confectioner's sugar, then roll again. Makes 3 dozen.

Coconut Cookies

1/4 cup butter
3/4 cup sugar
1 egg, well beaten

1 cup flour
1 cup coconut
dash of lemon juice or extract

Cream butter and sugar together. Add beaten egg, flour and coconut to form stiff dough. Add lemon juice or extract. Drop by spoonfuls on well-greased cookie sheet. Flatten slightly with fork. Bake in 350 degrees until cookies begin to brown. Remove from oven and allow to cool. Frost with lemon icing and sprinkle tops with coconut. Makes about 2 dozen. A blue ribbon cookie!!

Cherry Drop Cookies

1 pkg. cherry cake mix
1/2 cup oil
2 Tbsp. water
2 eggs

few drops red food coloring
1 cup chopped english walnuts
quartered maraschino cherries

Blend cake mix, oil, water, eggs, and food coloring. Stir in nuts. Drop by spoonful onto an ungreased cookie sheet. Top each cookie with a quarter of a maraschino cherry. Bake at 350 degrees for 10 - 12 minutes. Cool on cookie sheet 1 minute. Makes 4 - 5 dozen.

Applesauce Raisin Cookies

1 pkg. spice cake mix
1/2 cup oil
1/2 cup applesauce

1 egg
1 1/2 cups seedless raisins

Combine all ingredients. Drop onto ungreased cookie sheet by spoonfuls. Bake 12 - 15 minutes at 350 degrees. Lift off cookie sheet as soon as you take from the oven.

Lemon Crisps

1 pkg. lemon cake mix
2 eggs
1 tsp. lemon extract

Decoration: sprinkles, red/green sugar
crystals or pecan halves

Combine all ingredients and mix well. Drop by teaspoonful onto an ungreased cookie sheet. Top each cookie with choice of decoration. Bake at 350 degrees for 10 - 12 minutes. Cool on cookie sheet for 1 minute. Makes 4 - 5 dozen.

Maple Lace Cookies

1/2 cup maple syrup
1/3 cup butter

1/2 cup finely chopped pecans
1/2 cup unbleached flour

Boil maple syrup and butter together for 1/2 minute. Let cool to room temperature. Add flour and nuts; mix well. Drop by teaspoonfuls onto greased baking sheets, allowing at least 3 inches between cookies. Bake at 325 degrees for 8 - 10 minutes. Cool on baking sheet for 30 - 60 seconds and remove very carefully, using a spatula. Makes 24 cookies.

Peanut Chews

1/2 cup white corn syrup
1/2 cup sugar
3 Tbsp. honey

6 oz. chunky peanut butter
3 cups corn flakes

Blend corn syrup, honey and sugar together in sauce pan. Bring to low boil and boil until sugar is dissolved. Stir in peanut butter and remove from heat. Stir in corn flakes. Drop by spoonfuls onto waxed paper. Cool and serve.

Peanut Butter Cookies

1/2 cup sugar	1 tsp. vanilla
1/2 cup brown sugar	1 egg
1/2 cup shortening or margarine, softened	1 3/4 cup flour
1/2 cup crunchy peanut butter	1 tsp. baking soda
2 Tbsp. milk	1/2 tsp. salt
Hershey's kisses	

Cream sugars and shortening, then add peanut butter. Add remaining ingredients and mix well. Make into 1 inch balls. Place on ungreased cookie sheet 2 inches apart. Bake at 375 degrees for 10 - 12 minutes. While hot, place Hershey's kiss in middle of each cookie, press down and turn slightly. Let cool.

No Bake Fudgies

2 cups sugar	1/2 cup butter
2 1/2 Tbsp. cocoa	1/2 cup peanut butter
1/2 cup milk	2 cups oatmeal

In large saucepan, combine sugar and cocoa. Add milk, stirring until smooth. Add butter and bring to boil over high heat. Boil 2 minutes. Remove from heat. Add peanut butter, stirring until melted. Stir in oatmeal and mix well. Drop from teaspoon onto waxed paper or spread in a buttered baking dish. Cool thoroughly then cut into squares.

Minnesota Mail Carrier Cookies

1 cup shortening	1 cup coconut
2 cups brown sugar	1 cup dry oatmeal
1 tsp. baking soda	1 cup dates or raisins
2 Tbsp. warm water	1/2 cup nut meats
3 eggs, well beaten	2 1/2 cups flour

Dissolve baking soda in warm water, and then combine all ingredients. Drop by teaspoonfuls onto baking sheet and bake at 400 degrees.

ESP Cookies

1 egg
1 cup sugar

1 cup peanut butter
24 hershey kisses

Mix egg, sugar and peanut butter together. Form into walnut size balls. Bake at 350 degrees for 10 minutes. Remove from oven, place 1 kiss on each and press down. Bake 1 1/2 minutes more.

Butterscotch Cookies with Burnt Butter Icing

1/2 cup butter
1 1/2 cups brown sugar
2 eggs, beaten
2 1/2 cups flour
1/2 tsp. baking powder
1 tsp. baking soda
1/2 tsp. salt
1 cup sour cream

1 tsp. vanilla
2/3 cup walnuts

Burnt Butter Icing:
6 Tbsp. butter
1 1/2 cups powdered sugar
1 tsp. vanilla
1 Tbsp. hot water

Cream butter, add sugar gradually and cream thoroughly. Blend in the beaten eggs. Add dry ingredients to the creamed mixture alternately with sour cream. Blend in nuts and vanilla. Drop by spoon on greased baking sheet. Bake 10 to 15 minutes at 375 degrees. When cookie is cool, spread with icing. To make icing, melt the butter and keep over heat until golden brown. Blend in powdered sugar. Add vanilla and stir in hot water until the icing is of right consistency to spread smoothly.

Oatmeal Filled Cookies

1 cup brown sugar
3/4 cup shortening
2 cups oatmeal
2 cups flour
1 tsp. vanilla
1 tsp. salt
1/2 cup sour milk with 1 tsp. baking soda
1 egg

Date Filling:
1 lb. dates pitted and chopped
1/2 cup brown sugar
1/2 cup water

Mix all ingredients and chill before rolling. Use date or raisin filling. To make filling, mix all ingredients, cook until thick, and cool.

Cherry Winks

1/3 cup shortening
1 tsp. grated lemon peel
1 tsp. vanilla
1/2 cup sugar
1 well beaten egg
1 1/2 Tbsp. milk
1 cup enriched flour

1/4 tsp. salt
1/4 tsp. baking soda
1/2 tsp baking powder
3/4 cup chopped raisins
1/2 cup chopped walnuts
1 1/2 cup crisp wheat flakes, crushed
candied cherries

Thoroughly cream shortening, lemon peel, vanilla and sugar. Add egg and milk, beat thoroughly. Add sifted dry ingredients. Stir in raisins and nuts. Drop from teaspoon into crushed wheat flakes, toss lightly to coat. Arrange on greased cookie sheet. Top with piece of candied cherry. Bake at 400 degrees, about 12 minutes.

Shortbread Cookies

1 1/2 cups butter, softened
3/4 cup sugar

1 Tbsp. vanilla, almond, or lemon extract
3 cups flour

In large bowl, beat butter, sugar and extract until creamy. Add flour, beat on low speed until well mixed. Divide dough into thirds, press each portion into a 1/2 inch thick disk. Wrap in plastic wrap. Chill 30 minutes. Roll each third on a floured board, one at a time, until 1/8" thick. Cut out shapes with cookie cutters. Place on ungreased baking sheet. Bake at 350 degrees for 12 - 15 minutes. Makes 4 1/2 dozen cookies.

Ting - a - Ling

1 lb. milk chocolate
2 squares unsweetened chocolate

6 cups cornflakes

Melt chocolate in double boiler, add cornflakes and mix well. Put small quantities on wax paper and allow to harden.

Gypsies

6 oz. pkg. chocolate chips
6 oz. pkg. butterscotch chips

1 can chow mein noodles (5 1/2 oz.)
1 can spanish nuts (10 oz.)

Melt chips and add noodles and nuts. Drop by teaspoonfuls and let harden.

Wheaties Coconut Cookies

1 cup shortening / butter
1 cup brown sugar
1 cup white sugar
2 eggs
2 cups moist coconut
2 cups flour

1 tsp. baking soda
1/2 tsp. baking powder
1/2 tsp. salt
2 cups Wheaties
1 tsp. vanilla

Cream the shortening and gradually add sugar and eggs. Mix coconut and flour, baking soda, baking powder and salt. Then add the Wheaties and vanilla. Drop by teaspoon onto greased cookie sheet and bake 10 to 12 minutes in 350 degree oven.

Angel Cookies

1/2 cup white sugar
1/2 cup brown sugar
1 cup butter or margarine
1 tsp. baking soda
1 egg

1 tsp. vanilla
2 cups flour
pinch of salt
1 tsp. cream of tartar

Mix all ingredients together. Make round balls. Press down with glass after dipping glass in water, then sugar. Bake at 350 degrees for 10 to 12 minutes.

Dropped Filled Cookies

2 cups sugar
1 cup shortening
3 eggs
1/3 cup hot water
1 tsp. baking soda

1 tsp. vanilla
3 1/4 cups flour
1 small pkg. dates
1/2 cup water
1/2 cup brown sugar

Mix together sugar, shortening, eggs, vanilla and flour. Dissolve baking soda in hot water and add to the other ingredients. Cook and simmer the dates, water, and brown sugar until thick. Drop cookie dough on greased cookie sheets. Spoon filling on top of each cookie and then cover with a little more dough. Don't use too big proportions. Bake at 375 degrees for 10 -12 minutes.

Farmeretts

1 cup butter
1/2 cup dark brown sugar
1/4 cup white sugar
2 egg yolks

2 cups flour
1/2 tsp. baking soda
1 tsp. cream of tartar
1 cup coconut

Mix together butter, brown & white sugar, egg yolks, flour, baking soda, cream of tartar and coconut. Drop by spoon on ungreased cookie sheet and bake at 350 degrees for 25 minutes.

No Bake Chocolate Cookies

2 cups sugar
1/2 cup butter or margarine
1/2 cup milk
1 tsp. vanilla

2 cups oatmeal
6 Tbsp. cocoa
1/2 cup chopped nuts

Mix together the sugar, butter, milk and vanilla in a pan and boil for 1 1/2 minutes. Combine together the oatmeal, cocoa, and nuts. Pour sugar mixture over oatmeal mixture. Mix well and drop by teaspoon on wax paper.

Brown Sugar Cookies

1/2 cup brown sugar
1/2 cup white sugar
1 cup butter or margarine
1 egg
1 tsp. vanilla
2 cups flour

1/2 tsp. baking soda
1 tsp. salt
1/2 cup finely ground nuts
1 cup brown sugar
1/2 cup cream
1 cup powdered sugar

Cream together sugar and butter. Blend in egg and vanilla. Mix together flour, baking soda, salt and nuts. Add to sugar mixture. Chill dough 20 minutes. Shape into balls, roll in sugar and press flat with a glass. Bake on ungreased cookie sheet at 350 degrees for 10 -12 minutes. Boil 1 cup brown sugar and cream for 4 minutes stirring constantly. Remove from heat and blend in powdered sugar. Beat until smooth and frost cookies.

Brownie Meringues

2 egg whites
dash salt
1/2 tsp. vinegar
1/2 tsp. vanilla

1/2 cup sugar
6 oz. semi-sweet chocolate bits,
    melted and cooled
1/2 cup chopped walnuts

Beat egg whites with salt, vinegar and vanilla until soft peaks form. Gradually add sugar, beating to stiff peaks. Fold in chocolate and nuts. Drop from teaspoon onto greased cookie sheet. Bake in 350 degree oven for about ten minutes. Makes 3 dozen cookies.

Double Chocolate Nuggets

2 1/2 cups chocolate cake mix
    (can use the small Jiffy cake mix)
1/4 cup oil

1 egg
1/2 cup chocolate bits

Mix cake mix, oil and egg. Stir in chocolate bits. Drop from teaspoon onto greased cookie sheet, about 2 inches apart. Bake at 350 degrees for 10 - 12 minutes. Makes about 4 dozen cookies.

Polka Dot Cookies

2 cups flour
1/2 tsp. salt
1 tsp. baking powder
1/4 tsp. baking soda
1/2 cup butter or margarine
1/2 cup sugar
1/2 cup chopped pecans

1/2 cup brown sugar
1 egg, beaten
1 tsp. vanilla
1/4 cup milk
1 cup chocolate bits
1/2 cup chopped maraschino cherries

Mix flour, salt, baking powder and baking soda. Cream butter and sugars together. Blend in egg and vanilla. Add dry ingredients and milk. Stir in pecans, chocolate bits and cherries. Drop by rounded teaspoon onto greased cookie sheet. Bake at 350 degrees for 10 - 12 minutes. Makes about 4 dozen cookies.

Butterscotch Quickies

12 oz. butterscotch pieces
1/2 cup peanut butter

2 cups corn flakes
1 cup flaked coconut

Melt butterscotch pieces and peanut butter in top of a double boiler over hot but not boiling water. Stir frequently until pieces are melted and mixture is smooth. Remove from heat. Add corn flakes and coconut and mix well. Drop by teaspoonful onto wax paper. Chill until set.

Happy Dream Cookies

2 eggs, separated
2/3 cup sugar
1/2 cup walnuts

1/2 cup peanut butter chips
1 tsp. vanilla

Beat two egg whites until creamy. Gradually add sugar until stiff and forms peaks. Fold in walnuts and peanut butter chips. Add vanilla. Drop by teaspoonful onto cookie sheet lined with tin foil. Put them in oven preheated to 375 degrees, turn off oven and go to bed. Happy dreams!

Cinnamon Sugar Cookies

1 cup shortening
2 cups sugar
3 eggs, beaten
1 tsp. vanilla
1 cup sour cream
5 cups flour

1 tsp. salt
3 tsp. baking powder
1/2 tsp. baking soda
1 1/2 cups chopped walnuts
3 Tbsp. sugar
1 tsp. cinnamon

Cream sugar and shortening. Add vanilla, sour cream and eggs. Mix thoroughly. Add flour with baking powder, baking soda and salt. Add nuts. Drop batter from a spoon onto a greased cookie sheet. Press flat. Sprinkle mixture of cinnamon and sugar onto cookies, gently pressing mixture into dough. Bake 15 minutes at 350 degrees. Makes 6 dozen cookies.

Jammer Cookies

1 cup butter
1/2 cup sugar
2 1/2 cups flour
strawberry or raspberry freezer jam

frosting:
1 cup powdered sugar
2 tsp. almond flavoring
hot water

Cream butter and sugar. Stir in flour. Mix with hands. Don't use all the flour at once as it may get too stiff. Shape into 4 long rolls on a large cookie sheet. Indent in center with edge of your hands and spread with jam in center. Bake 20 - 25 minutes at 300 degrees until very lightly browned. Mix frosting ingredients to desired consistency and frost cookies and cut in angles while warm.

Bird Nests

12 oz. butterscotch bits
5 oz. can chow mein noodles

1 cup chopped salted peanuts
1 bag small jelly beans

Melt butterscotch bits in a pan over low heat. Add noodles and peanuts to the melted bits and stir. Drop large spoonfuls of mixture onto wax paper. Shape each nest with your fingers. Put 4 or 5 jelly bean "eggs" into each nest. Chill in refrigerator. Makes about 15 nests.

Chocolate Chip Kiss Cookies

9 oz. Hershey's kisses
1 cup butter, softened
1/3 cup sugar
1/3 cup packed light brown sugar

1 tsp. vanilla extract
2 cups flour
1 cup mini chocolate chips
chocolate topping

Heat oven to 375 degrees. Remove wrappers from chocolate pieces. In large mixing bowl, beat butter, sugar, brown sugar, and vanilla until well blended. Add flour, blend until smooth. Stir in small chocolate chips. Mold scant tablespoon dough around each chocolate piece, covering completely. Shape into balls, place on ungreased cookie sheet. Bake 10 to 12 minutes or until set. Cool slightly, remove from cookie sheet to wire rack. Cool completely. Drizzle topping over each cookie. About 4 dozen cookies.

Pineapple Sponge Cookies

1/3 cup shortening	1 1/3 cups flour
2/3 cup sugar	1/2 tsp. baking soda
1 egg	1/4 tsp. salt
1 tsp. lemon extract	1/2 cup crushed pineapple

Cream shortening with sugar; beat in egg. Sift flour with baking soda and salt and add to creamed batter. Fold in pineapple, (drain some of the juice out), lemon flavoring and mix lightly. Drop by teaspoonful onto a lightly greased cookie sheet and bake at 375 degrees for 12 -15 minutes.

Dreamy White Chip Orange Cookies

2 1/4 cups flour	1/2 cup packed brown sugar
3/4 tsp. baking soda	1 egg
1/2 tsp. salt	2 to 3 tsp. grated orange peel
1 cup butter, softened	2 cups white vanilla chips
1/2 cup sugar	

Combine flour, baking soda and salt in small bowl. Beat butter, granulated and brown sugar in large mixer bowl until creamy. Beat in egg and orange peel. Gradually beat in flour mixture. Stir in vanilla chips. Drop dough by rounded Tbsp. onto ungreased baking sheets. Bake in preheated 350 degree oven for 10 to 12 minutes or until edges are light golden brown. Let stand for 2 minutes; remove to wire racks to cool completely.

Potato Chip Cookies

1 cup shortening	2 cups flour
1 cup white sugar	1/2 tsp. salt
1 cup brown sugar	1 tsp. baking soda
2 eggs	2 cups oatmeal
1 tsp. vanilla	2 cups crushed potato chips

Mix all ingredients together. Raisins, chocolate chips or nuts may be added to cookies. Drop by teaspoon on ungreased cookie sheet. Bake at 375 degrees 10 to 15 minutes. Makes 6 dozen.

Refrigerator Cookies

1 cup white sugar
1 cup brown sugar
1 1/2 cups margarine
3 eggs

5 to 6 cups flour
1 tsp. baking soda
2 tsp. cinnamon
1 cup chopped nuts

Mix all ingredients together. Shape in rolls and freeze. Slice and bake in 350 degree oven for 12 to 15 minutes.

Chocolate Drop Cookies

1 cup sugar
1/2 cup shortening
1/2 tsp. salt
1 egg
2 sq. chocolate, melted
1/2 cup milk

2 cups raisins
1 cup walnuts
1 1/2 tsp. vanilla
1 3/4 cups flour
1 tsp. baking powder

Mix ingredients one by one. Drop by spoonful onto greased cookie sheet. Bake at 350 degrees until light brown.

Grandma's Oatmeal Chocolate Chippers

1 cup shortening
1 cup sugar
1 cup brown sugar
2 eggs
2 cups flour

1 tsp. salt
1 tsp. baking soda
2 cups rolled oats
1 cup chocolate chips

Cream shortening and sugar; add eggs and beat well. Sift flour, salt and baking soda. Add to creamed mixture. Mix well. Stir in oats and chocolate chips. Shape in 1 inch balls.. Place on ungreased cookie sheet 2 inches apart. Flatten with glass dipped in sugar. Bake at 375 degrees for 8 to 10 minutes or until light brown.

Roasted Pecan Clusters

3 Tbsp. butter
3 cups pecan pieces

3/4 lb. (6 squares) chocolate or almond bark

Melt butter in a jelly roll pan. Spread pecans evenly in pan. Bake at 300 degrees for 30 minutes, stirring every 10 minutes. Melt bark squares in top of a double boiler, remove from heat, and stir until smooth. Cool 2 minutes, add pecans, and stir until well coated. Drop by teaspoonfuls onto waxed paper. Before serving, let cool completely. Makes about 3 1/2 dozen.

Fattigman

6 egg yolks
3 egg whites
6 Tbsp. sugar
flour

6 Tbsp. cream
2 Tbsp. melted butter
6 cardamon seeds

Beat egg yolks and whites together until thick and lemon colored, add sugar and continue beating, add cream and beat again. Blend in butter, cardamom and flour enough to make a dough suitable for rolling. Roll thin as paper, cut in diamond shape and fry in hot shortening 2 or 3 minutes, or until a golden brown.
NOTE: If a deep fat thermometer is used, heat fat to 370 degrees.

Pecan Pie Bars

Crust:
2 1/2 cups flour
1 cup cold butter
1/2 cup sugar
1/2 tsp. salt

Filling:
4 eggs
1 1/2 cups white Karo syrup
1 1/2 cups sugar
3 Tbsp. butter, melted
1 1/2 tsp. vanilla
2 1/2 cups pecans, halves or chopped

Beat together all ingredients for the crust until mixture resembles fine crumbs. Press firmly in greased 15 x 10 pan. Bake 20 - 23 minutes at 350 degrees, or until golden brown. To make filling, beat eggs, syrup, butter and vanilla until well blended. Stir in pecans and pour over hot crust. Bake 25 minutes or until filling is firm around edges and slightly firm in center. Cool.

Frosted Peanut Marshmallow Crispy Treats

1/4 cup butter
10 oz. marshmallows
1/2 cup peanut butter
5 cups Rice Krispies cereal

1 cup peanuts
6 oz. butterscotch chips
6 oz. chocolate chips

Melt (microwave) butter in large mixing bowl until melted. Add marshmallows, toss to coat, and microwave until melted and smooth when stirred. Blend in peanut butter. Immediately add cereal and peanuts. Toss until well coated. Press mixture into greased 9 x 13 pan. Melt butterscotch and chocolate chips together until smooth when stirred. Pour over cereal and spread to cover. Chill.

Toffee Squares

4 1/2 cups oatmeal
1 cup brown sugar
3/4 cup butter, melted
1/2 cup dark corn syrup

1 Tbsp. vanilla
1 tsp. salt
12 oz. chocolate chips
2/3 cup chopped nuts

Combine oatmeal, brown sugar, butter, corn syrup, vanilla and salt. Mix well. Press firmly into well-greased jelly roll pan. Bake at 450 degrees for 12 minutes. (Mixture will be brown and bubbly.) Cool thoroughly. To remove from pan, loosen edges, invert pan, and tap firmly. Melt chocolate chips and spread on bars. Sprinkle with nuts. Chill until chocolate sets. Store in refrigerator.

Yummy Bars

1 stick butter
2 cups graham cracker crumbs
6 oz. pkg. chocolate chips
6 oz. pkg. mint or butterscotch chips

1 can sweetened condensed milk
1 cup chopped nuts
1 cup coconut, optional

Melt 1 stick butter, pour in 9 x 12 inch pan. Add graham cracker crumbs, chips and nuts, layering in order. Pour milk over the top. Bake at 350 degrees for 20-25 minutes. Let cool and cut in bars. (Can put 1 cup coconut in before chocolate chips.)

Bear Squares

6 cups crisp rice cereal (7 1/2 oz.)
4 cups miniature marshmallows (6 oz.)
1/4 cup smooth peanut butter
3 Tbsp. margarine

1/2 cup candy-coated chocolate pieces
   (like M & M's)
24 bear-shape chocolate graham cookies

Lightly grease a 9 x 13 pan. Mix cereal and 1 cup marshmallows in a large bowl. Put peanut butter, margarine and the remaining marshmallows in a saucepan. Stir over low heat until completely melted and smooth. Immediately pour over cereal mixture and stir until well blended. Mixture will leave sides of bowl and form a ball. Transfer to prepared pan and press into an even layer. While still warm, scatter candies over top, then press them down gently. Stick bear-shaped cookies waist deep into cereal mixture, spacing them about 1 1/2 inches apart. Let cool before cutting between bears into squares. Makes 24 squares. These freeze well.

Orange Maple Pecan Bars

4 cups graham cracker crumbs
1 cup confectioner's sugar
1/3 cup frozen orange juice concentrate,
   thawed

1/4 cup maple flavor pancake syrup
1/4 cup margarine, melted
1 1/2 cups pecans, chopped
Decoration: confectioner's sugar

Line a 9 x 13 pan with foil, letting ends extend above pan on two sides. Mix cracker crumbs, confectioner's sugar, orange concentrate, syrup, margarine and 3/4 cup of the pecans in a large bowl until blended. Transfer to prepared pan and press into an even layer. Gently press remaining nuts on top. Dust with confectioner's sugar. Using foil ends to lift onto cutting board, cut in bars. Lift off foil. Makes 24 squares. These freeze well.

Cream Cheese Layer Bars

1 1/2 cups graham cracker crumbs
1/4 cup sugar
1/3 cup butter, melted
8 oz. cream cheese
1/2 cup sugar

1 egg
1/4 cup flaked coconut
3/4 cup chopped nuts
6 oz. chocolate chips

Combine crumbs, sugar and butter; press onto bottom of 9 x 13 pan. Bake at 350 degrees for 5 minutes. Combine cream cheese, sugar and egg, mixing until well blended. Spread over crust. Sprinkle with remaining ingredients. Press lightly into surface. Bake at 350 degrees for 25 - 30 minutes or until lightly browned. Cool.

Cheesecake Bars

2 cups unsifted flour
1 1/2 cups packed brown sugar
1 cup cold margarine or butter
1 1/2 cups quick-cooking oats
2 (8 oz.) pkgs. cream cheese, softened

1/2 cup sugar
3 eggs
1/4 cup milk
1 tsp. vanilla
1/4 cup lemon juice from concentrate

Combine flour and brown sugar. Cut in margarine until crumbly. Stir in oats. Reserving 1 1/2 cups mixture, press remainder into a greased jelly roll pan. Bake 10 minutes at 350 degrees. Meanwhile, in large mixer bowl, beat cheese and sugar until fluffy. Add eggs, beat well. Add milk and vanilla, then lemon juice. Beat well. Pour over crust. Sprinkle with reserved mixture. Bake 25 minutes or until lightly browned. Cool. Refrigerate.

Baby Ruth Bars

2/3 cup melted margarine
4 cups quick oatmeal
1 cup brown sugar
1/4 cup corn syrup
1/4 cup crunchy peanut butter

1 tsp. vanilla
6 oz. chocolate chips
6 oz. butterscotch chips
2/3 cup peanut butter
1 cup salted peanuts

In large mixer bowl combine margarine, oatmeal, brown sugar, corn syrup, crunchy peanut butter and vanilla. Pour in greased 9 x 13 baking dish and pat down good. Bake 12 minutes at 400 degrees. In medium saucepan melt chocolate and butterscotch chips and 2/3 cup peanut butter. Add peanuts. Spread over crust and let cool.

Lemon Pudding Squares

2 cups flour
1 cup butter
1 1/2 cups powdered sugar
16 oz. cream cheese

6 oz. pkg. instant lemon pudding
4 cups milk
1/2 tsp. fresh lemon juice
16 oz. Cool Whip

For the crust, mix flour and butter and press into 9 x 13 cake pan. Bake at 375 degrees for 12 - 15 minutes. Blend powdered sugar and cream cheese, and spread on cooled crust. Prepare pudding according to pkg. directions. Add lemon juice. Pour on top of cream cheese. Let set. Spread Cool Whip on top. Chill thoroughly.

Zucchini Brownies

1/2 cup shortening
1/2 cup cocoa
1 1/2 cups sugar
2 eggs
1 tsp. vanilla
1/2 cup finely chopped zucchini

1 cup flour
1/2 tsp. baking soda
1/2 tsp. baking powder
1/8 tsp. salt
1/2 cup chopped walnuts

Cream shortening, and beat in cocoa, sugar, vanilla and eggs. Add zucchini, and beat well. Add flour, baking soda, baking powder and salt, and beat well. Stir in nuts. Pour into a greased and floured brownie sheet. Bake at 350 degrees for 25 minutes. Cool and cut into squares.

Old Fashioned Brownies

1 cup butter
3 squares unsweetened chocolate
2 cups sugar
4 eggs

1 tsp. vanilla
1 cup flour
1/2 cup chopped nuts

Melt butter and chocolate in saucepan. Remove from heat and add remaining ingredients, whipping them in with a fork. Bake in greased and floured 9 x 13 pan at 350 degrees for 20 - 25 minutes. Frost.

Peanut Butter Brownie Bars

6 eggs
3 cups sugar
1 1/2 cups brown sugar (firmly packed)
1 cup peanut butter
1/2 cup shortening

1 Tbsp. vanilla
4 cups unsifted flour
1 1/2 Tbsp. baking powder
1 1/2 tsp. salt
1/2 cup peanuts

Combine eggs, sugars, peanut butter, shortening and vanilla. Blend thoroughly. Add dry ingredients and mix only until mixture is smooth. Spread dough in 2 greased cookie sheets or 3 13x9x2 greased cake pans. Sprinkle with nuts. Bake in moderate oven at 350 degrees for 25 minutes. Cool and cut.

Blond Brownies

2 cups flour
2 tsp. baking powder
1/8 tsp. salt
1/2 cup butter or margarine

2 cups brown sugar
2 eggs
1 tsp. vanilla
1 cup chopped pecans

Combine flour, baking powder and salt. Melt butter. Remove from heat and stir in sugar. Add eggs and vanilla. Stir until mixed well. Stir in dry ingredients and add pecans. Spread in greased 9x13 baking pan. Bake 20 to 25 minutes at 350 degrees. Do not overbake.

Marbled Brownies

1 pkg. Duncan Hines brownie mix
3 oz. cream cheese
3 Tbsp. butter or margarine
1/2 tsp. vanilla

1/4 cup sugar
3 eggs
1 Tbsp. flour

Beat together cream cheese and butter. Add the sugar, 1 egg, flour and vanilla. Beat until smooth and set aside. Empty brownie mix and chocolate flavor packet into bowl. Add 2 Tbsp. water and 2 eggs. Mix by hand about 50 strokes. Pour half the brownie batter in a greased 9" square pan. Pour all the cream cheese mixture over the brownie batter. Spoon the remaining brownie batter here and there over the cream cheese batter. Pull knife through batter in wide curves to create a swirled appearance. Bake at 350 degrees for 35 minutes. Cool and frost with Milk Chocolate Frosting.

Chocolate Mint Brownies

1 cup sugar
1/2 cup butter, softened
4 eggs, slightly beaten
1 cup flour
1/2 tsp. salt
1 can (16 oz.) Hershey's syrup
1 tsp. vanilla
1/2 cup nuts, chopped

2 cups powdered sugar
1/4 cup butter, softened
2 Tbsp. milk
1/2 tsp. peppermint extract
4 drops green food coloring
1 cup chocolate chips
6 Tbsp. butter, softened

Mix and bake the first 8 ingredients in a greased jelly roll pan at 350 degrees for 20 minutes, (edges crisp). Cool. Mix the next 5 ingredients to make the frosting. Let the frosting set a few minutes before spreading on the brownies. Melt the chocolate chips and add the 6 Tbsp. softened butter to the hot chocolate. Spread on top of the frosting. Refrigerate.

Sour Cream Raisin Bars

1 3/4 cups oatmeal	4 egg yolks
1 3/4 cups flour	6 oz. sour cream
1 cup butter	3 Tbsp. corn starch
1 cup brown sugar	1 1/2 cups sugar
1 tsp. baking soda	2 cups raisins

Mix oatmeal, flour, butter, brown sugar and baking soda. Press into 9 x 13 pan, saving some of the crumbs for the top of the bars. Mix together the egg yolks, sour cream, corn starch, sugar and raisins. Put on top of crust. Sprinkle remaining crumbs on top. Bake at 350 degrees for 10 - 15 minutes.

Corn Flake Dream Bars

1/4 cup butter	1 tsp. vanilla
1/2 cup brown sugar	1/4 tsp. salt
1 cup flour	1 cup shredded coconut
2 eggs	1 cup chopped nuts
1 cup brown sugar	1 cup corn flakes

Cream butter and 1/2 cup sugar. With a pastry blender or fork, work in the flour. Press mixture evenly and firmly over bottom of large greased glass pan and bake in 350 degree oven for 12 minutes, or until delicately browned. Beat eggs until light and add 1 cup sugar gradually. Add vanilla and salt and beat thoroughly. Fold in shredded coconut, corn flakes and chopped nuts and spread evenly over baked crust. Return to oven and bake 25 minutes longer. Cut while warm.

Chewey Walnut Bars

2 cups brown sugar	1/2 tsp. baking soda
2 tsp. vanilla	1/2 tsp. salt
2 eggs	2 cups coarsely chopped walnuts
1 cup flour	

Combine brown sugar, vanilla and eggs. Beat until smooth. Combine and sift flour, baking soda and salt, add to sugar mixture, blend. Fold in walnuts. Place in greased 9 x 13 pan. Bake in 350 degrees for 25 - 30 minutes. Cool in pan and cut into bars. Makes 24 bars.

Hello Dolly Bars

1/2 cup butter
1 cup graham cracker crumbs
1 cup chocolate chips

1 cup flaked coconut
1 cup walnuts
15 oz. can sweetened condensed milk

Melt butter in 9x13 pan sprayed with Pam. Sprinkle other ingredients on top in order given. Bake 30 minutes at 350 degrees.

Mixed Nut Bars

1 1/2 cups flour
1/2 cup margarine, soft
1/4 tsp. salt
3/4 cup brown sugar

1 small can mixed nuts
6 oz. pkg. butterscotch chips
1/2 cup light Karo syrup
2 Tbsp. butter

Mix flour, margarine, salt, and brown sugar. Press with fingers in a 9x13 pan, and bake at 350 degrees for 10 minutes. Cool. Spread on a can of mixed nuts. Melt butterscotch chips, Karo syrup, and butter over low heat. Pour over nuts. Bake ten minutes more. Cool and cut.

Fudge Nut Bars

1 cup butter
2 cups brown sugar
2 eggs
1 tsp. vanilla
2 1/2 cups flour
1 tsp. salt
1 tsp. baking soda

3 cups oatmeal
1 cup chopped nuts
2 (6 oz.) pkg. chocolate chips
15 oz. can sweetened condensed milk
1 Tbsp. butter
1/2 tsp. salt
1 tsp. vanilla

Cream butter, brown sugar and eggs. Add vanilla, flour, baking soda, salt, and oatmeal. Melt in double boiler the chips, condensed milk, butter, salt and vanilla. Press 2/3 of dough mixture on 10 x15 greased cookie sheet. Spread with chocolate mixture and l cup chopped nuts and put remaining 1/3 dough on top. Bake at 350 degrees for 25 -30 minutes.

Matrimonial Bars

2 cups rolled oats	Pinch of salt
1 cup flour	1 cup water
1 tsp. baking powder	1/2 lb. dates
3/4 cup brown sugar	1/2 cup sugar
3/4 cup shortening	1 tsp. vanilla

Put together oats, flour, baking powder, brown sugar, shortening, and salt like pie crust. Pat half of mixture in bottom of pan. Use other half to put over filling. The filling is made of the other ingredients. Boil them and pour over bottom layer. Bake in oven at 350 degrees for 30 minutes...no more!! Makes 20 bars.

Lemon Bars

2 cups flour	2 cups sugar
1 cup margarine	4 Tbsp. lemon juice and grated rind
1/2 cup powdered sugar	4 Tbsp. flour
4 eggs	1 tsp. baking powder

Mix flour, margarine and powdered sugar and pat in bottom of 9x13 pan. Bake 20 minutes at 350 degrees. Mix other ingredients together and pour over hot crust. Return to oven and bake another 25 minutes. Frost with thin coating of powdered sugar frosting thinned with lemon juice.

Marble Squares

1/2 cup butter or margarine	3 cups plus 2 Tbsp. flour
6 Tbsp. sugar	1/2 tsp. baking soda
6 Tbsp. brown sugar	1/2 tsp. salt
1/2 tsp. vanilla	1/2 cup chopped walnuts
1/4 tsp. water	6 oz. semi-sweet chocolate pieces
1 egg	

Cream butter, sugar, brown sugar, vanilla and water. Beat in egg. Sift and mix in flour, baking soda and salt. Add walnuts and blend in. Spread in greased 9 x 13 cake pan. Sprinkle chocolate pieces on top and bake at 375 degrees for one minute. Run a knife through batter to marble-ize. Bake 12 - 14 minutes longer. Cool and cut into squares.

Triple Layer Chocolate Bars

1 1/2 cups graham cracker crumbs
1/2 cup cocoa
1/4 cup sugar
1/3 cup butter or margarine, melted
14 oz. can sweetened condensed milk
1/4 cup flour

1 egg
1 tsp. vanilla
1/2 tsp. baking powder
3/4 cup chopped nuts
12 oz. semi-sweet chocolate chips

Combine crumbs, 1/4 cup cocoa, sugar and butter. Press firmly on bottom of greased 9x13 pan. In large mixer bowl, beat sweetened condensed milk, flour, remaining 1/4 cup cocoa, egg, vanilla and baking powder. Stir in nuts. Spread evenly over crust. Top with chocolate chips. Bake 20 to 25 minutes at 350 degrees or until set. Cool and serve.

Coconut Crunch Pretzel Bars

1 box German chocolate cake mix
1/2 cup crushed pretzels
1/2 cup butter, melted
1 egg
1/4 cup sugar
1 cup dark corn syrup

2 eggs
1 cup pecans, chopped
1 cup butterscotch chips
2 1/4 cups coconut
6 oz. chocolate chips

Combine cake mix, pretzels, melted butter and egg. Mix until well blended. Press in bottom of greased 9x13 pan and bake at 350 degrees for 15 minutes or until crust puffs and appears dry. Cool 5 minutes. Combine sugar, corn syrup and 2 eggs. Mix at low speed until well blended. Stir in remaining ingredients. Spoon evenly over partially baked crust. Bake an additional 30 - 40 minutes or until edges are deep golden brown. Cool 10 minutes, then loosen edges with knife. Cool and cut into bars.

Butter Pecan Turtle Bars

2 cups flour
1 cup brown sugar
1/2 cup softened butter
1 cup whole pecans

1/2 cup brown sugar
2/3 cup butter
6 oz. chocolate chips

Mix the first three ingredients with an electric mixer. Pat into a 9 x 13 pan. Sprinkle with pecans. Boil for l minute: 1/2 cup brown sugar and 2/3 cup butter. Pour hot mixture over the pecans and crust. Bake at 350 degrees for 20 minutes. Sprinkle chocolate chips on top and allow 2 minutes for chips to melt. Spread to cover. Cool before cutting.

Mississippi Mud Bars

1 cup butter or margarine
2 cups sugar
1/2 cup cocoa
4 eggs
1 tsp. vanilla

1 1/2 cups flour
1 1/2 cups chopped pecans
3 1/2 oz. flaked coconut
7 oz. jar marshmallow cream
chocolate frosting

Cream together butter, sugar and cocoa in a bowl until light and fluffy. Add eggs and vanilla. Beat 2 minutes at a medium speed. Blend in flour. Stir in coconut, pecans and spread into a greased 10 x 15 jelly roll pan. Bake at 350 for 30 minutes. Remove from oven and spoon marshmallow creme over all. Let stand 5 minutes. Spread carefully with a spatula. Frost with chocolate frosting while bars are still warm. Cool before cutting.

Candy Bar Bars

1 lb. box powdered sugar
2/3 cup sweetened condensed milk
1/2 tsp. vanilla
1/2 tsp. almond extract

12 oz. chocolate chips
12 oz. butterscotch chips
1 lb. chopped peanuts

Combine powdered sugar, milk, vanilla and almond extract in a large bowl. Mix thoroughly, using hands to knead. Roll mixture between two sheets of plastic wrap to form a 9 x 13 rectangle. Chill in refrigerator. Meanwhile, melt chocolate and butterscotch chips in top of a double boiler. Stir in peanuts. Spread 1/2 of chocolate mixture in the bottom of a buttered 9 x 13 pan. Carefully place fondant layer on top. Spread remaining chocolate mixture on top. Refrigerate until firm. Remove from refrigerator 10 minutes before cutting. Store in refrigerator.

Reeses Bars

1/3 box graham crackers, crushed
1 cup margarine, softened
6 oz. chocolate chips

1 box powdered sugar
1 cup peanut butter

Mix together all ingredients except chocolate chips, and pat in a greased 9 x 13 pan. Melt chocolate chips and spread over top. Refrigerate until set. Cut into squares.

Date Bars

1 1/2 cups flour
1/2 tsp. baking soda
1/2 tsp. salt
1 cup brown sugar
1 1/2 cups rolled oats
1 cup butter, melted
1 cup chopped walnuts

Filling:
1 lb. dates, chopped
1 cup water
1 cup sugar
1/2 tsp. vanilla

Sift flour, baking soda and salt. Mix with sugar, oats, butter and walnuts until mixture is crumbly. Press half of the mixture in a greased 9 x 13 pan. Cook dates, water and sugar on low heat, stirring constantly until thick. Cool. Spread over first layer and top with remaining crumb mixture. Bake at 325 degrees for 35 minutes. Cut into squares.

Mound Bars

2 cups crushed graham crackers
1/4 cup powdered sugar
1/2 cup butter, melted

1 can sweetened condensed milk
3 cups flake coconut
1 large size Hershey bar

Mix together graham crackers, powdered sugar and butter. Pour into a greased 8 x 12 inch pan. Bake 10 minutes in 350 degree oven. Mix together milk and coconut. Spread on cracker base. Bake 10 minutes. Melt Hershey bar and spread on bars when done.

Creamed Nut Caramels

2 cups white sugar
1 cup white Karo syrup
2 cups whipping cream
1/3 cup butter

1 tsp. vanilla
pinch of salt
chopped nuts if desired

Cook sugar, syrup, and 1 cup whipping cream for ten minutes. Add another 1 cup whipping cream slowly. Cook 5 more minutes. Then add butter, a small amount at a time. When thermometer reaches 230 degrees, lower heat and cook to 245 degrees. Remove from stove as soon as it reaches 245 degrees. Add pinch of salt and vanilla. Mix gently. Nuts may be added to mixture. Pour in 9 x 13 pan. Cool. Then cut in squares and wrap in wax paper. Keeps well a long time if you find a good hiding place.

Norwegian Spiced Nuts

2 cups mixed salted nuts
1 egg white

1 cup sugar
1/2 tsp. cinnamon

Slightly beat egg white with fork until frothy, then add sugar and beat. Add cinnamon.
Pour this over nuts and mix until nuts are completely coated with sugar mixture. Spread
out on a brown paper covered cookie sheet. Bake at 325 degrees for 25 - 30 minutes.
Watch closely as they burn easily. Break apart.

Microwave Peanut Brittle

1 cup raw peanuts
1 cup sugar
1/2 cup white syrup
1/2 tsp. salt

1 Tbsp. butter
1 tsp. vanilla
1 tsp. baking soda

Combine peanuts, sugar, syrup and salt. Microwave on high 5 minutes. Stir. Microwave
3 more minutes. Add butter and vanilla. Microwave 2 more minutes. Add soda, stir until
foamy. Pour onto cookie sheet sprayed with non-stick spray. Break when cool.

Marshmallow Cream Candy

2 cups brown sugar
1/4 cup milk

1 tsp. butter
1/2 lb. marshmallows, cut up

Mix sugar, milk and butter, and boil to soft ball stage; beat in marshmallows until creamy.
Pour into small buttered pan and cut in squares.

Fudge Mallow Candy

12 oz. pkg. chocolate chips
1 cup any style peanut butter

6 1/4 oz. pkg. miniature marshmallows

Melt chocolate pieces with peanut butter over low heat, stirring until smooth. Fold in
marshmallows. Pour into greased 9' square pan. Chill until firm. Cut into squares. Makes
approximately 2 dozen.

Quick Nut Fudge

1 lb. powdered sugar
1/2 cup cocoa
1/4 tsp. salt
6 Tbsp. margarine

4 Tbsp. milk
1 Tbsp. vanilla extract
1 cup chopped pecans or walnuts

Put all ingredients except nuts in double boiler (can cook in T-Fal!!) Stir until smooth. Stir in nuts. Spread in buttered 9x5 pan. Cool. Cut in squares.

Peanut Butter Fudge

1 lb. margarine
2 cups creamy peanut butter
8 Tbsp. cocoa

8 tsp. vanilla
2 lb. powdered sugar

Melt margarine and peanut butter until smooth over medium heat. Remove from heat and add cocoa and vanilla. Mix this until well blended, then gradually add powdered sugar. Mix until well blended. Spread in greased 9 x 13 pan. Let it become completely cold, then cut into desired pieces. Makes about 5 lbs.

No Fail Fudge

4 1/2 cups sugar
12 oz. can evaporated milk
1/2 stick margarine (1/4 cup)
1 tsp. vanilla

16 marshmallows, quartered
1 lb. milk chocolate*
12 oz. milk chocolate chips
chopped nuts, optional

Combine marshmallows, milk chocolate and chocolate chips, and set aside until needed. Mix together sugar, milk and margarine. Bring to a rolling boil and continue cooking for 5 minutes, stirring constantly. Remove from heat and stir in chocolate mixture. Stir until all is melted and mixed well. Add vanilla and nuts, if desired. Pour onto lightly greased cookie sheet, cool, and cut.

* I buy two of the 7 oz. Hershey bars and finish out the 1 lb. requirement with either smaller bars or another 2 oz. of chocolate chips.

Divinity Fudge

3 cups sugar
1/2 cup corn syrup
3/4 cup water
1/2 tsp. salt

2 egg whites
1 tsp. vanilla
chopped nuts

Combine first three ingredients. Place over low heat until sugar is dissolved. Cover and boil for 3 minutes only. Uncover and boil until it spins a thread. Take off heat and let stand while beating egg whites. Add salt and vanilla to stiffly beaten whites. Pour boiled mixture slowly into egg whites and beat until just ready to lose its sheen. If nuts are used, stir them in and drop by teaspoonfuls onto wax paper.

Two Ingredient Fudge

12 oz. semi-sweet chocolate pieces

3/4 cup sweetened condensed milk

Melt chocolate pieces in double boiler over hot but not boiling water. Remove from heat and stir in sweetened condensed milk until well blended. Spoon into a greased 8" square pan. Chill until set and cut into squares.

Holiday Fudge

4 1/2 cups sugar
1 can evaporated milk, (large can)
5 Tbsp. butter
1 pint marshmallow cream

2 pkgs. German Sweet chocolate
2 pkgs. chocolate chips
2 cups chopped nuts

Place sugar, milk and butter in pan. Bring to rapid boil. Boil 6 minutes, stirring constantly. Add German chocolate, chocolate chips and marshmallow cream, and stir until chocolate is melted. Add chopped nuts. Pour into greased pan and chill. Makes 5 pounds.

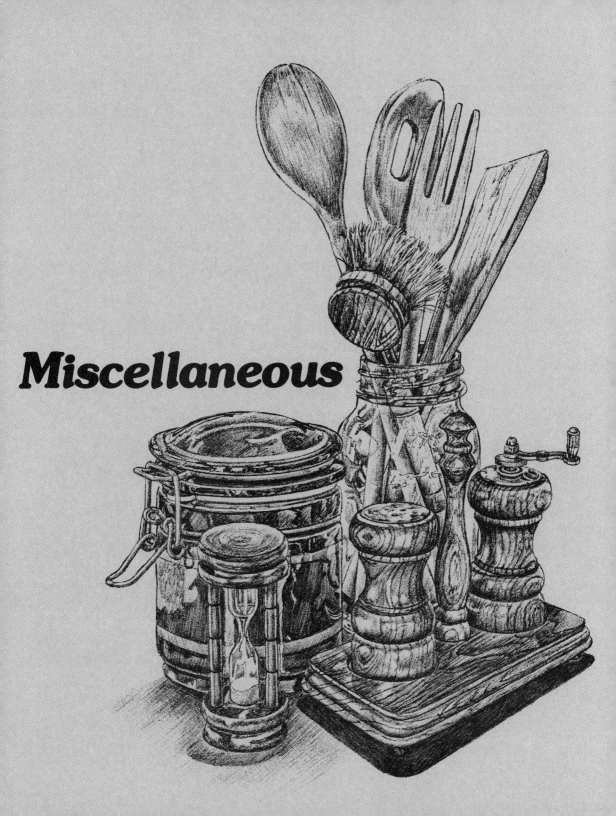

Miscellaneous

Miscellaneous

Strawberry Freezer Jam

3 cups mashed strawberries
4 cups sugar

3/4 cup water
1 pkg. Sure Jell

Mix sugar and fruit. Let stand ten minutes. Boil water and Sure Jell for 1 minute. Add fruit and stir three minutes. Put in glass jar, leaving 1/2 inch at the top. Cover with lids. Stand at room temperature for 24 hours. Put in freezer. Keeps in refrigerator for three weeks or use right out of freezer. Great on toast or ice cream.

Refrigerator Rhubarb Jam

4 cups cut-up rhubarb
4 cups sugar

8 3/4 oz. can crushed pineapple
3 oz. pkg. strawberry jello

Combine rhubarb, sugar and pineapple with syrup in large kettle. Bring to a boil, reduce heat and simmer 15 minutes or until rhubarb is tender. Remove from heat and stir in jello until dissolved. Pour into jars, seal, and store in refrigerator. Makes 3 pints.

Strawberry Rhubarb Jam

5 cups rhubarb
4 cups sugar

6 oz. box strawberry jello

Put cut up rhubarb, sugar and jello in large bowl. Stir well. Let stand overnight. Using large T-Fal pot, bring to full boil. Cook 15 minutes, stirring often. Pour into jars. Seal when cool.

Baked Bananas

8 or10 large bananas
Lemon Sauce:
1/2 cup sugar
1 cup boiling water
1 Tbsp. cornstarch

2 Tbsp. butter
1 1/2 Tbsp. lemon juice
1/8 tsp. nutmeg
salt to taste

Mix cornstarch and sugar; add water gradually, stirring constantly; boil 5 minutes; remove from fire; add butter, lemon juice and nutmeg. Pour Lemon Sauce over bananas in casserole dish. Bake 12 to 15 minutes, or until bananas begin to get soft.

Orange Sherbet

15 oz. orange jello
1 qt. sugar
1 qt. orange juice

1/2 cup lemon juice
1 gallon milk

Heat orange juice to boiling. Dissolve jello and sugar in hot juice. Cool. Add lemon juice and milk. Place in freezer. When half frozen, beat thoroughly and then freeze.

Chocolate Sauce

9 sq. bitter chocolate
3/4 cup water
3 cups sugar

1 1/2 cups white corn syrup
3 cups evaporated milk
1 Tbsp. vanilla

Melt chocolate over hot water. Add water slowly. Stir until smooth. Add sugar and syrup. Cook until a soft ball is formed when tested in cold water. Remove from heat; add milk and vanilla.

Hot Butterscotch Sauce

1 cup packed brown sugar
1/4 cup half & half

4 Tbsp. butter
2 Tbsp. light corn syrup

Combine all ingredients and stir to mix. Microwave on high for 2 minutes, until it boils. Stir. Pour into a sterile pint jar, cover and store refrigerated for up to 1 month. Makes 1 cup. Try this on ice cream, cake, or over plums or nectarines.

Maple-Nut Sauce

1 cup butter
6 cups sugar
2 cups water
1 1/2 cups corn syrup

1 pint evaporated milk
2 Tbsp. maple extract
1 lb. nut meats, chopped

Melt butter; add sugar, water and syrup and boil until soft ball forms. Remove from heat. Slowly add milk, flavoring and nuts.

Peanut Butter Sundae Sauce

2/3 cup packed brown sugar
1/2 cup half & half

1 Tbsp. honey
3/4 cup peanut butter

Using a 1 quart sauce pan, heat brown sugar, half & half and honey to boiling. Stir constantly. Remove from heat and stir in peanut butter. Blend until smooth. Serve warm over yogurt, ice cream, waffles or pancakes.

Caramel Sauce

3 lbs. brown sugar
2 1/2 cups sugar
2 cups water

2 cups corn syrup
1 tsp. salt
1 cup cream

Heat sugars, water, salt and corn syrup to boil. When soft ball forms, cook slightly and stir in cream.

Gruyere Cheese Sauce

4 Tbsp. flour
4 Tbsp. butter
3 cups half & half
1 1/2 cups gruyere cheese, grated

milk for thinning
salt to taste
white pepper to taste

Melt butter in saucepan and add flour to make roux. Add half & half gradually, stirring constantly, and thin with milk to desired thickness. Add cheese and stir until melted and season to taste with salt and pepper. Serve hot over chicken kiev or chicken breasts.

Easy Dressing

1 lb. bag croutons
4 1/2 cups celery
1 medium onion
1 stick butter
3 cups chicken broth

1 1/4 cups half & half
salt
pepper
poultry seasoning
garlic powder

Combine all ingredients in 3 quart casserole. Bake 1 hour at 350 degrees covered and 15 minutes uncovered.

Oyster Stuffing for Turkey

1/2 cup chopped celery
1/2 cup chopped onion
1/4 cup butter
6 to 8 cups dry bread crumbs
1 Tbsp. chopped parsley
3 cups chopped oysters

1 bay leaf
1 tsp. poultry seasoning
salt and pepper
2 beaten eggs
1 3/4 cups milk and oyster liquid
10 - 12 lb. turkey

Cook celery and onion in butter until soft but not brown. Add crumbs and parsley and mix thoroughly. Add oysters, bay leaf, seasonings and eggs. Add enough liquid to moisten and mix. Remove the bay leaf. If you prefer a rich dressing, add more butter. Then stuff bird lightly and truss.

Orange Chicken Glaze

2 cups orange concentrate
2 cups margarine

1 Tbsp. ginger
2 Tbsp. dry mustard

Cook all ingredients together until butter is melted. Brush on chicken after chicken has baked for 1/2 hour. Cook another 15 minutes and brush second time. Let set 10 minutes in hot oven.

Cherry Sauce for Pork

24 oz. jar cherry preserves
2 Tbsp. red wine vinegar
1/8 tsp. cinnamon
1/8 tsp. nutmeg

dash cloves
2 Tbsp. cornstarch
2 Tbsp. water
1/4 cup slivered almonds

Combine the preserves, wine vinegar, cinnamon, nutmeg and cloves. Heat to boiling. Mix the cornstarch and water together and stir into preserves mixture. Boil one minute. Add slivered almonds. Add water to make 2 1/2 cups. Use 1/4 cup per serving.

Chutney

tomatoes	dill
onion	salt
green pepper	pepper

Mix all ingredients and let this set for a while.

Watermelon Pickles

3 cups sugar	1 tsp. ground cloves
2 cups vinegar	2 tsp. cinnamon
1 cup water	rind from 1 watermelon

Clean all pink from the watermelon rind and remove the green outer skin. Cut into chunks. Cook the rind in salt water until tender (1 tsp. salt to 1 qt. water). Drain. Mix all remaining ingredients and cook watermelon in the syrup until the rind becomes clear in the syrup.

Low Calorie Beet Pickles

1/2 cup white vinegar	1 Tbsp. artificial sweetener
1/2 tsp. salt	1 can (16 oz.) beets
1 tsp. mixed pickling spice	

Heat beets slowly in their own juice. Drain, reserving 1/2 cup juice. Heat vinegar, beet juice, salt and spices. Simmer on low heat for 10 minutes. Cool. Add artificial sweetener and pour over beets. Refrigerate.

Spicy Pickled Beets

small beets	1 tsp. allspice
2 cups sugar	1 Tbsp. cinnamon
2 cups water	1 tsp. cloves
2 cups vinegar	

Select small beets. Cook until tender and then dip into cold water. Peel off skins. Then make the syrup with the remaining ingredients. Pour over beets and simmer 15 minutes. Pack into sterilized jars and seal.

Danish Pickled Beets

1/2 cup white vinegar
1/2 cup water
1/2 cup sugar

1 tsp. salt
1/8 tsp. pepper
2 cups thin-sliced beets

Boil vinegar, water, sugar, salt and pepper for 2 minutes. Place beets in a deep bowl. Cover with marinade. Cool, cover and refrigerate.

Cranberry Relish

3 oz. plus 2 Tbsp. cherry jello
1 cup hot water
1 cup cold water
1 1/4 cups sugar
20 oz. can crushed pineapple, drained

1 orange, peeled
1 apple, peeled
12 oz. fresh cranberries
1/2 cup chopped pecans or walnuts
1/2 cup finely chopped celery

Using a food grinder, grind the apple, orange and cranberries. Mix 1/2 cup sugar with ground cranberries and fruit. Mix 3/4 cup sugar with jello and hot water and stir until jello is dissolved. Add cold water. Add cranberry mixture, nuts, celery and pineapple. Mix well. Chill. Note: This freezes well also.

Peanut Butter Popcorn

2 qts. popped corn
1/2 cup sugar
1/2 cup light corn syrup

1/2 cup peanut butter
1/2 tsp. vanilla

Combine sugar and corn syrup. Cook to a rolling boil. Remove from heat. Add peanut butter and vanilla. Stir until peanut butter is melted. Pour over popcorn and stir until well coated.

HANDY FOOD MEASUREMENTS

Almonds, slivered: 2 oz. bag = 1/2 c.
Apples, diced or sliced: 1 lb. = 3 med.
    = 2 3/4 c.
Apricots, dried: 1 lb. = 3 c. = 4 1/2 c. cooked
Apricots, fresh: 1 lb. = 5 to 8 med.
    = 2 1/4 c. sliced
Asparagus, fresh: 1 lb. = 16 to 20 spears
    = 2 c. cooked
Bananas: 1 lb. = 3 to 4 med. = 2 c. sliced,
    1 1/3 c. mashed
Beans, dry: 1 lb. = 2 1/2 c. (1 c. dry =
    2 1/4 c. cooked)
Beans, green, fresh cut: 1 lb. = 3 c.,
    2 1/2 c. cooked
Beans, green, frozen: 9 oz. pkg. = 1 2/3 c.
Beans, green, canned: 15 oz. can = 1 2/3 c.
Berries (except strawberries): 1 lb. = 2 c.
Bread crumbs, from day-old bread:
    2 slices = 1 c.
Bread crumbs, canned, dry: 10 oz. can
    = 2 1/2 c.
Broccoli, fresh, cut 2-in. length: 1 lb. = 6 c.
    (including 4 c. florets)
Broccoli, fresh, chopped: 1 lb. = 4 1/2 c.
Cabbage, fresh, shredded: 1 lb. = 4 c.,
    med. head is 2 lb.
Carrots, sliced: 1 lb. = 8 - 9 large = 4 c. sliced
Cauliflower, fresh: 1 lb. = 1 1/2 c.
Cauliflower, frozen: 10 oz. = 2 c.
Celery, chopped: 1 rib = 3/4 c.
Cheese, cottage: 1 lb. = 2 c.
Cheese, shredded: 4 oz. = 1 c.
Cherries, canned: 1 lb. = 1 3/4 to 2 c.
Cherries, maraschino: 10 oz. = 45 cherries
Chicken, bone-in breast, cooked, cubed:
    1 lb. (2 med.) = 1 1/2 c.
Chicken, skinless, boneless breast, cooked,
    cubed: .6 lb. (2 med.) = 1 1/2 c.
Chicken meat, canned, drained: 5 oz. can
    = shy 1/2 c.
Chocolate chips: 1 c. = 6 oz.
Cocoa powder, unsweetened: 8 oz. can = 3 c.
Coconut, flaked or shredded: 7 oz. bag
    = 2 2/3 c., 1 cup = 2.7 oz.
Coffee, ground: 1 lb. = 5 1/2 c. = 88 tsp.

Cool Whip: 8 oz. = 3 1/2 c.
Cornmeal: 1 lb. = 3 c. (1 c. uncooked
    = 4 1/2 c. cooked)
Crackers, graham: 1 lb. box = 66 singles or 33
    doubles = 4 c. crumbs
Crackers, saltine: 1/2 lb. = 88 singles
Crackers, saltine, crumbs: 28 singles = 1 c.
Cream, heavy, whipped: 1 c. cream
    = 2 c. whipped
Egg whites (large eggs): 1 c. = 8 to 10 whites
Flour, all-purpose, sifted: 1 lb. = 4 c.
Flour, all-purpose, unsifted, spooned:
    1 lb. = 3 1/2 c.
Flour, cake, sifted: 1 lb. = 4 3/4 c.
Flour, whole wheat, unsifted, spooned:
    1 lb. = 3 1/3 c.
Garlic, minced: 1 med. clove = 1/2 tsp.
Gelatin, unflavored: 1/4 oz. env. = 2 tsp.
Ginger root, peeled, chopped: 2 oz. = 5 Tbsp.
Grapes, seedless: 1 lb. = 2 1/2 c.
Honey: 1 lb. = 1 1/3 c.
Juice, canned: 46 oz. can = 5 3/4 c.
Ketchup: 1 lb. = 1 2/3 c.
Lemon juice: 6 med. lemons = 1 c. juice
Lemon zest, grated: 1 lemon = 2 to 3 tsp.
Mandarin oranges: 15 oz. can = 100 sections
Marshmallows: 10 oz. bag = 40 large
Marshmallow: 1 large = 10 miniature
Milk, nonfat dry, reconstituted: 1 lb. (3 1/4 c.
    powder) = 17 c. milk (3/8 c. powder
    = 2 c. liquid)
Mushrooms: 8 oz. = 3 c. sliced =
    1 c. sliced sauteed
Oatmeal (uncooked): 1 lb. = 5 1/2 c.;
    1 c. uncooked = 1 3/4 c. cooked
Olives, ripe, large, pitted: 6 oz. can drained
    = 45 olives
Onions, green, cut in 1-in. lengths: 4 onions
    (1/2 bunch) = 1 c.
Onions, coarsely chopped: 1 lb. = 3 large =
    2 1/2 c. (1 c. = 1 1/4 large)
Orange juice: 3 med. oranges = 1 c.
Orange zest, grated: 1 orange = 1 Tbsp.
Parsley, chopped: 1 bunch = 1 1/3 to 1 1/2 c.
    chopped (1/4 c. = 6 or 7 stems)

Pasta: 1 lb. = 4 to 5 c. uncooked = 8 c. cooked
Peaches, canned, sliced: 16 oz. can = 1 3/4 to 2 c.
Peaches, fresh, sliced: 1 lb. = 4 med. = 2 c.
Pears, fresh, sliced: 1 lb. = 4 med. = 2 c.
Peas, fresh, in pod: 1 lb. = 1 1/4 c. shelled
Peas, frozen: 10 oz. = 2 c.
Peanut butter: 18 oz. jar = 2 c.
Pecans, chopped: 2 oz. bag = 1/2 c.
Pepper, green, diced: 1 med. = 1 c.
Pineapple, canned, chunks and crushed: 20 oz. can = 2 1/2 c.
Pineapple, canned, chunks: 20 oz. can = 50 chunks
Pineapple, canned, slices: 20 oz. can = 10 slices
Pineapple, fresh, cubed: 2 lb. = 1 med. = 3 c.
Potato chips, crushed: 1 c. packed = 1/2 c. crumbs
Potatoes: 1 lb. = 3 med. = 2 1/4 cooked, 1 3/4 c. mashed
Prunes, dried, pitted: 1 lb. = 2 1/4 c. = 4 c. cooked
Pumpkin, canned: 16 oz. can = 2 c.
Raisins: 1 lb. - 2 3/4 c. (1 c. = 6 oz.)
Rhubarb, fresh, diced: 1 lb. = 3 1/2 c. = 2 c. cooked
Rice, brown: 14 oz. pkg. = 2 c. = 8 c. cooked
Rice, quick-cooking or converted: 14 oz. pkg. = 2 c. = 8 c. cooked
Rice, regular: 1 lb. = 2 1/4 c. raw = 6 3/4 c. cooked (1 c. raw = 3 c. cooked)
Rice, wild: 1 lb. = 3 c. raw = 11 to 12 c. cooked
Shallots, chopped: 1 med. = 3 to 3 1/2 tsp.
Shrimp, tiny, canned, drained: 4 oz. can = 1 c.
Spinach, fresh: 12 oz. bag, stems removed = 5 c. = 1/2 c. chopped and cooked
Spinach, frozen, chopped: 10 oz. pkg. = 1 1/8 c.
Strawberries: 1 lb. = 1 3/4 c. sliced
Sugar, brown, packed: 1 lb. = 2 1/4 c.
Sugar, granulated: 1 lb. = 2 1/4 c.
Sugar, powdered, unsifted: 1 lb. = 3 3/4 c.
Tomatoes, canned whole, chopped: 28 oz. can = 1 1/3 c. tomatoes, lots of liquid
Tomatoes, fresh, chopped: 1 lb. = 3 med. = 3 c.
Tuna, canned, drained: 6 oz. can = 1 c.
Vanilla wafers, crushed: 28 = 1 c. crumbs
Walnuts, chopped: 2.5 oz. bag = 1/2 c.
Water chestnuts, sliced: 8 oz. can = 1 c.
Zucchini, sliced: 4 (bratwurst size) = 4 c.

Emergency Substitutions:

If you don't have . . . . substitute . . . . .

1 c. **buttermilk** = 1 c. milk + 1 Tbsp. lemon juice (wait 5 min.)

1 c. sifted **cake flour** = 1 c. minus 2 Tbsp. sifted all-purpose flour

1 oz. **unsweetened chocolate** = 3 Tbsp. unsweetened cocoa + 1 Tbsp. butter

1 oz. **unsweetened chocolate** = 1 2/3 oz. semisweet chocolate and reduce sugar in recipe by 2 tsp.

1 oz. **semisweet chocolate** = generous 1/2 oz. unsweetened chocolate + 1 Tbsp. sugar

1 Tbsp. **cornstarch** = 2 Tbsp. flour

1 c. light **corn syrup** or **honey** = 1 1/4 c. sugar + 1/3 c. liquid

1 clove **garlic** = 1/4 tsp. garlic powder

1 c. **half and half** = 7/8 c. milk + 1/3 c. melted butter

1 Tbsp. fresh **herbs** = 1 tsp. dried herbs

1 c. whole **milk** = 1/2 c. evaporated milk + 1/2 c. water or 1 c. skim milk + 2 tsp. melted butter

1/4 c. chopped **onions** = 1 Tbsp. dried minced onion or 1 tsp. onion powder

1/2 c. **wine** (in desserts) - 1/2 c. fruit juice

1/2 c. **wine** (in cooking) = 1/2 c. broth

Sources: Handbook of Food Preparation of the American Home Economics Association; Al Sicherman's kitchen

NAPKIN FOLDING

THE FAN

Fold the napkin in half. Starting on the shorter side, pleat in 1-inch accordion pleats all the way to the top. Slip one end into a glass and allow the other end to open up.

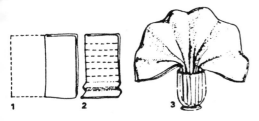

THE OXFORD

Fold the napkin into thirds. Fold the sides to the center. Fold down the top left and right corners. Fold up the bottom edge. Turn the napkin over, tuck one side into the other and stand it upright.

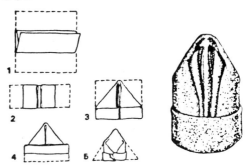

THE SCARF

Fold the napkin into quarters. Fold it in half diagonally. Pleat each half. Slip through a napkin ring or tie with a ribbon.

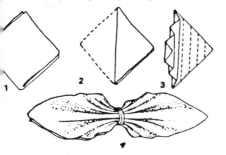

THE BONAPARTE

Fold the napkin in half diagonally. Fold the bottom left and right corners to the top, forming a diamond. Fold the bottom corner up, leaving about 1 inch at the top and lay the napkin flat.

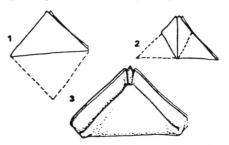

THE DIAGONAL STRIPE

Fold the napkin into quarters with the free corners at the top right. Roll down the top flap halfway. Tuck the second and third flaps under it, making 3 equal stripes. Turn back the sides and lay the napkin flat. Insert a card or flower for decoration.

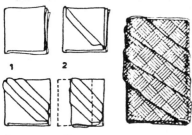

THE KINA

Fold your Square napkin in half and in half again, creating a small square. Fold your new square in half, creating a triangle. It does not matter what side is up, but begin to accordion fold from one side to the other. Each one of these folds should be about 1 inch wide. Now hold the bottom and open out the pleats and arrange in your favorite glass.

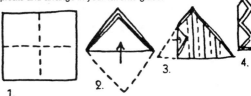

THE HAVANA

Fold the napkin into quarters with the free corners at the bottom. Fold the top flap up one half. Fold each of the remaining flaps up to within 1 inch of the previous flap. Fold back the sides and lay the napkin flat.

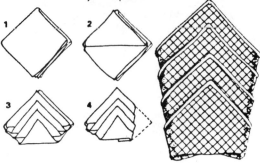

THE SURPRISE PACKAGE

Fold the napkin into quarters with the free corners at the top. Fold the bottom and side corners to the center. Turn the napkin over and fold the first flap down halfway. Insert a surprise.

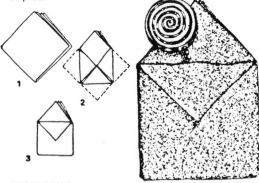

THE PYRAMID

Fold the napkin into quarters. Fold it in half diagonally. Bend the napkin in the middle and stand it upright.

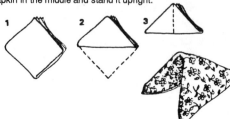

BASIC BOW

Beginning with your flat napkin, bring all four corners to the center. Crease. Bring left and right corners to the center again. Flip over left to right, so the smooth side is up. Bring the top and bottom points to the center. Keeping the points together, pinch the sides from the left and right.

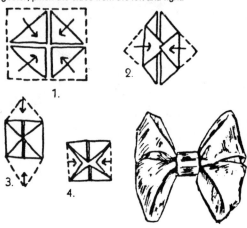

THE BISHOP'S HAT

Fold the napkin in half diagonally to form a triangle. Fold the left and right corners up to meet at the top point, forming a diamond. Fold the bottom corner up, leaving about 1 inch at the top. Fold the corner back to the bottom edge. Turn the napkin over and bring each of the sides back, tucking one into the other. Stand the napkin upright and tuck each of the flaps into the cuff, or let the flaps fall out to the sides for a flower effect.

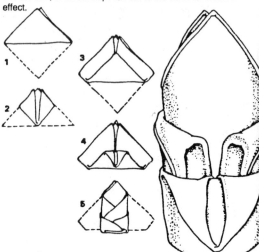